TO THE DIGGINGS!

MOUNT ALEXANDER GOLD-DIGGERS AT EVENING MESS.

TO THE DIGGINGS!

A Celebration of the 150th Anniversary
of the Discovery of Gold in Australia

– GEOFF HOCKING –

Lothian
BOOKS

Forest Creek, Mount Alexander
engraving by Thomas Ham, *The Gold Digger's Portfolio*, 1854
(PRIVATE COLLECTION)

– CONVERSION TABLE –

One ounce (1 oz) = 28.3 grams
One pound (1 lb) = 0.454 kg
One ton = 1.02 tonnes

One inch (1 in) = 2.54 cm
One foot (1 ft) = 30.5 cm
One yard (1 yd) = 0.914 metres
One mile = 1.61 km

One penny (1d) = approx. 1 cent
One shilling (1s) = 10 cents
One pound (£1) = $2

Money values quoted in text cannot be equated using direct conversion.
To gain an approximation of present values (2000) any amount should be multiplied by a factor of 30:1.

(FRONT ENDPAPER)
Gold Diggings, c. 1848.
Photograph by John Kerr Hunter, c. 1848
(LA TROBE PICTURE COLLECTION,
STATE LIBRARY OF VICTORIA)

(PART TITLE)
*Mount Alexander Gold-diggers
at Evening Mess*
Engraving from *London Illustrated News*, 1852
(CASTLEMAINE ART GALLERY & HISTORICAL MUSEUM
COLLECTION)

(BACK ENDPAPER)
**Miners at the Red, White & Blue
Mine, Bendigo**
Unknown Photographer, c. 1910
(PRIVATE COLLECTION)

(TITLE PAGE)
*Old Ballarat, as it was in the summer
of 1853 to 54*
Oil painting by Eugène von Guérard, 1884
(BALLARAT FINE ART GALLERY COLLECTION)

Thomas C. Lothian Pty Ltd
11 Munro Street Port Melbourne, Victoria 3207

Copyright © Geoff Hocking 2000
First published 2000

National Library of Australia
Cataloguing-in-Publication data:

Hocking, Geoff, 1947–.

To the diggings.
Includes Index.
ISBN 0 7344 01140.

1. Gold mines and mining – Victoria – History.
2. Gold mines and mining – Australia – History.
3. Victoria – History. 4. Australia – History.
I. Title. 994.5

Design by Geoff Hocking
Colour reproduction by DigiType/Art Preparation, Bendigo
Printed in Singapore by Tat Wei Printing Packaging Pte Ltd

CONTENTS

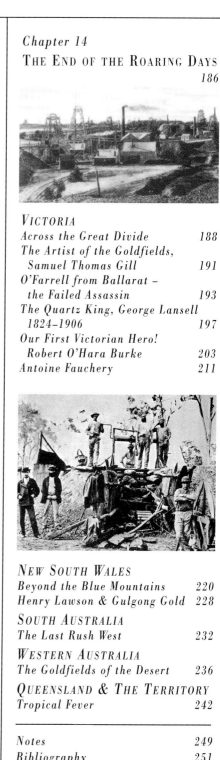
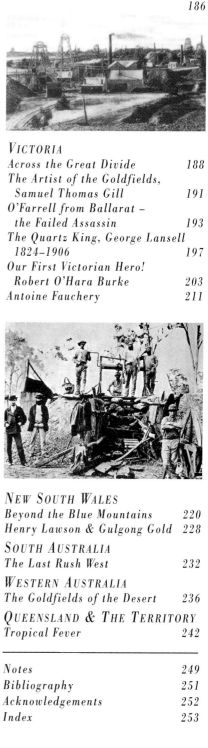

High and Dry
Lithograph from *Mountains and Molehills* by Frank Marryat, 1853
(COURTESY OF THE BANCROFT LIBRARY, UNIVERSITY OF CALIFORNIA, BERKELEY)

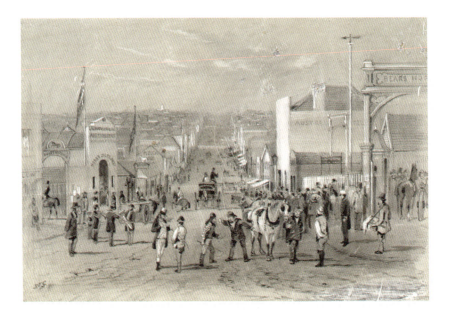

Bourke Street, Melbourne
Watercolour by S. T. Gill, 1853
(LA TROBE PICTURE COLLECTION, STATE LIBRARY OF VICTORIA)

The buildings that lined the San Francisco streets were not at all like the bark huts and mudstone shacks that characterised the early Australian diggings.

Maybe the Californians thought they were going to stay in the West, whereas the adventurers on the Antipodean fields were only there for the easy gold – to get rich and get out as quickly as they could.

There were plenty who did make it rich on the Australian diggings, and who stayed to invest their gold in the elegant mansions and great public buildings that still stand today.

INTRODUCTION

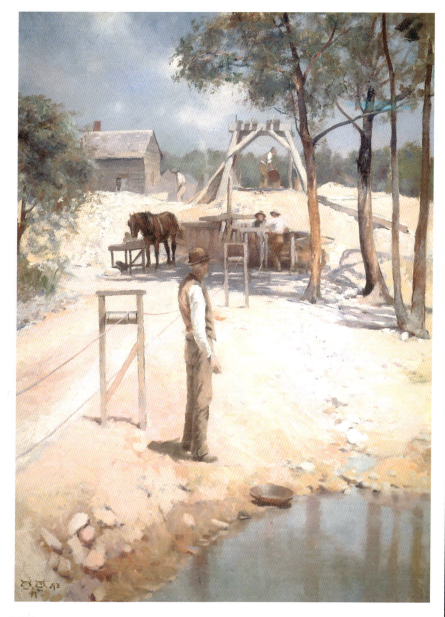

Mining scene, Creswick
Oil by Walter Withers, 1893
(*Ballarat Fine Art Gallery*)

This painting by Australian Impressionist artist, Walter Withers, shows a whip on the Creswick diggings in Central Victoria.

A whip was a horse-drawn pulley system that was used to raise and lower men and ore up and down the shaft.

The horse would walk away from the shaft when pulling the bucket to the surface, and would walk backwards when lowering.

Diggers would rely upon a steady horse to ensure safety in this operation.

I WAS BORN IN BENDIGO, in Chum Street, Golden Square, only a few metres from 'Fortuna', the magnificent home of George Lansell, the Quartz King of the Victorian goldfields.

My first schooling was at Specimen Hill Primary, a small rural school perched on a rise of quartz-strewn, gravelled ground overlooking the valley through which the Bendigo Creek runs after heavy rains. I can clearly remember we picked up specks of gold from the school playground on mornings after such a downpour.

Later, I was moved to Golden Square Primary, a larger school closer to the bed of the creek, right next door to the Golden Square Methodist Church, which was an imposing, spired building with a large mezzanine gallery that encircled the body of the interior, such was the size of the congregation of hearty-voiced Cornishmen who had rushed onto the Bendigo diggings after the discoveries there in 1851.

My great-grandfather was one of these stout and faithful Cornishmen who, as it seems, along with half the population of that coastal corner of Britain, had migrated to the colonies, eager to dig and tunnel their way to glory on the diggings.

I grew up among the landscape of the diggings, the names of the streets around recalling the 'roaring days' – Panton, Hargraves, Chum, Booth, Barnard, MacKenzie. We wandered along the gullies whose names honoured the diggers who had toiled there a century before – California Gully, Sailor's Gully, Long Gully, Job's Gully, Peg Leg, Adelaide, Tipperary, Golden Gully, and New Chum Gully, which ran opposite our home.

The diggers had recreated the idea of London in the dust and the mud of the goldfields – Pall Mall, Charing Cross, Park Lane were names given to meandering tracks that soon became the centre of this bustling town.

As children, we played on the great dumps of crushed quartz sand that stood as stark reminders of the extensive subterranean mining ventures that made Bendigo and the central Victorian goldfields among the richest places on earth. Up until the middle of the twentieth century tall steel poppet legs straddled the city; they dominated the skyline, strung out in long lines from north to south, tracing the reefs that ran deep below the surface. The mines of central Victoria were rich indeed, and some of the owners and shareholders were the richest men of all.

My maternal grandfather, Fred Cronin, was born on the diggings, the son of poor Irish settlers from Cork. When he was young he was mates with mining magnate George Lansell's son Leonard; together they would muck about in the boats on the wide ornamental lake that nestled in front of Len's place, also in Chum Street. When Fred was a man he worked for Lansell at the Little 180, the great Hustler, and the Red, White and Blue, driving the steam engines that hauled the cages up and down the shafts. In later years several of his sons, my uncles, also worked in the mines until the closure of the last in the 1940s.

The Duke of Cornwall Mine, at Fryerstown near Castlemaine, was typical of the hundreds of ventures financed by speculators and investors.

The square sandstone building, with its tall chimney, is also typical of similar engine houses on the Cornish tin-mines and those found around Burra, in South Australia.

When the migrants came they brought their traditions with them. In all of these places the famous 'pastie' can be found in abundance. The true Cornish pastie has a thick rolled crust, formed when the pastry is folded over its filling. The pastry was an excellent insulator, and pasties would stay warm for many hours. As the miners would not have been able to wash the grime from their hands before taking their crib (lunch) they would hold this crust while eating, and it was then discarded.

Some cooks would fill one half of the pastie with meat and vegetables, the other with apple or other stewed fruits, making the single pastie a two-course meal in itself.

(Castlemaine Art Gallery & Historical Museum Collection)

The Old England Hotel, Barker's Creek

(PRIVATE COLLECTION)

Kentish-born, John Hopkins Walter built his hotel in 1862, after the railway passed through Barker's Creek.

Charles Richard Ladd moved his family from the Avoca diggings, and took over the licence of the Old England on 20 July 1889. The Ladds only stayed in Barker's Creek for another two years, when they moved up to Bendigo to try their luck there.

The Old England is on the western side of the railway line. Specimen Gully, where in October 1851 Worley and Peters found the first gold of the Mt Alexander rush, is on the other side of the line, just a few hundred metres into the bush.

This valley had been at the heart of Dr Barker's Ravenswood Run, a vast sheep-grazing run, typical of the holdings taken up by scores of squatters following the opening up of the district by Major Mitchell's expedition of 1836.

By the middle of November 1851, it was estimated that 67,000 ounces of gold had been taken in Victoria. 10,000 ounces were sent down to Melbourne by escort on 27 September.

By Christmas 1851 250,000 ounces of gold had been taken from the central Victorian region.

Fred married eighteen-year-old Alice Ladd, whose family was among the first at Carisbrook; she always claimed that her father was the first white child born on those diggings, and, given her advanced years when she made these claims, we had no reason at all to doubt her. When her father decided to try his luck on the diggings they moved to Barker's Creek, just outside Castlemaine, and not far at all from Specimen Gully, where the first gold was found on the Mt Alexander diggings. My great-grandfather was, for a short while, the publican of the Old England Hotel, which still stands beside the Midland Highway.

As we grew up we were enmeshed in the culture of the diggings. The mines may have long gone, the 'roaring days' a faint echo, but our lives in the 1950s were little different to that enjoyed, and at times endured, by our grandparents. We attended the same schools, the same churches, sang the same hymns, and I am sure heard much the same sermons. We entertained ourselves the same way, with Sunday School picnics, and church teas, in large groups of boisterous relatives who all seemed to live in the same area. We walked in and out of people's houses, knew everybody, and if we weren't related to them, someone we knew was.

The diggings ran a current through all of our lives. Every now and again, generally after inclement weather, the local paper would carry a report of someone's backyard disappearing, or half of the roadway collapsing, or a schoolyard opening up to reveal a shaft or tunnel long forgotten. As the towns developed, the Municipal Councils undertook to cap and seal the open shafts that littered the landscape; some were concreted over, but most were sealed with timbers and covered with earth, and every now and again one fell in, reminding us of our heritage.

My paternal great-grandfather had first gone to America with his family, and several of his brothers stayed on at the mines in Montana,

Map of the early Bendigo goldfields, c. 1852

(COURTESY FRANK CUSACK, BENDIGO)

Victorian Government Surveyor, William Swan Urquhart, mapped the goldfields in 1852.
This map was based on his survey.

Diggers on Rout [sic] ***to Deposit Gold***
Lithograph by S. T. Gill, 1852

(REX NAN KIVELL COLLECTION, U1018
BY PERMISSION, NATIONAL LIBRARY OF AUSTRALIA)

A pair of determined diggers stride purposefully through the bush to Melbourne to pay their gold into the Treasury.

With rifles at the ready and their mongrel between them, they look the type to brook no interruption to their purpose.

There were many, however, who had lost everything they carried as they made their way through the black and gloomy forests to and from the diggings. Some poor fellows were found stumbling, days later, back onto the diggings with little more than the shirt on their backs, the miscreants who had robbed them of their gold dust no doubt living it up in the nearest bush-inn or grog shop.

John Sherer recalls:

Gangs of mounted bush-rangers, masked, and with pistols, are infesting all the roads, stopping the travellers, and even the gold transports … two men from Geelong were also attacked by three mounted diggers, who took all their gold-dust, money, and fire-arms, and bound them to trees. This happened in the broad light of day.

– John Sherer, *The Gold Finder of Australia*, p. 16.

a sister in California. The great diaspora of the Cornish was never considered equal to that of the Irish, who fled their homeland after the potato famine, were forced out by the British or carried away on convict ships. The Cornish migrated of their own accord, ready for great adventure, and eager to build a prosperous future through honest, hard work.

At one stage Bendigo seemed an outpost of the Duchy of Cornwall. The predominance of the nuggety little 'cousin Jacks' and 'Jennys' on the Bendigo diggings was unparalleled anywhere in the country. Others in Bendigo who showed no allegiance to the ancient Kings of Cornwall, would, when asked their religion, simply answer – 'not Methodist'.

Bendigo has always had a large Irish population, and its Roman Catholic Cathedral was one of the last Gothic-styled churches built in the world. If any of our family were in hospital for one reason or another it was an act of proud defiance to refuse the attentions of any of the 'brides of Christ' on their hospital rounds. The family surname, Cronin, attracted the attention of the nuns, but the Protestant Irish, like the Cornish, were pretty good at holding their own. Lessons learnt in the class-ridden old country took generations to understand in the new.

Although Australia prides itself on the spirit of mateship born on the diggings, it was such division and lack of fraternity that also led to the battles fought there.

The rush to California in 1848 had attracted large numbers from around the world, including hundreds from Australia, to the west coast of America. When New South Wales announced the discovery of goldfields there, the migration was largely internal, attracting diggers from the other Australian colonies of South Australia, Victoria and Van Diemen's Land, and back from California.

When the news of gold in Victoria was broadcast the unexpected news of gold in the 'south countrie' created almost unbelievable excitement worldwide. It seemed that the whole of the country was littered with nuggets, and the greatest rush of all was on. Gold mining suddenly became a serious business. This was worth leaving home for, leaving all behind and being born anew in the free spirit of the colonies.

When professional miners arrived, the diggings took on a different hue. The spirit of the adventurers and the wild colonial boys was

The Forest Creek Diggings,
Mount Alexander, Port Phillip
London Illustrated News, 1852

(Castlemaine Art Gallery
& Historical Museum Collection)

displaced by the earnest diligence of experienced mining men. The diggers at Bendigo were certainly among the best of these.

There was always a large and permanent Chinese population in Bendigo. When I was studying at the School of Mines I clearly remember the Chinese-born father of one of my teachers, as he took his daily stroll, up from the Chinese quarter in Bridge Street, past the school, and on into Bendigo. We used to buy fireworks from him in his dark, timber and verandahed store, filled with all sorts of strangely, fascinating oriental goodies – kites, weird vegetables, brightly coloured clothing, and of course rows and rows of penny bungers, catherine wheels, tom thumbs and rockets.

I stood and watched in Bridge Street the day a bulldozer ran through his shop and stripped the street bare of the Chinese houses. I rummaged through the rubble looking for anything of value that may have escaped the dozer's blade, but it was all gone. Today, descendants of the original Chinese families have built a museum to house the ceremonial dragons of which Bendigo is so proud; they have created a beautiful Chinese garden across the creek, and proudly honour the contribution their forefathers made to the spirit of the diggings.

In the 1960s I watched a workman hack into the great 50-foot-long oregon timbers of the Deborah Mine. He was claiming the metal pulley housings for scrap. The poppet legs of that mine are one of the few that still stand today, the rest of it has long gone, the crushing battery,

Illustrations such as this, when reproduced in the popular papers of the time, did much to stir the adventurous soul of many an English office boy, counter clerk or wage-hand. The idea of travel to the colonies was canvassed widely in the popular press; and gold was the currency that made the adventure possible.

The Great Extended Hustler's Mine, Sandhurst, The Shafts and Surface Works
Engraving from *Illustrated Australian News*, 20 May 1873

(LA TROBE LIBRARY PICTURE COLLECTION, STATE LIBRARY OF VICTORIA)

Once these poppet-legs dominated the landscape across the Victorian goldfields.

There was a romanticism about these steel giants, each one bearing the name of the company that had come together to finance the deeper search for gold: Hustlers; Red, White and Blue; Deborah; Hercules; New Moon; Nell Gwynne; New Chum; Napoleon – and many more. These were the names that underwrote our lives.

Even though the mines have long gone, the same names appear on street signs, or new housing estates, or shopping malls; each a constant reminder of the heritage left to us by the energies of our fore-fathers.

Share Certificate, issued by the Abe Lincoln Tribute Company, New Chum Sandhurst (Bendigo)

(PRIVATE COLLECTION)

After three to four years the alluvial gold was played out, but it didn't herald the end of the diggings – the investors moved in instead.

The diggers went from a freewheeling itinerant band to investors, partners, shareholders or employees in the scores of mining companies that issued scrip from Queensland to Kalgoorlie.

The mining exchange became the new hive of frantic activity, where speculators rushed to join in the second gold boom.

the winding shed, the engine house – even the sand dumps have almost disappeared beneath housing estates.

While we may be proud of the magnificent public buildings, the ornate Victorian iron lacework, and the stories of the wealth that came from the soil, the diggers of the first rush laid the foundation of both the cities of today and the lives we are now living.

In the humble honesty of the miner's cottage we preserve the memories of our forefathers; in the remnants of their forgotten shafts, the mullock heaps, the rusting, broken machinery overgrown in the bush, the stone walls, the creekbeds, the silent poppet-legs, we honour their lives.

While this book has been written in celebration of the 150th anniversary of the discovery of gold in Australia, it also attempts to honour the memory of those who came in the early days, to understand the relationship between events on both sides of the Pacific, and the political and social changes that followed the opening up of Australia through the currency of gold.

CHAPTER 1

GOLD! GOLD! GOLD!

IN 1842 SOME NUGGETS OF GOLD were discovered by Francisco Lopez in the San Francisquito Canyon in California. Oddly enough, little attention was paid to Lopez's discovery. The earth remained undisturbed until the great rush six years later. But the discovery of gold in this valley in 1846, and the great rush that followed, were almost overshadowed by the constant warring over this territory by the two nations that contested it, the United States and Mexico.

The West had long been a prize unattainable to the Americans. The British held the key to Oregon, and the only other way into California was blocked by the Rockies. Mexico and the slave-owning southern states of America had little empathy with the northern states' attempts to spread liberal ideals across the whole continent. 'The fulfilment of our manifest destiny to overspread the continent' was the opinion of the *United States Magazine and Democratic Review* in

Gold Mining at Sutter's Mill, Coloma (El Dorado County, California)
Oil by an unknown artist, c. 1855 (detail)
(COURTESY OF THE BANCROFT LIBRARY, UNIVERSITY OF CALIFORNIA, BERKELEY)

In this painting of Sutter's unfinished Mill at Coloma in the valley where the first gold had been found, a pair of California '49ers take their rest in the shade of a timber-framed building. One leans against his bed-roll and cradle, the other strikes a pose characteristic of all working men, leaning on his pick.

James W. Marshall

(COURTESY OF THE BANCROFT LIBRARY, UNIVERSITY OF CALIFORNIA, BERKELEY)

James Marshall found the gold that ushered in the Californian goldrush.

John Charles Frémont

(COURTESY OF THE BANCROFT LIBRARY, UNIVERSITY OF CALIFORNIA, BERKELEY)

Frémont was the adventurer and explorer who made several expeditions into the Far West before the goldrush. With Sutter and other Californian Americans, he helped lead the Bear Flag revolt that eventually laid the foundations for the conquest of California.

Portrait of John A. Sutter

(COURTESY OF THE BANCROFT LIBRARY, UNIVERSITY OF CALIFORNIA, BERKELEY)

It was on his ranch at New Helvetica (Sutter's Fort) that the first gold of the California rush was found.

July 1845. Resentment of the interference of foreign nations intent on preventing the annexation of Texas led to a resolution in the House of Repres-entatives on 5 January 1846 to end Anglo-American occupation of Oregon. Belief in America's 'manifest destiny' was, in part, the justification for the invasion and eventual capture of California.

The 'Americans' in the Mexican province of California had long sought to take control of the domain they felt was rightly theirs. Although the first non-native landholder in California, John Sutter, had prospered following a grant from the Mexican government of 45,000 acres of the Sacramento Valley just west of the Sierra Nevada, he conspired with renowned explorer, John Charles Frémont, and others who had an interest in California, to take the territory from the Mexicans.

Throughout the early months of 1846 the Americans and the Mexicans were involved in a stand-off, sizing each other up over the Rio Grande. After a large squad of Mexican soldiers surrounded a scouting party of American dragoons, killing 11, wounding 5 and cap-turing the remaining 47, the United States declared war on Mexico.

Frémont, and fellow-travellers of the 'Bear Flag Revolution', immediately saw the opportunity to press home Anglo-European defiance of Mexican rule over California. They captured a large mob of horses belonging to the Mexican Army bound for Sutter's Fort, and took Governor Vallejo prisoner, holding him at the Fort. The Bear Flag of the newly proclaimed Republic of California flew for the first time on 14 June 1846. Frémont was chosen as leader of the new republic on 5 July.

The Republic of California was shortlived. On 7 July an American naval vessel steamed into Monterey, captured the capital, claimed all of the territory for the United States and raised the Stars and Stripes flag in Yerba Beuna on the 8th (Yerba Beuna was renamed San Francisco on 30 January 1847). The Bear Party recognised the

inevitable and wisely joined the Union, and the Stars and Stripes flew over Sutter's Fort the following day.

Sometime later Sutter engaged carpenter James Marshall to construct a timber mill at Coloma on the American River (near what is now known as Sacramento City) to supply much-needed timber for a flourmill he was also building, and to supply the needs of the growing township of San Francisco.

On 24 January 1848 Marshall found some small nuggets of dull yellow metal glinting in the tail-race of the partly-built mill. Believing it to be gold Marshall took the nuggets to Sutter's Fort.

Sutter recounts the occasion when he was first shown Californian gold:

> It was a rainy afternoon when Mr Marshall arrived at my office in the Fort, very wet, and I was surprised to see him, as he was down a few days previous ... I [had] sent up to Coloma a number of teams with provisions, mill irons, etc., etc. He told me then that he had some important and interesting news which he wished to communicate secretly to me.[1]

When they were alone, and with doors locked behind them, Marshall took a rag from his pocket and

> began to show me this metal, which consisted of small pieces and specimens, some of them worth a few dollars; he told me that he had expressed his opinion to the labourers at the mill, that this might be gold; but some of them were laughing and called him a crazy man ... after having proved the metal with aqua fortis, which I found in my

Coloma (El Dorado County, California)
Hunter & Co.'s Express, c. 1848

(COURTESY OF THE BANCROFT LIBRARY, UNIVERSITY OF CALIFORNIA, BERKELEY)

This engraving shows Coloma, where Sutter's Mill was sited, after the establishment of a sizable town in the valley where the first gold had been found.

Sutter's Mill is shown on the right.

CALIFORNIA REPUBLIC

Sam Brannan

(COURTESY OF THE BANCROFT LIBRARY, UNIVERSITY OF CALIFORNIA, BERKELEY)

Mormon leader Brannan's exultant ride through the streets of San Francisco shouting 'Gold! Gold! Gold from the American River', ushered in the Californian goldrush.

(OPPOSITE)

The Bear Flag was created by William L. Todd, and the wife of John Sears, who tore a strip from a red petticoat and sewed it along the edge of a piece of light brown muslin.

Todd then drew a star in the upper left corner and a crudely formed grizzly bear to its right.

Brick dust, linseed oil and venetian red paint were used to draw this design, with the words California Republic lettered beneath in black. Some believe that the star was in solidarity with the Texans who were also at war with Mexico, and the stripe reminiscent of the stripes in the American flag.

It seems that the designers of the Bear Flag revolution desired empathy with all sides. Even Governor Vallejo was keen to throw in his lot with the Americans, eventually taking a seat in the California legislature.

apothecary shop, likewise with other experiments, and read the long article 'gold' in the *Encyclopedia Americana*, I declared this to be gold of the finest quality, of at least 23 carats.[2]

At the time Marshall's discovery was kept quiet as a goldrush to California was the last thing Sutter wanted. After several years of upheaval and hostility, the war with Mexico was drawing to an end, and the Americans were poised to take control of all the territories of New Mexico, California and the Rio Grande border of Texas. 'The fulfilment of our manifest destiny' began in earnest as hundreds of American settlers from the East took the great wagon trails to the West in search of farming lands.

It was almost four months later, on 12 May 1848, that Sam Brannan, a storekeeper at Sutter's Fort, rode through the streets of San Francisco waving a gold-filled glass jar over his head, shouting 'Gold! Gold! Gold from the American River'. Gold fever infected all of the United States, and turned the attention of the world towards the American territory of California. California was once again invaded, but this time the 'army' carried picks and shovels, and was intent on an entirely different prize.

California Here We Come!

The cry of 'Gold' reached right across the North American continent, it carried across the oceans, and was heard loudly along the eastern seaboard of Australia, across the mountains and into the bush. Gold enticed thousands to cross the hostile American heartland to the hills of Sacramento, and across the open seas to the frontier port of San Francisco, eager for their great adventure. California was the first to experience the mass migration to its shores that became the hallmark of subsequent gold discoveries.

Although the discovery of gold on the American River had been reported in the *Californian* as early as 15 March 1848, the news was not widely believed. The *California Star* also reported the discovery of gold on 25 March, but this item provoked little interest, as the new territory of California was more intent on its potential for investment and development than with the haphazard lottery of finding gold.

On 29 May the *California Star* reported that

the whole country from San Francisco to Los Angeles, and from the seashore to the base of the Sierra Nevadas, resounds to the sordid cry of

GOLD, GOLD, GOLD! while the field is left half-planted, the house half-built, and everything neglected but the manufacture of shovels and pickaxes.

The streets of most Californian towns emptied of their men, the farms were deserted and the ports left idle as hundreds of men, shouldered their picks and shovels and headed for Sutter's Fort.

On 10 June the *Star* added to the excitement:

Spades, shovels, picks, wooden bowls, Indian baskets [for washing], etc., find ready purchase, and are frequently disposed of at extortionate prices ... the probable amount taken from these mountains since the first of May last, we are informed, is $100,000, and which is principally in the hands of the mechanical, agricultural and laboring classes.

The newspaper also added that it was forced to cease publication as all its staff had taken off for the diggings.

The news continued to spread throughout California, but there it stopped. It was not until later in June that ships left anchored in San Francisco Bay could gather a working crew to sail back to the eastern seaboard. They carried the news of the find, and samples of the yellow metal, and with it the stories of ready wealth that soon became the stuff of legend.

The 1848 presidential election dominated the news in the eastern states up until 15 September, when the following small item from the Pacific coast appeared in one of the New York papers:

Captain John Sutter
(COURTESY OF THE BANCROFT LIBRARY, UNIVERSITY OF CALIFORNIA, BERKELEY)

Sutter's hopes were dashed by the loss of 'his' California and were ultimately destroyed by the great influx of diggers in the autumn of 1848.

The discovery on the American River, which ran through his holding, changed his fortunes forever, as most of his labourers soon deserted him for the diggings.

His sawmill was never finished and, although he had invested over $25,000 in his flourmill, that also brought him no reward. In fact, by the 1850s all that remained of Sutter's Fort was the central building. Its walls (two and a half feet thick, and fifteen to eighteen feet high) were all that withstood the onslaught of the goldrush.

The fort, which had been a haven for immigrants, and had offered hospitality to explorer John Frémont and mountainman Kit Carson, became just another relic of California before the rush.

Sutter had seen his vast empire taken from him bit by bit, first by miners, then by squatters, and finally his claim to his Mexican title was denied by the American government.

Captain Sutter was declared bankrupt in 1852.

Sutter's Fort
(COURTESY OF THE BANCROFT LIBRARY, UNIVERSITY OF CALIFORNIA, BERKELEY)

The American Flag can be seen flying over the main building of the fort.

SUTTERS FORT.

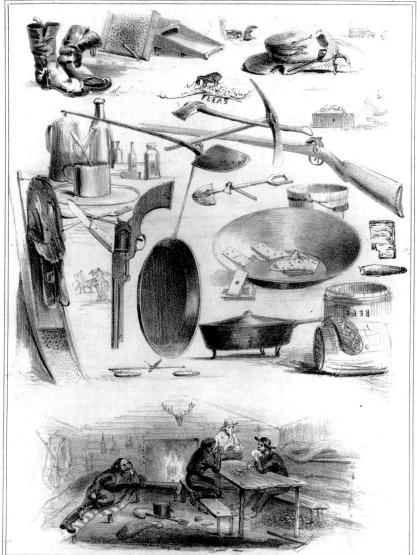

MINERS COAT OF ARMS.

Lith. & Pub. by Britton & Rey San Francisco

Miners' Coat of Arms
Britton & Rey, (lithographer
& publisher), 1856

No matter where the miners went,
the kit was much the same.

This American lithograph shows an
extensive array of boots, hats, cooking
equipment, a puddling cradle, pick and
shovel, and the indispensable firearms.

The Colt revolver became the weapon
of choice from California to Castlemaine;
light, reliable and affordable, the Colt
saved the life of many a miner, but also
took the lives of countless others.

It is often recorded in the diaries and
letters of diggers on the Australian
goldfields that, upon return from work
in the shafts all day, they would fire their
pistols before retiring, and would
do the same on awakening next
morning.

The barrage of pistol shots was like
the deafening roar of a great battle, but
the diggers needed to ensure that their
powder was dry and the pistols clean
and ready for action, lest they were
needed in defence of their owners in
any emergency.

INTERESTING FROM CALIFORNIA –
We have received some late and interesting intelligence from California.
It is to the 1st of July … It relates to the important discovery of a very
valuable gold mine. We have received a specimen of gold.

On 17 September the *Herald* correspondent 'Piasano' reported that
the entire population had gone to the mines, many to return a few days
later with hundreds of dollars in dust and nuggets. Spades and shovels
sold for $10 apiece. Blacksmiths were making $240 a week. Why, even a
child could pick up three dollars worth of gold in a day from the trea-
sure streams.

Every seaport as far south as San Diego, and every interior town, and
nearly every rancho from the base of the mountains in which the gold
has been found … has become suddenly drained of human beings.
Americans, Californians, Indians and Sandwich Islanders, men, women

and children, indiscriminately … there are at this time over one thousand souls busied in washing gold, and the yield per diem may be safely estimated at from fifteen to twenty dollars.

After the arrival of the Royal Mail Steamship *Europa* in London on 10 October, the editor of the *Times* scanned the papers on board for news from the United States. He discovered an item full of almost-unbelievable accounts of the success of the American goldfields, but concluded his report on page 4 of his paper with the following caution:

> the placer sand is said to be so rich, that if exported to England or the United States, it would be very valuable. Consequent upon this excitement, the price of provisions has increased enormously. We need hardly observe that it is necessary to view these statements with great caution.

The British, although defeated in the War of Independence a century earlier still maintained a strong and influential political presence and a feeling of propriety over its former colony. They openly distrusted 'the wily Yankee', and warned against rushing to the American diggings to 'swell the anti-British party in the United States'. Meanwhile, the British continued to expand their Empire. Although it stood alone in a world hostile to its monarchy, Britain believed in its right to influence the affairs of other nations.

At the same time all of Europe was in turmoil; the French people had risen and swept away the monarchy of King Louis Philippe; Austria and Hungary were at war; Italy was tearing itself apart in an attempt to become one nation, province was fighting against province, city-state against city-state, people across Europe were demanding the same rights for all citizens.

> **13 October 1849:** *The constitution for the State of California is approved by convention in Monterey. 'Eureka' is approved as the motto of the State of California.*
>
> **December 1849:** *The population of San Francisco was estimated at 100,000, 35,000 having arrived by sea, 42,000 overland, and 3000 sailors who had deserted their ships.*

Panoramic View of San Francisco, c. 1851
(CALIFORNIAN STATE LIBRARY COLLECTION)
Ships left at anchor in the bay.

Wherever gold was discovered, the closest port saw hundreds of ships left untended, crews absconded, heading for the diggings as quickly as they stepped ashore.

It was the same two years later when diggers rushed to Australian ports. In Port Phillip Bay (Melbourne) ships' captains requested that passengers be carried ashore in light craft or on pilots' boats so they could lie at anchor a mile from shore. They feared that they would lose their crews and be unable to make the return journey to their home port.

At one stage captains and shipowners offered premium wages to encourage sailors, or anyone who was interested, to crew the ships back from Australia.

Few were interested, the lure of gold was too enticing, and ships lay at anchor for months on end.

Ship's captains had even requested that the gaols be opened to allow some prisoners to serve out their sentences as crew aboard a returning ship.

Pull Away Cheerily! The Gold Diggers Song, by Harry Lee Carter, George Henry Russell and Henry Russell
Engraved music sheet
London Musical Bouquet Office, c. 1848
(COURTESY OF THE BANCROFT LIBRARY, UNIVERSITY OF CALIFORNIA, BERKELEY)

This music sheet shows a small mining operation in California. Three diggers are working their cradle, while women and children look on.

The diggings inspired artists, song writers, performers and writers to celebrate the great event, such was the seductive nature of this phenomenon that captured the imagination of the entire world.

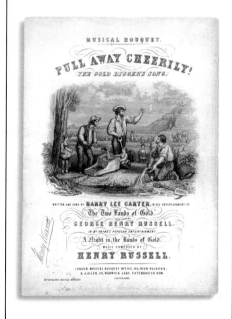

The Republic or the Economy?

Over half a million British had been transplanted to Canada, and thousands to other colonies all around the globe. With the end of transportation of convicts to Australia in 1840, the continued agitation of the Irish for freedom from British rule, the widespread devastation of cholera in almost all over-populated western Europe, Britain was determined to maintain security across its widespread domain.

The discovery and subsequent appeal of the California goldfields was seen by the British government as an opportunity to rid the British Isles of some of its unwanted population, yet it was also concerned about the large number of English who might leave the Empire entirely, through migration to America, a country over which Britain no longer had any constitutional influence.

Britain continued to hold an ambivalent attitude towards the Americans. In early November 1848 the *Times* scoffed at the reports of great finds in California, and went on to denounce the goldfields as a delusion:

> The discovery of gold in the Sacramento, like that of communism on the Seine, has produced a confusion of rank and a startling degree of equality ... even politics have disappeared and republicanism ceased to be preached for the moment ... we must hear more of this El Dorado before we bestow upon it ... our serious consideration.

The *Times* remained sceptical of the so-called Eldorado of California:

> There was need of many mines to gild the Mexican war, and to pay its expenses. These acquisitions have cost the Union twenty-five millions of

Gold Digging in California
(Courtesy of the Bancroft Library, University of California, Berkeley)

This extraordinary engraving shows all the forms of mining used in the extraction of gold on the California diggings in the one scene.

At the left a puddling machine in action, panning in the foreground, at the rear a horizontal tunnel has been driven into the hillside, while a vertical shaft has been dug in the centre, beneath the windlass, which was also a common feature on the Australian diggings.

The 'long tom' being used by the miners in the centre right was not so familiar on the early Australian diggings. It was an extended form of open-ended puddling box, over which water was washed. Perhaps the severe lack of water on the Australian diggings made this device impractical, but similar systems of water races as shown in the background were employed in Australia after the alluvial gold had largely disappeared and company mining took over.

The first rocking cradle in California was used by Isaac Humphreys soon after he had seen the gold that had been found at Sutter's Mill.

Gold dust had been sent to him in San Francisco for analysis. He confirmed the validity of the find, and set off immediately for the American River. Humphreys improvised a rocker, based on a design he had seen in use on another goldfield.

(Opposite)
Map of mining region of California, 1855
Californian Pictorial Lettersheets, Britton & Rey (lithographer & publisher)
(Courtesy of the Bancroft Library, University of California, Berkeley)

our money. If in the course of twenty years, the principal and interest be repaid by the dust collected from the rivers of California, the Union may deem itself most fortunate.

News items positive about the diggings were relegated to lesser pages of the paper. The *London News* made the cynical observation:

> that Brother Jonathon had taken California for its fine harbours and tallow trade, when, lo and behold. He found gold.

The fear of republicanism was at the heart of most British attitudes towards the Californian diggings. If wealth could be readily accumulated by ordinary people, what impact would that have on the ruling classes? If those people gained economic power, how could the born-to-rule aristocracy manage to keep the population in its appointed place? If thousands of British subjects migrated to California, became wealthy and adopted American ways, what was the future for the rule of the monarch? What would be the influence, then, of the 'new Yankee' on the political aspirations of those at home and those already agitating in other colonies.

This same fear was expressed some years later by Earl Grey, the British Secretary of State for the Colonies, when he advised Charles Joseph La Trobe, the Governor of the Australian Colony of Victoria:

> there is a spirit abroad which must be carefully watched and promptly brought under control if this colony is not to parallel California in crime and disorder ... a sense of importance and independence arising from unexampled prosperity.[3]

Events soon got in the way of political point-scoring. By November 1848 the diggings had proved so successful that the USS *Lexington* was able to leave San Francisco with $500,000 of gold bound for the east coast and the United States Mint. In December a Lt Lucian Loeser carried a tea-caddy holding 230 ounces (6.5 kg) of Californian gold into the Washington War Department, where it caused considerable excitement. President Polk, confirmed the reports of the Californian discoveries in a message to Congress on 5 December: 'the accounts

MAP
OF THE
MINING REGION
OF
CALIFORNIA.
1855.

Lithog.d & publd by Britton & Rey
SAN FRANCISCO.

CITY OF SAN FRANCISCO.

Taken from the high ground back of the city – It will be seen that S. F. is situated in a natural basin on a hill side running towards the bay. there is much more shipping

of the abundance of gold are of such an extraordinary character as would scarcely command belief were they not corroborated by the authentic reports of officers in the public service'.

In Australia a Sydney newspaper of 31 August 1849 reported:

> there is now a shortage of farm labour in NSW, as many men, often recently arrived migrants, have gone to California to try their luck on the diggings. There were many doubters when reports of California gold reached Sydney late last year, but they were followed up by some samples, and the exodus began. Letters received in Australia tell of an up-river journey of 60 miles and a land journey of 70 miles until the diggings are reached. The work is hard and dangerous, and the living rough.

The diggings in California attracted all types of nefarious and shady characters; hundreds left the eastern seaboard of Australia for California, where the pickings were thought to be easy and the rule of law not yet established, including old lags, the refuse of Britain's prison hulks, and more latterly those from the cells of Van Diemen's Land (Tasmania), known as Vandemonians, and many a notorious bushranger appeared in San Francisco far from the long arm of British Law. The 'Sydney Ducks', as they were sometimes known, caused such a problem that vigilante groups were soon established to protect the citizens of San Francisco. Those who kept to their old tricks suffered summary justice, without recourse to the niceties of trial by jury, gasping their last breath with their feet swinging just above Californian soil. In the early days the diggers took matters into their own hands, frontier life had given them that freedom, and they took the opportunity to govern themselves as they saw fit.

City of San Francisco (California)
Engraving by J. Clark, 29 May 1850

This engraving shows sailing ships moored in San Francisco Bay.

By this time 'The Queen of the Pacific' (as San Francisco had become known) had grown into a bustling, substantial seaport. It boasted several hotels, churches, schools, hospitals and banks, as well as saloons, gambling halls and brothels.

It was close to the port that Levi Strauss first established his dry-goods store at 90 Sacramento Street. Here he was able to 'capture' the miners almost as they first stepped ashore, ready to be kitted out before they set off for the diggings.

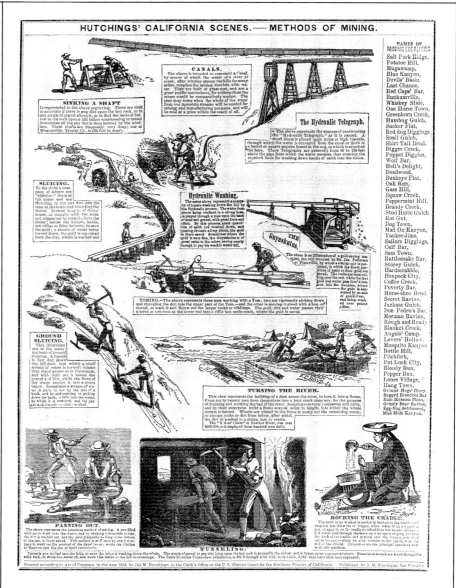

Hutchings California Scenes –
Methods of Mining
Engraved from drawings by
Charles Christian Nahl
J. M. Hutchings, San Francisco, c. 1855

(COURTESY OF THE BANCROFT LIBRARY,
UNIVERSITY OF CALIFORNIA, BERKELEY)

This detailed engraving shows the various methods of mining employed on the California diggings; hydraulic washing, sluicing, panning, tunnelling, the building of flumes, long toms; and a Chinese miner with a washing cradle or puddler, as they were known on the Australian diggings.

The long list at the right of the image carries the names of several of the notable diggings in California. Names such as Red Dog Diggings, Grizzly Bear Ravine, Rattlesnake Bar, Stud Horse Gulch, Hang Town, Mad Mule Canyon and Buckeye Flat reflect the penny westerns that were so popular in the eastern states at the time.

The success of the Californian goldfields saved the Western world from a devastating depression. The economies of Europe were struggling after months of war and revolution, while the end of the Mexican War had seen the cancellation of contracts, as the American Army shed its forces onto a struggling labour market, swelling the ranks of the already half-employed.

The excitement of the goldfields boosted demand for tools, for food and clothing, for transportation, for the planning of permanent townships, and the mobilisation of the hearts and minds of an otherwise dispirited people.

Merchants on the east coast of the United States also geared up to benefit from the demands of the diggers out west. Remarked one New Yorker in December 1848:

any person strolling along our docks cannot help being struck with the quantity of merchandise of all kinds, which is marked for shipping from this port alone, of which not less than $400,000 have been sent within the last thirty days.

A Road Scene in California, 1856
Anthony & Baker, engraver;
Wide West Office, publisher

*(COURTESY OF THE BANCROFT LIBRARY,
UNIVERSITY OF CALIFORNIA, BERKELEY)*

A group of Indian men, women and children, Chinese labourers, prospectors, miners and pioneers make their way to the diggings.

Plans were laid for a railway to connect the east with the west, and goods were obtained from up and down the states. Philadelphia shipped hundreds of tons of flour, while the prices of clothing skyrocketed following the shipment of old stocks from Baltimore to the Pacific Coast. It was comparatively easy for merchants on the east coast of Australia to supply the Californian West, and merchants in Sydney made the most of every opportunity, the prices of picks, shovels and other mining equipment went through the roof as Sydneysiders shipped their stocks to California.

Go West Young Man!

The journey to the goldfields was not an easy one. New Yorker William Swain wrote to his family and friends back east from 'the Diggings' in California on 6 January 1850:

> tell all whom you know that are thinking of coming that they have to sacrifice everything and face danger in all its forms, … thousands have laid and will lay their bones along the routes to and in this country. Tell all that death is in the pot if they attempt to cross the plains and hellish mountains …[4]

Road to the Diggings
Tinted lithograph
Read & Co., London, 15 February 1857

*(REX NAN KIVELL COLLECTION, S7454
BY PERMISSION, NATIONAL LIBRARY OF AUSTRALIA)*

Eugene Ring wrote of his experience crossing to California via Panama,

> that it was a fight for self from start to finish … the restraints of home were thrown off. No need of the mask of social life here, and men were reckless and natural …

Travelling from the paved streets of New York to the seemingly primitive Panama isthmus must have been quite a shock for the venturer unused to a 'natural' environment.

Placer Mining at Foster's Bar, California

Oil on millboard by Ernest Narjot, c. 1851

(COURTESY OF THE BANCROFT LIBRARY, UNIVERSITY OF CALIFORNIA, BERKELEY)

The waterwheel was one of the constant features of all the goldfields.

This painting by French artist, Narjot, shows miners digging in the banks of the river, feeding the sluice-boxes that washed the earth in the hope that nuggets would be revealed.

A Native American can be seen in the foreground leaning against a boulder, arrows slung across his back, his hunting bow in his right hand.

The Indians were the losers in the rush to the diggings that overtook their home-lands, destroying their hunting grounds and despoiling the river salmon runs that they had managed effectively for generations.

There were several tribes in the Sierra foothills when the rush began – the Maidu, Nisenan, Koukow, Miwok, Pomo and Yokuts – and a government report as early as 1848 recorded that half of the diggers were Indians. However, they were soon displaced by Europeans, and were exploited as cheap labour for these American settlers, who treated them just as the Hispanics had done before the rush.

Their population declined from 150,000 before 1845 to less than 30,000 in 1870. Syphilis, cholera, measles, smallpox and other epidemic diseases contributed heavily to this decline.

> I sat on the counter of a store in Jackson one evening, when a Digger Indian came in with several ounces of nuggets tied up in a rag.
>
> He put the package in one bowl of the scales and laconically spoke the word 'raisin'. The storekeeper leisurely walked around the counter, found a box of raisins and returning to the scales began dropping raisins, one at a time, as if they were too precious to part with, into the other bowl of the scale. When the raisins balance the gold, he emptied them into a paper bag which he handed to the Indian who departed satisfied.
>
> – *The Autobiography of Charles Peters; Miners in the Sierra.*

But later, after he had some success at the diggings he wrote again to his family still advising them to 'stay at home, for if my health is spared, I can get enough for both of us'.

He assures his family he has no regrets about venturing to the gold-fields. He remarks that, in fact, he had put on fifteen pounds in weight since leaving the East, and that he even seemed to grow in height, although he was suffering an attack of rheumatism, a complaint not uncommon among miners who spent half their days up to their knees in muddy water:

> I have not seen the hour yet when I regretted starting for California, nor have any one of our party ever regretted that we undertook the enterprise. I have seen hard times, faced the dangers of disease and exposure and perils of all kinds, but I count them as nothing if they enable me to place myself and my family in comfortable circumstances. [5]

Twenty-one-year-old Eugene Ring, another New Yorker, who had left his family behind and set off for the diggings in 1848 by way of Panama and South America, wrote of his first night on the trail:

> By sunset we had reached a country more rolling and more covered with trees and verdure ... we made our first camping out. Seated on the ground around a crackling blaze, we passed the saucepan and boiled tea around, and felt ourselves borderers indeed. The tent was spread over the branches of a fallen tree for those to sleep under who wished; but John and I feeling above such effeminacy, of which a Boone or a Crockett would be ashamed, wrapping our blankets around us and lay down with our feet to the remains of the fire and watched the stars ... until sleep closed our eyes. [6]

Bar Room in the Mines

Long Tom.   Lith & Published by Britton & Rei S F^a

This view of a simple, single-roomed saloon on the Californian goldfields shows miners taking their recreation after hard labour at the diggings.

They are seen here drinking (a common and extremely popular pastime) and playing cards.

Miners at work in a gully using a long sluice (long tom), shovels and picks.

As on the Australian diggings, the miners here in California preferred to work in teams, sharing the labour and the rewards. They teamed together for mutual protection, often as a result of sharing the long journey from either the eastern states or from the other side of the world.

The diggings were a huge 'melting pot' where mateships were formed among most unlikely companions, thrown together by circumstance rather than by design.

He also recorded his first view of the diggings around Coloma where the first gold had been found:

> In the centre of the valley through which runs the North Fork were clustered the various contrivances of buildings that made up the place, from a blanket hung across two poles, to a frame house. On the banks of the river and in the stream were the miners engaged in the different operations of gold washing. At the lower-end of the town on a bend of the river stood the 'Mill', celebrated as the spot where gold was first discovered, and beyond, the waters of the river hurried on.[7]

The exploits of the American West with its heroes, mountainmen, cowboys and Indians gripped the imagination of the mid-nineteenth-century desk-bound easterners who had looked on the goldfields as both a great Western adventure and a validation of their manhood. 'The West' entered the American psyche, just as the bushranger was to capture the imagination of Australian diggers several years later.

California Forty-Niner
Quarter-plate daguerrotype

(COLLECTION, AMON CARTER MUSEUM, FORT WORTH, TEXAS)

The art of photography was in its infancy in 1849, and it was such a novelty for the diggers that they rushed to have their images recorded to send back to their loved ones in the eastern cities.

This California Forty-Niner looks the epitome of the then popular idea of the western frontiersman: bushy-bearded and bold, with his bowie-knife thrust rakishly in his belt.

What would his family back east have made of this cavalier image? The rush to the diggings wrought great changes in such one-time office clerks, farm-hands and factory workers.

A pair of Colt pistols

Samuel Colt had done more to ensure 'that the West was won' than any 'gun-shootist', soldier or Indian fighter. His revolving chamber pistols were to become the weapon of choice on the goldfields, both in the United States and in Australia.

The revolutionary pistol had been in use by the US Army in California in the war with Mexico, and the pistols were favoured by the western rangers in their battle with the Comanche Indians.

The pistols came to the Australian gold-fields, where they were used by troopers, diggers and bushrangers alike.

The pistol at top is an 1851 Colt Navy which was more than likely lost by a Californian digger near Vaughan Springs, in Central Victoria. It was found in a creek-bed, the site of extensive sluicing operations by George Cox almost a century later.

An 1849 Colt 'Baby Dragoon' or 'Pocket Navy' is shown below. This lighter pistol was carried up to the Forest Creek diggings in 1851 by Castlemaine pioneer, George Yandell.

(COURTESY, DOUG MILLS, CASTLEMAINE — 1851 NAVY; FELIX CAPPY, CASTLEMAINE — 1849 POCKET NAVY)

For the native-born New Yorker, that first night around the campfire under starry skies was the stuff of penny novels, not of everyday experience.

Eugene Ring writes of an encounter with a Native American later on in his travels:

> as we neared each other I saw that he was a tall powerfully built man, the scantiness of his costume showing off his proportions to excellent advantage … an old red flannel shirt that would have reached the knees of a short man; carved reed passing through the lobe of each ear, and dangling against his neck, a bundle of arrows slung on his back, and a bow in his hand … I was remarkably attentive to his every point, movement and expression … particularly as I knew that in this section there had been much fighting between the miners and Indians; and many murders committed by the latter … he showed me the strength and force of his bow; which I offset by a sight of my Colts revolver for which he seemed to show a profound respect.[8]

The ship was built for Samuel Hall of East
Boston, who also owned the *Surprise*,
Gamecock and *John Gilpin*.

Hall claimed that the *California* would
'fully equal them in speed' and promised
that 'a very quick trip may be relied
upon'.

A Great Business Opportunity

With the diggings not yet two years old, steamboats were plying
the rivers, making four trips a day up the Sacramento River as far
as Yuba City. The creek where William Swain was camped had 'no
more than six houses built on it [when he had arrived]. Now, within a distance of ten miles, 150 dwellings are built'. In a letter of
16 January 1850 he added:

> The 'redskin' who four months ago roamed in his nakedness, the
> undisputed lord of these mountains and valleys, may be seen on the
> hilltops gazing with surprise upon the scenes below – the habitations,
> the deep-dug channels and the dams built. The sound of the labour-
> er's ax, shovel, pick and pan are sounds new to his ear, and the sight
> one to which his eye has never been accustomed.[9]

On the diggings money was certain to be made in the mines but
the merchants who supplied the miners made the most of all.
Swain finished his letter with the postscript: 'P.S. An onion in the
mines is worth a dollar, and boots $40 per pair. I have paid $8 for
a jar of pickles'. As on the Australian diggings, all kinds of goods
could be had, for a price, and most were ready to pay.

Among the many enterprising characters the women of California, like Mary Jane Caples, figured proudly:

> I concluded to make some pies and see if I could sell them to the
> miners for their lunches, as there were about one hundred men on
> the creek, doing their own cooking – there were plenty of dried
> apples and dried peeled peaches from Chili, pressed in the
> shape of a cheese ... so I bought fat salt pork and made lard, and my
> venture was a success. I sold fruit pies for one dollar and
> a quarter a piece, and mince pies for one dollar and fifty cents. I some-
> times made and sold a hundred in a day.[10]

Montez appears spelt with a 'z' in most
American references to her, but in
Australia her name was spelt Montes.
The reason is unknown, but much of what
is known of her life is almost unbelievable
anyway. The woman who was referred
to in the British press as 'La Belle
Horizontale' probably had much to put
behind her when she left for Australia in
1855.

Lola's House in Grass Valley
(COURTESY OF THE BANCROFT LIBRARY, UNIVERSITY OF CALIFORNIA, BERKELEY)

Lola arrived on the California diggings in 1853, where she established a saloon in the rough-and-ready mining town of Grass Valley.

Here the diggers certainly appreciated her ample charms and all the trappings of European elegance that she brought with her.

The saloon was furnished with Louis XVI cabinets, ormolu mirrors, gold leaf and jewellery, a large deep-red-topped billiard table with dragon-carved legs.

She had Kanaka houseboys and a pet bear was kept for the entertainment of her guests – numbered among them were senators, governors and millionaires, and, of course, the diggers, who adored her.

Lola left California for the diggings in Australia after her house burnt to the ground in 1855. She died penniless on the streets of New York in 1861.

Another sold some jewellery she didn't particularly value for $20: with this jewelry she purchased onions which she sold on arriving here for eighteen hundred dollars … she also brought some quinces & made quite a nice profit on them.[11]

While her husband was at his claim, Luzena Stanley Wilson used her time profitably:

I determined to set up a rival hotel. So I bought two boards from a precious pile belonging to a a man who was building the second wooden house in town. With my own hands I chopped stakes, drove them into the ground, and set up my table. I bought provisions at a neighbouring store, and when my husband came back at night he found, mid the weird light of the pine torches, twenty miners eating at my table. Each man as he rose put a dollar into my hand and said I might count him a permanent customer. I called my hotel El Dorado.[12]

There were also plenty of women who plied the oldest trade in the book, and dancers and entertainers such as the notorious Lola Montez were in great demand, card players being most popular:

In one corner a coarse-looking female might preside over a roulette-table, and perhaps in the central and crowded part of the room a Spanish or Mexican woman would be sitting at monte [a card game popular with Mexican gamblers] with a ciga-rita in her lips, which she replaced every few moments with a fresh one. In a very few fortunate houses, neat, delicate and sometimes beautiful French women were every evening to be seen in the orchestra. These houses, to the honour of the coarse crowd be it said, were always filled.[13]

Few women toiled at the diggings, although many had travelled from the East with their husbands; many had also sent their husbands ahead, looking to join them once they had become settled. One such women waited for three years for her husband, and then decided to pack up her children and set out to join him. When she finally arrived in the mining town of Jackson, she discovered that he had died just three months earlier. The journey out was rough enough, without turning straight around and heading back East, so she stayed, and took over the running of the store her husband had established, eventually becoming one of the success stories on those diggings.

Miners and Sluice Boxes
Quarter plate daguerreotype by Isaac Wallace Baker. c. 1850
(OAKLAND MUSEUM CALIFORNIA COLLECTION)

The miners destroyed the environment in the search for gold. They dammed rivers, cut down forests, diverted streams and turned the earth upside down in the relentless search for gold.

The Sierra foothills had been a pleasant green and wooded environment before the miners ripped it apart.

This scene is reminiscent of the photograph of the Forest Creek diggings (Australia) taken in 1858 by Antoine Fauchery (see page 211).

A devastated landscape was often all that was left after the miners moved on.

Baker in Front of Batchelder's Daguerreian Saloon
Quarter-plate daguerreotype, by Isaac Wallace Baker
(OAKLAND MUSEUM OF CALIFORNIA COLLECTION)

Perez Mann Batchelder arrived in Sonora, California, in 1851. The miners were very interested in the new medium of photography and were eager to have the exploits recorded wherever they could. Batchelder took his studio onto the goldfields where he was able to maximise his business opportunities.

This photograph shows Isaac Baker, one of Batchelder's business partners, in front of his 'Daguerreian Saloon'.

Chinese Gamblers, San Francisco

(Courtesy of the Bancroft Library, University of California, Berkeley)

– Californian Chinese –

The discovery of gold in California drew shiploads of Chinese away from their homeland, which had been through years of drought, then floods and often violent political rebellion.

Compared to the migrant ships that carried diggers from Europe, the 60-day Pacific crossing for the Chinese was likened to the journey to the Southern states of slave ships from Africa. The conditions aboard the Chinese vessels were extremely unpleasant.

When the Chinese landed in California they faced both discrimination and open hostility from the European diggers. Although they were at first small in number, they were regarded by the authorities as valuable contributors to the frontier society; they were always extremely hardworking. As their numbers grew and they spread across the goldfields, their European counterparts sought to force them back into the towns.

When, in 1852, Governor John Bilger declared that 'the Chinese were a menace to the state', anti-Chinese activity was almost sanctioned by government. Heavy licence fees and taxes were levied on the 'Celestials' in an attempt to drive them from the diggings.

However, the population of over 20,000 Chinese in California was not that easily dismissed. Even though they were harassed by officialdom, burdened by discriminatory taxation, and even attacked and murdered by vigilante groups, they did not leave and remained to become an integral part of American society.

Women who worked as cooks, or who took to washing the clothes of the miners, could make an easy $30 a day. One washerwoman claimed she had earned 'nine hundred dollars in nine weeks', and on hearing this one miner commented that if such women were common 'a man might marry and make money from the operation'.

The Chinese on the Diggings

There had been Chinese in California for many years before the goldrush, and they had always been held in high regard, their services as labourer, carpenter, cook and agricultural worker always in demand. Before the goldrush the Governor of California had declared that he regarded the Chinaman as 'one of the most worthy of our newly adopted citizens'. However, after the surface gold declined, and when the thousands who had travelled across America from the eastern states arrived only to discover that the good times were over, they too fell back on the streets of San Francisco and other frontier towns looking for the work that the Chinese had long regarded as their own.

At the end of the 1840s there were only about 4000 Chinese in California. Only one year later the Chinese population had risen to 25,000, and it was not long before the government that had held them up as paragons of hard work and enterprise was to legislate to drive them away. By 1852 open resentment of the Chinese was the norm. The Europeans, the 'Americans', declared that California and its gold belonged to them. The cry of 'California for the Americans' preceded the cry of 'No Chinese – Roll up! Roll up!' that was to ring out across the Australian diggings a decade later.

Just as happened on the Australian diggings, the Americans levied unreasonable taxes on the Chinese in a vain attempt to drive them from the diggings and from the country. In San Francisco the city attempted to enact what was known as the 'pig-tail ordinance', which required all convicted Chinese prisoners to have their hair shorn to within an inch of their heads, an almost unbearable insult to the proud Chinese.

In 1868 a treaty was agreed between the United States and China to grant 'reciprocal exemption from persecution on account of religious belief'[15] and to give Chinese citizens in the US the same privileges as citizens of America in China. The Americans saw this as a betrayal of the American workers, and resentment of the Chinese grew.

Across California the miners took the law into their own hands – just as they had joined together against the 'Sydney Ducks' and 'The Hounds', a gang of hooligans and ruffians who had terrorised the streets of San Francisco in the early days – and set themselves up as judge and jury, passing sentence this time on the Chinese. They attacked the Chinese, destroying their business houses in the hope that they would leave the territory. As in all such activities, however, someone eventually went too far: one night in Los Angeles a group of Americans attacked and murdered nineteen Chinese by hanging and shooting, and stole over $40,000 worth of their property.

Gold! Gold! Gold! – and more

Only three years after the 1848 goldrush had invigorated the United States and captured the imagination of the world, attention shifted across the Pacific to the new diggings in the Antipodes.

Edward Hargraves was one of hundreds who had left Australia for the diggings in California. While gaining invaluable experience in the California rush, he became convinced of the likelihood of deposits of gold in Australia – the hills of Sacramento, where he had first tried gold digging in 1849, bore a striking similarity to the country around Bathurst in central New South Wales.

Hargraves left California in 1851 and returned to Australia. As he boarded the ship an American digger called out to him, 'There's no gold in the country you're going to, and if there is, that darned Queen of yours won't let you dig it'.

Hargraves removed his hat and, striking a defiant pose, rejoined, 'There's as much gold in the country I am going to as there is in California; and Her Most Gracious Majesty the Queen, God bless her, will make me one of her gold commissioners'.

Panorama of Virginia City
Photograph by Carleton E. Watkins, c. 1876
(COURTESY OF THE BANCROFT LIBRARY, UNIVERSITY OF CALIFORNIA, BERKELEY)

Watkins, a San Francisco photographer, went to the Comstock Lode near Virginia City, Nevada, in 1876.

The view shows the frontier town surrounded by waste sand dumps, (a sight familiar to the citizens of the Australian towns of Bendigo and Ballarat towards the end of the nineteenth century), steam and smoke belching forth from the engine rooms of the stamping mills.

The goldfields did little to enhance the natural environment. In Australia the legacy was of fine 'Victorian' towns, but in many cases the American West seemed to lose its towns as quickly as the gold ran out, becoming ghost towns once mining had ceased.

Watkins's photographs were prepared as stereoscopes, a popular viewing method in the late nineteenth century. Double images, mounted side by side on card, were inserted in a viewing holder 15 cm in front of a pair of magnifying binoculars. The effect on the image was to create a three-dimensional impression of the object in the photographs.

A double-mounted image is shown in full above.

Now's the time to change your
    clime,
Give up work and tasking,
And all who choose be rich
    as Jews,
Even without asking,
California's precious earth,
Turns the new world frantic,
Sell your traps, and take a birth,
Across the wild Atlantic.
Everyone who digs and delves,
All whose arms are brawny,
Take a pick and heil yourselves –
Off to Californy.

Digging Gold
Artist unknown, c. 1850
From *Californian Pictorial Lettersheets*

The five-verse poem accompanying this curious engraving coins the phrase 'Californicators' at the end of the third verse as a reference to being deceived by the false promise of the diggings.

He was soon proved right when, in the first months of 1851, he washed out some gold beyond the Blue Mountains near Bathurst. Before long the ships that once had carried diggers away from Australia's shores now brought thousands of eager diggers and adventurers back to the great 'antipodean El Dorado'.

Gold had also been found in Montana as early as 1851, and again in 1858. The first really big discovery was at Bannack in 1862, and on 26 May 1863 the discovery at Alder Gulch once again fired the imagination of those in the south, but the gold rush to Montana was never to achieve the same legendary status as California's.

The finds were made at the same time as the news of Australian gold was first broadcast, and the biggest rush only a few months after the outbreak of the American Civil War.

While the discoveries of the late 1850s may have drawn miners back from the rush to Australia, the war that raged across the south had a devastating impact on every American state, almost overshadowing the excitement of the new goldfields.

The Montana gold rush saw gold worth over $100 million taken from a 14-mile-long valley near Virginia City. The rush had all the hallmarks of the good old days of 1849, but the diggings had lost their innocence – in the bad, bad West the gunfighter was abroad, and the diggings had become a hard, brutal place of outcasts, deserters, rough-riders, those without future, without homes, without hope. As on the subsequent Australian diggings, the grog and the girls were close at hand, ready to take that gold and send the diggers, pockets emptied, back to their claims.

In January 1891 prospector Bob Womack struck the El Paso lode in the Cripple Creek field, south of Denver, Colorado. On 4 July Winfield Scott Stratton staked out the aptly named 'Independence' claim, one that eventually returned him millions, ensuring his title as one of the 'Bonanza Kings' of Cripple Creek.

On 12 August 1896 gold was found on the Klondike Creek on the north-western Canadian border with Alaska. It was almost a year before the news of this discovery reached the United States, and the cry of 'North to Alaska' echoed across the continent. Over the next three years over 100,000 prospectors and boomers rushed onto that freezing goldfield.

Towards the end of 1899 gold was discovered near Nome, but this rush left 30,000 desperate men starving and stranded there on the beaches only a few months later.

~ *CHAPTER 2* ~

FIRST GOLD IN AUSTRALIA?

Gold Diggings at Ophir
Engraving
Picturesque Atlas of Australasia,
(ed. Andrew Garran), 1888

(PRIVATE COLLECTION)

(OPPOSITE)

Edward Hargraves Discovers Gold
Engraving
Picturesque Atlas of Australasia,
(ed. Andrew Garran), 1888

(PRIVATE COLLECTION)

Hargraves set out for Bathurst on
5 February 1851, convinced that he would
find gold in the creeks and valleys that had
so reminded him of California.

He was taken to Lewis Ponds Creek,
a tributary of Summerhill Creek, where

I found myself in the country that I was
so anxiously longing to behold again.
The resemblance of its formation to that
of California could not be doubted
or mistaken. I felt myself surrounded
by gold …

RUMOURS OF THE DISCOVERY of specimens of gold had been circulating throughout the colonies for many years before the Australian rush began in 1851. In earlier times specimens of gold embedded in quartz had been displayed as curiosities in the shops of Sydney. They were considered 'queer stuff' that had been picked up by shepherds following their flocks.

As early as 1823 a convict working on a road gang near Bathurst was flogged for having a lump of rough gold in his possession. He was charged with the theft of a gold watch that had disappeared about the same time as he was showing his nugget. As he wouldn't reveal where he had found his gold, it was concluded that he had stolen the watch and melted it down. The poor fellow received 150 lashes as the reward for his 'discovery'. Others who had also found nuggets were quick to learn from this salutary lesson. Another shepherd who brought several pieces of gold to Sydney converted them to cash 'with as little ceremony as possible'.

An old prisoner named MacGregor, who had been assigned to a squatter up-country, displayed a piece of pure, waterworn gold on one of his visits to Sydney. He was ordered to show the spot where it had been found on his master's run, but refused to do so, obviously hoping to keep the secret for himself. He was in prison for debt when the rush began in 1851, and a party eager to take off for the diggings paid his debts and secured his release in return for showing them where he had found his gold. However, once near his old haunts MacGregor disappeared.

1839 – The Australian Alps

Count Paul de Strzelecki found gold in the Australian Alps in 1839. Although he believed that it existed there in large quantities, he was also advised to keep his discovery from public knowledge, as the authorities were fearful of the consequences if the large and often restless convict population became aware of the existence of gold in the colonies.

1840 – Strathloddon, Victoria

A nephew of William Campbell, the licensee of the Strathloddon Run, found gold at Campbell's Creek in 1840. Campbell, when shown a pannikin filled with 'clean, pure, heavy gold', demanded that it be kept a secret 'lest people should come and turn up the soil and the shepherds abandon their flocks'. He feared undesirables would overtake his sheep run.

1844 – Hartley, New South Wales

The Reverend W. B. Clarke showed the Governor, Sir George Phipps, some specimens of gold that he had found near Hartley. Upon seeing the yellow specks the Governor reacted in the same manner as had Campbell four years earlier in Victoria, exclaiming, 'Put it away, Mr Clarke or we shall all have our throats cut'.

1846 – Montecute, South Australia

Although some gold had been mined at Montecute as early as 1846, at this time South Australia's mining destiny lay in its rich copper deposits. When the rush to New South Wales and Victoria almost depleted South Australia of its menfolk, there were attempts to find goldfields in the hills around Adelaide. However, gold in any quantity was not discovered until diggers returning from Victoria tried their luck in the creeks of South Australia late in 1852.

February 1849 – Glenmona Station, Victoria

A shepherd boy, Thomas Chapman, started a small goldrush after he found gold at 'Glenmona', Messrs McNeil and Hall's station in the

Edward H. Hargraves, Australian Gold Discoverer, first found at Ophir, Feby. 12th 1851
Hand-coloured lithograph by George French Angas.
Printed by C. Goddard, Sydney, c. 1851
(Rex Nan Kivell Collection, U4111 By Permission, National Library of Australia)

Hargraves, a veteran of the 1849 rush to Sacramento, is credited with the discovery of 'Australian gold' around Bathurst in New South Wales.

He may have taken the credit as the first, but many others had also been successful around the same time.

After Hargraves had successfully tried his hand in Summerhill Creek, he left the district until after John Lister and brothers William and Charles Tom, whom Hargraves had previously instructed in panning methods, found the first payable gold at Ophir.

It was Hargraves, however, who made the announcement when he took Ophir gold in to show the Colonial Secretary, and it was Hargraves who received both recognition and eventually reward.

Lister and Tom contested Hargraves's claims, but were defeated. They tried again forty years later, and, finally, received the recognition that Hargraves had long denied them.

***Gold Escort from Bathurst Arriving
at the Colonial Treasury, Sydney,
on 21 August 1851***
Pen and wash drawing by William Caxton,
Engraved version published *Illustrated
London News*, 24 January 1852

*(REX NAN KIVELL COLLECTION, T2241
BY PERMISSION, NATIONAL LIBRARY OF AUSTRALIA)*

The excitement caused by the arrival in
Sydney of the Government Gold Escort
and mail containing gold is recorded in
this contemporary drawing by the English
artist, William Caxton.

Pyrenees, 100 miles north-west of Melbourne. He claimed to have found 350 ounces of gold, which he sold to Brentani, the jeweller, in Melbourne. He agreed to lead a party back to the spot, but ran away as they neared the station, obviously fearing the consequences of his actions when discovered by his employer.

The news still got out, and was reported in the *Argus* on 6 February. Governor La Trobe sent troopers to the station to prevent any trespass on the land, but were surprised to find thirty or forty men already at work. Unfortunately, the diggers had dug only one small hole, and were quickly sent packing, their bags empty. They concluded that the nugget sold to Brentani must have been some melted plate, and that there was no gold in Victoria at all. Thomas Chapman was not seen again.

12 February 1851 – Summerhill Creek, New South Wales

When the veteran of the California diggings, Edward Hargraves, announced his find in the *Sydney Morning Herald* on 15 May 1851, there were already several hundred diggers working at Summerhill Creek, near Ophir.

Although Hargraves is credited with the discovery of gold in Australia, it took several years before he was granted the reward he believed was justly due to him. He was not shy, however, when he considered how important his find was for New South Wales.

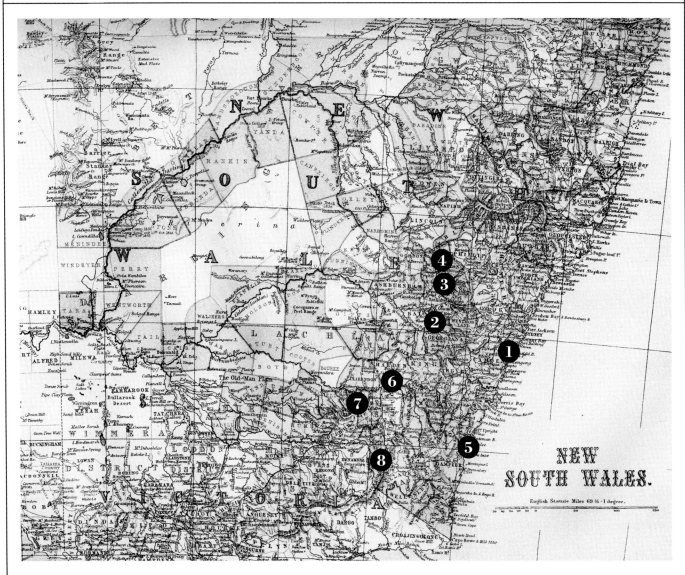

After he had washed out five panfuls of gravel from the creek-bed, finding gold in all but one, he had exclaimed to his companion:

> This is a memorable day in the history of New South Wales. For this day's work I shall be created a baronet, you will be knighted, and my old horse will be stuffed, put into a glass-case, and sent to the British Museum.[1]

His prophetic rebuff to the American digger several years earlier was fulfiled when he was made Gold Commissioner in Her Gracious Majesty's Colony of New South Wales soon after.

When the news broke that an Aboriginal shepherd boy working for Doctor Kerr, of Bathurst, had found a nugget in the Murroo Creek that weighed 2 hundredweight, the rush to these diggings took off in earnest. The *Bathurst Free Press* reported on 16 July 1851 that

> Bathurst is mad again. The delirium of gold fever has returned with increased intensity. Men meet together, stare stupidly at each other, talk incoherent nonsense and wonder what will happen next. A hundred-weight of gold is a phrase scarcely known in the English language. It is beyond the range of our ordinary ideas.*

Map of New South Wales, 1878
From *The History of Australia* by David Blair, McGready, Thompson and Niven, Glasgow, Melbourne & Dunedin, 1878
Lithograph by W. & A. K. Johnston, Edinburgh
(*La Trobe University, Bendigo, Library Collection*)

KEY:

1. Sydney
2. Bathurst
3. Hill End
4. Gulgong
5. Tilba Tilba
6. Young (Lambing Flat)
7. Temora
8. Kiandra

Cradling and Panning

Engraving by W. Hatherall, from *Cassell's Picturesque Australasia*, 1889

(PRIVATE COLLECTION)

James Esmond was the first to use a rocking cradle on the Creswick diggings.

Esmond had been in California and adapted the techniques he had seen in use there to the Victorian field.

---

* While nuggets of such size were certainly unknown on the Californian diggings, they were quite common in Australia.

The rush to the Colony of New South Wales that followed Hargrave's discovery echoed the rush to California, and again filled Australia with excitement. Just as in California, homesteads were left deserted, farms abandoned and towns emptied of men, the ships that had carried diggers from the east coast of Australia across the Pacific to California now headed south again, rushing the diggers home, while thousands of others poured across Australia's colonial boundaries, heading for the goldfields.

Victoria had been separated from colonial rule by New South Wales on 11 November 1850, and it was only six months later that Hargraves announced his discovery. So many able-bodied men left Victoria for New South Wales that La Trobe (now the Governor of the new Colony of Victoria) posted a reward for the discovery of Victorian gold in the hope of reversing the depopulation of the newly proclaimed colony.

From then on, it seemed that every itinerant shepherd, every farmboy, carrier or journal-bound office clerk spent their idle moments dreaming of discovering gold.

June 1851 – Clunes, Victoria

Clunes claims to be the site of the first discovery of gold in Victoria, even though there is evidence of gold found elsewhere earlier. William Campbell (of Strathloddon Run) claimed to have found gold as early as 1840 at Campbell's Creek, near Castlemaine, years before Hargraves had made his discovery at Summerhill Creek in New South Wales.

The news of the Californian diggings had encouraged Campbell to do some further exploring of his own. He had examined geological reports from California and concluded, in much the same way as Hargraves, that gold should be found in similar country. On a visit to fellow-squatter Donald Cameron's station, 'The Clunes', he investigated a large quartz vein and concluded 'that it was the most likely place I knew to find gold in'. At this time Campbell did little to

MAP OF THE ROADS to all GOLD MINES in VICTORIA.
Showing the Cross Roads from one Mine to another, with indications of various Stations.
Divided into Squares of ten Miles, to easily calculate the distance of any New Mines when discovered

Lithographed by J. B. Philp.

further his investigation until on a later visit he encouraged Cameron and others to accompany him on a 'search for gold'.

> In the course of a few minutes I had the satisfaction of having the correctness of my expressed opinions verified by the discovery of a gold mine in Australia, on the exact spot where I said I thought it would be found.[2]

It became known later that Campbell had found rich golden stone on Donald Cameron's station as far back as March 1850, but the find was concealed until Campbell announced his discovery in a letter to Mr James Graham, 'a prominent public man in Melbourne', where he stated that, on 10 June 1851, 'within a radius of 15 miles of Burbank [near Clunes], on another party's station, he had procured specimens of gold'.[3]

Just as so many other discoveries before them had been kept secret, they also kept this one to themselves for fear of the consequences for the squatter if his run were to be overtaken by diggers. Under pre-emptive rights Cameron had ownership of the land on which his homestead was built, so at least that was safe from digging, but the rest of Clunes was open for exploitation if the news got out.

Map of the Roads to all the Gold Mines in Victoria, showing the Cross Roads from one Mine to another, with indications of various Stations. Divided into squares of ten miles to easily calculate the distance of every new mine when discovered.
Lithograph by James B. Philp, c. 1853
(LA TROBE PICTURE COLLECTION, STATE LIBRARY OF VICTORIA)

This map clearly indicates the major goldfields of central Victoria; from the left showing Ballarat, Mt Alexander, Mt Korong, Bendigo, McIvor and then the Ovens in the upper right.

Although this map is clearly not to scale, the information contained would have served the diggers well on such a journey unaided by signage.

From the memoirs of Mary Ann Berry:

On the way [there] we saw, near springs a great herd of kangaroos bounding along. We arrived on 15th August '53. I think it highly probable that I was the first white woman to set foot in that part … There was a terrible bushfire on the 9th January, 1854. We had to take the children and stores to a place of safety, and burn a patch round the tents, by which we managed to save them.

Father's bad luck was persistent, as the holes he sank were duffers. Eventually he sold one claim for £1; the purchaser secured £500 of gold from it!

Mrs Berry was the daughter of John Mason, who was associated with the first discovery of gold at the head of Creswick Creek.[4]

From *Creswick Memoirs* (collected 1908–12), first published in the *Creswick Advertiser* in 1940.

– J A M E S   E S M O N D –

James Esmond had returned to Australia from America on the same ship as Edward Hammond Hargraves, finder of the first gold in NSW, accompanied by the brother of James Marshall, who had found the first gold in California.

Esmond claimed to have been the first to use a puddler in Victoria.

When the rush to the goldfields in New South Wales caused a mass migration from Victoria, spreading panic across the colony, Cameron decided that his discovery should be made known, hoping to stem the rush to the north. The announcement was made to the Mining Committee in Melbourne on 8 July 1851, and within days 'a rush of diggers was soon upon the ground, where they remained working until a richer mine was discovered near Buninyong'.

Once the rush was on and the shepherds had become diggers, and the diggers were turning up the soil, the claimant to be the first to have discovered gold on any field where the government could levy a licence fee was entitled to receive a good reward. Campbell's reticence, and later claim, led to confusion, as there were others who were sure that they had been the first.

James William Esmond, a veteran of the Californian diggings who had returned to Australia on the same ship as Hargraves, was erecting a building on another station nearby. German physician-turned-prospector, Dr George Bruhn, was looking for gold in the Pyrenees when he saw specimens at Cameron's station that he was informed had come from Clunes. In the course of his travels he told Esmond. Esmond put the experience gained in 1849 to work, and he, too, found gold at Cameron's station on or about 28 June 1851.

Although it seems that it was Campbell who made the first discovery at Clunes, Esmond was the first to work the claim. All three – Campbell, Bruhn and Esmond – were rewarded.

July 1851 – Anderson's Creek, Warrandyte, Victoria

At almost the same time, Louis John Michel and a small party of prospectors found gold at Anderson's Creek, north-east of Melbourne, near Warrandyte. Henry Frencham, who was to feature prominently in a later discovery at Bendigo, was also in this party.

20 July 1851 – Mt Alexander, Victoria

From the *Argus*, 8 September 1851:

> Dear Sir,
> I wish to publish these few lines in your valuable paper that the public may know that there is gold found in these ranges about four miles from Dr Barker's home station, and about a mile from the Melbourne road, at the Southernmost point of Mount Alexander, where three men and myself are working. I do this to prevent parties getting us into trouble, as we have been threatened to have the constables fetched, for being on the ground. If you will have the kindness to insert this in your paper that we are prepared to pay anything that is just, when the Commissioner comes.
> In the name of the party,
> John Worley,
> Mount Alexander Ranges, September 1, 1851.

Three shepherds and a bullock driver were working in the outer reaches of Dr Barker's Ravenswood No 1. Run in the rolling foothills of Mt Alexander in central Victoria. In July they found some small nuggets of dull yellow metal in the creeks at what was eventually known as Specimen Gully, the first gold discovery on what became the Mt Alexander goldfields. However, when two of them, John Worley and Christopher Peters, returned to the homestead and showed the specimens to the overseer, they were treated with derision.

Although gold had been discovered at nearby Clunes some months earlier, it was the announcement of their find in the *Argus* newspaper on 8 September that sparked the biggest rush of all to the Australian

Mount Alexander
News Letter of Australasia,
No. 75, November 1862
(CASTLEMAINE ART GALLERY
& HISTORICAL MUSEUM COLLECTION)

The mountain was named by Major Mitchell, who passed this way in September 1836. When Mitchell wrote in his journal on 30 June 1836, 'As I stood, the first European intruder on the sublime solitude of these verdant plains', he had no inkling of the great invasion that was to destroy this solitude for ever.

South Australian Police Commissioner Alexander Tolmer, travelling through here in March 1852, described the hustle and bustle he had observed on these diggings:

> Let the reader imagine thousands of bearded, un-couth looking men, dressed in dirty short jumpers, with trousers the colour of yellow ochre, busily at work – some filling carts with gold-impregnated earth, and carting it to the bank of the creek, lined with cradles, where washers were in full operation.
>
> The cradles were placed lengthwise with the water which was at the time of the thickness of cream, and of a yellow colour. Those who worked the cradles, held the handles with one hand, and with the other broke the lumps of earth with a stick, and stirred up the contents, keeping the cradles constantly rocking, whilst others stood by with ladles of some kind, and kept baling water continuously into them.
>
> Others again were carefully washing into large tin dishes, the deposits that had fallen through the sieves of the cradles and onto the boards beneath
> — Alexander Tolmer, *Reminiscences of an Adventurous and Chequered Career at Home and in the Antipodes,* 1882

Tolmer's South Australian Gold Escort carried the first gold back to Adelaide in November 1851 (see page 169).

THE GOLD-FIELDS OF AUSTRALIA : BALLARAT.

The Gold-fields of Australia, Ballarat
Wood engraving published *London Illustrated Times,* 8 July 1865, after a watercolour by George Rowe

(REX NAN KIVELL COLLECTION, U4951 BY PERMISSION, NATIONAL LIBRARY OF AUSTRALIA)

It is obvious that Mr Hiscock's discovery at Buninyong, by attracting great numbers of diggers to the neighbourhood, was the cause of the discovery of Ballarat. Ballarat is, in fact, upon the same range, and at no great distance

– so concluded the committee in 1853 conferring upon Hiscock his reward of £1000.[5]

A young man left his native shores,
For trade was bad at home;
To seek his fortune in this land
he crossed the briny foam;
And when he went to Ballarat.
It put him a glow.
To hear the sound of the windlass,
And the cry 'Look out below'.

– From 'Look Out Below' by Charles Thatcher.

diggings. Mt Alexander and Forest Creek were the diggings that captured the imagination of 'new chums' the world over.

The Castlemaine field was to become the richest alluvial field the world had ever seen. By the middle of November it was estimated that 67,000 ounces of gold had been taken from the district. Ten thousand ounces were sent to Melbourne by escort on 27 September.

By Christmas 1851 250,000 ounces of gold had been taken from the central Victorian region. Major Mitchell had crossed through the region in 1836, which was described by him as 'Australia Felix' a richly pastured land. The thousands of diggers who plundered Mitchell's dream following the discoveries of 1851 laid the foundations of a society, based not on agriculture and sheep-herding but on quartz, iron and steam.

8 August 1851 – Buninyong and Ballarat, Victoria

Before the goldrush, Ballaarat (later spelt Ballarat) was an almost forgotten outpost of the Yuille brothers' sheep-run. Buninyong was at the centre of several runs taken up by squatters in 1838. The first settlement began there in 1841 when timber splitters and teamsters settled their families in the valley. There were over fifty families in the area, with shepherds and timber-cutters on the lonely outreaches of the runs.

A hut, built by pioneer George Gabb, served as a hotel, and Campbell and Woolley moved their store next to it. A blacksmith soon joined them, and in 1844 Dr Power set up his medical practice. In 1847 the Learmonths sponsored the building of a church and schoolroom, and the Presbyterian Minister, Rev. Thomas Hastie, became the first clergyman and teacher in the district. At this time Buninyong was the largest inland township in Victoria. It could have become an important trading centre but for Hiscock's discovery on 2 August 1852.

Rev. Hastie later described the peaceful valley before the rush where he 'often passed the spot on which Ballarat is built … and there could not be a prettier spot imagined'.[6]

Mr George Inness, a resident of Buninyong since 1845, informs me that he discovered gold in July of that year at the Black Hill, Ballarat, but he kept the circumstance a secret. His movements were watched however by Hiscock the blacksmith, who was in the habit of sharpening the miner's picks. Hiscock some time afterwards began prospecting on his own and found gold at Hiscock's. If Inness' statement is correct the existence of gold was known in Victoria much earlier than is generally supposed – C. W. Langtree (1888).[7]

Thomas Hiscock is given the credit for the discovery of the Ballarat goldfields. In early August 1851, while he was searching for a lost cow, he picked up a piece of gold-studded quartz. Within a few days he had washed out two and a half ounces of gold from the gravels in the area around the Yarrowee Creek. Some of the diggers heading for Clunes, only 27 miles to the north, heard the news and diverted to Buninyong – and a rush was on.

Ballarat in 1851, as viewed from Bath's Hotel
The Discovery of Gold – 1851, engraving from *Victoria and Its Metropolis*,
(PRIVATE COLLECTION)

Hundreds on hundreds of tents were clapped down in the most dusty and miserable of places; and all the ground was perforated with holes, round or square, some deeper, some shallower, some dry, some full of water.

All between the holes the hard, sand-coloured clay lay in ridges, and you had to thread your way carefully amongst them if you did not mean to fall in.

Still horrider stenches from butchers' shops and garbage pits: the scene thickened, and tents after tents, stores and bark-huts crowded upon you like a great fair.

The discoverer of the first gold on the Ballarat diggings, Thomas Hiscock, was born in Berkshire, England, in 1809. With his wife Phoebe, and their two sons, Thomas and John, they sailed from London aboard the *Caroline* arriving in Geelong in 1841.

On arrival he was able to obtain work as a blacksmith, and in 1844 moved his family up to the growing settlement at Buninyong, where he was a general storekeeper and blacksmith.

After gold had been found in New South Wales, the government of Victoria offered a reward for a similar find in the new colony. Unbeknown to Hiscock when he made his discovery in August, James Esmond had had similar success in Clunes just weeks before.

Hiscock communicated his find to the editor of the *Geelong Advertiser* on 10 August, and they urged the government to reward both men as the discoverers of Victorian gold. Hiscock eventually was awarded £1000.

Only a few years after his discovery at Buninyong, he was visiting the rush at Mt Alexander when he caught a cold, which developed into inflammation of the lungs, 'from which he was unable to rally'; he died on 25 July 1855 at the early age of 46 years.

– T H O M A S   H I S C O C K –

When the first Commissioner came onto these diggings to collect the first licence fees, the early Buninyong yield was very poor, and the disappointed diggers were either unable to pay or saw no reason to give what they had to the government. Most of the diggers simply vanished into the bush.

On 18 August 1851 the government proclaimed legislation granting the Crown rights to all gold found on Crown lands, while at the same time ruling that it was illegal to be found searching for gold without a licence. A fee was set at 30 shillings a month, imposed on all male adults on the goldfields, whether engaged in mining activity or not. It was this fee, introduced on 1 September that was eventually to cause this and the subsequent Governor so much trouble.

As Commissioner Armstrong patrolled these disappointing diggings, a crowd of diggers took refuge in Mother Jamieson's Inn, maybe the first inkling that the Ballarat diggers were unlikely to bow to the demands of the government officials. Among them was John Dunlop, a seventy-year-old veteran of the Battle of Waterloo, and a young Irishman, James Regan. They slipped quietly away from the Inn, and made their way into the darkly wooded forest. They trekked along the White Horse Range on Yuille's Ballarat station, until they came upon a small hill on the northern edge of the run. Towards the end of August Dunlop and Regan panned the first gold of the Ballarat diggings in a creek running south from the foot of this hill, a tributary of the Yarrowee. The point, known later by the misnomer of Poverty Point, was one gully away from the more aptly-named Golden Point, where over 20,000,000 ounces of Ballarat gold were later found.

Within six weeks there were 2000 tents near Golden Point, with over 10,000 men encamped there, and the din from the rocking of the cradles could be heard over three miles away. Antoine Fauchery recorded the scene:

No doubt the place I am passing through was not considered rich enough to be worth working; but a hundred paces further on still, the holes are closer together, and about ten minutes after finding these first traces of gold-seeking, at the top of a plateau at the extremity of which the road ends, the horizon widens and I am overlooking 'The Ballarat Gold Fields'.

The sun is declining. At my feet I can just manage to see the diggers' tents scattered about. Workers, with pick and shovel on their shoulder, fan out in all directions. Fires are lit at different points, and my heart

Diggers on the Road to Bendigo

Engraving from the *Picturesque Atlas of Australasia* (ed. by Andrew Garran) 1888

(PRIVATE COLLECTION)

Melbourne Morning Herald,
20 December 1851

We are assured by eye witnesses on whom we rely that two successful miners in their respective sprees acted thus: – One placed a 5 pound note between two slices of bread and butter, and remarking that he relished a costly sandwich, deliberately ate it. The other equally lucky (and we presume equally glorious) lighted his pipe with a 5 pound Bank of Australia note, remarking at the time to the company present that he did not care a .... for money.

We believe him.

grows heavy at the thought that here I am, alone once more, about to enter a new sphere. The barking of dogs warns me that it would be imprudent to venture here at this hour, and, rolled up in my blanket, and stretched out at the foot of a tree, I put off until tomorrow my first appearance on this stage.[9]

Between 21 September and 31 December 1851, 30,323 ounces of gold from this field were carried by the gold escorts to Melbourne.

When the news of the rush to Ballarat reached England early in 1852, hundreds of experienced coal and tin miners from Cornwall, Scotland and Wales set out on the six-month-long voyage. They landed in Port Phillip, only to be told that Ballarat was played out. When they arrived on the diggings, they found them almost deserted.

October 1851 – Sandhurst (Bendigo), Victoria

When 24-year-old William Johnson from Sydney picked up from the Bendigo Creek a bit of slate with a small spur of gold imbedded, he showed it to the shepherd, old Ben Hall. After examining the slate, Hall threw it away.

The area around a chain of waterholes where Golden Gully met the Bendigo Creek was frequented by sheep-herders. However, it was not until Margaret Kennedy and her companion, Mrs Farrell, had gone to the Bendigo Creek and constructed a 'mia-mia' (an Aboriginal-style hut, resembling a tent, made from sticks and bark) while their husbands were away that any serious investigation of the potential of the creek was attempted.

Specks of gold had been picked up at various times. The squatters were well aware of the impact a gold find would have on their prospects, so they tried to keep any news of gold from the shepherds and the shearers until the sheds had been cleared. It was impossible, though, to keep a lid on the rumours of gold discoveries in central Victoria, particularly as such news had so long been awaited. The news of the find on Dr Barker's Ravenswood No.1 Run on the

Christopher and Theodore Ballerstadt sold their claim on the Victoria Reef, Bendigo, to George Lansell, who later became known as the 'Quartz King' of Bendigo.

Lansell built his mansion, 'Fortuna', on the site of Ballerstadts' original house.

Ballerstadts' claim was one of the first to have been worked on Bendigo.

(LA TROBE PICTURE COLLECTION, STATE LIBRARY OF VICTORIA)

From *The Annals of Bendigo, 1867*

– MARGARET KENNEDY –

– HENRY FRENCHAM –

foothills of Mt Alexander rapidly made its way into every shepherd's hut across the rolling valleys. Mrs Kennedy and Mrs Farrell had been to Forest Creek, and observed for themselves the method of gold panning there.

Kennedy's husband was overseer of the Ravenswood Station and Patrick Farrell was a cooper employed by Gibson and Fenton to construct barrels for tallow, as Fenton's flocks were scabby and he had decided to boil them down after the shearing had finished.

Farrell had no work at the beginning of September, so after obtaining some rations he said he was going down to Forest Creek but, unknown to Fenton and Gibson, he turned back for the Bendigo Creek. Farrell, his wife and Margaret Kennedy were quite successful in their endeavours, stashing away quite sizable number of nuggets. But just as Worley and Peters had learnt at Specimen Gully only months before, itinerant shepherds panning for gold on the squatter's run enjoyed little favour from the authorities.

The well-known chain of waterholes was not necessarily an isolated or lonely spot. By all records there seemed to have been people coming and going all the time. William Sandbach and his brother, who also worked on Gibson and Fenton's station, shearers' cook Johnson, John Ross, shepherd Ben Hall, hut-keeper Charles Asquith, someone named O'Donell, Fenton, Robinson and James Ross were all in and out of the district, with one eye on the sheep and another in the gullies.

Mrs Kennedy feared that 'they would be murdered some night, as it was known they had gold', so they armed themselves in their primitive shelter. One night, listening to the sounds of the bush outside, they heard footsteps trampling through the bush. Patrick Farrell had loaded his pistol with cooper's rivets, and Mrs Kennedy took up a rusty old bayonet, while Mrs Farrell armed herself with a tomahawk as her husband fired off a shot into the night. 'We will fight for it', he declared, but it appears that the shot had frightened the intruder away. It was only after this event that Farrell went off to Forest Creek and obtained digging licences for them all.

Returning to the sheep run some weeks later, the shearer's cook, Johnson, again saw Mrs Kennedy and Mrs Farrell with their skirts hitched up, knee-deep in clay, filling tin cans with gold. He also observed old Ben Hall scooping up a billycan of gold, letting the pieces trickle slowly through his fingers, and exclaiming, 'This is better than shepherding, boys!'

Kangaroo Flat
Watercolour by George Rowe, 1857
(COLLECTION – BENDIGO ART GALLERY)

This painting by Rowe shows a scene familiar to all who ventured onto the diggings. Tents line the meandering creek, and the immediate landscape is denuded of trees as the diggers cleared almost all the land around for shaft timbers, firewood and building materials.

It took almost a century before the vegetation returned to these valleys, but the great stands of box and ironbark eucalypt were gone forever. Only scrub and stringybark grew in their place.

The creek-beds became the site for villages, then the towns, and English trees soon lined the streets, irrevocably changing the nature of this ancient landscape.

It has long been debated who actually made the first discovery at Bendigo, but Mrs Kennedy and Mrs Farrell were probably at the right place at the right time. So, it appears, was the journalist and avid prospector, Henry Frencham, and his party of Robert Atkinson and fellow-reporter James Ogilvie Ross, who had followed the creek from the White Hills, picking up gold as they went, and were now prospecting very close by. By this time Frencham was quite an experienced prospector, and had been scouring the creeks around the White Hills north of Mt Alexander, making his way along the creek on the Ravenswood Run, picking up 'specs' as he went.

At the same time Fenton and Gibson were also prospecting in a nearby valley, convinced that they too had found the first gold in the Bendigo area.

After Frencham also saw Kennedy and Farrell hard at work, he dispatched one of his party, the one-armed Henry Byass, to Forest Creek to seek out Captain Harrison, to report that gold was discovered on the Bendigo Creek. The announcement was made as Byass posted bills across the diggings along Forest Creek, that 'women were getting quart-pots of gold on Bendigo Creek'.

February 1852 – Beechworth, Victoria

Gold had been discovered as early as 1846 in circumstances almost exactly the same as the find at Sutter's Mill in California in the same year. It was not until the rest of Victoria was overwhelmed by gold fever that any serious discovery was made.

The first recorded discovery of gold in Beechworth was near one of the outlying shepherd's huts on David Reid's 'Wooragee' station, a large sheep run that soon became the centre in the north-east of the same frantic activity that was happening further south.

*Spring Creek Diggings,
Beechworth, 1867*

The Woolshed Diggings
Oil by A. W. Eustace, 1856

The Woolshed diggings were on David
Reid's 'Wooragee' station. As often
happened, the activities of the miners
forced the squatters to look elsewhere
for land suitable for their investment.

Reid left 'Wooragee' and took up
grazing at Barnawatha station.

I was at my station at Wooragee [afterwards known as Gemmel's station]. In the evening, two young men came and asked to stay for the night. I got into a conversation with them, and they mentioned that they had been with Mr Smyth surveying the mountains on geodetic work, and that they had been discharged. They said to me, 'This looks like gold country'.

I asked them if they knew anything about gold, and they said they had been to the California diggings, and that if they had the tools they would try that part of the country … My shepherd, a man called Howell … asked to be allowed to go with the two men … On the third day after they started, they discovered gold on the creek in front of the outstation hut, that stood where Beechworth now stands.

The three men sunk some shallow holes two to three feet deep on the edge of the creek, and washed the stuff on the rock in a dish. Howell returned and mentioned the matter to me. Then the news got about that gold was found in the creek, and men came from Albury and from Wangaratta … They sank alongside the first claims, and got good gold. Then a great rush set in, and men came from all parts.[10]

Reedy Creek, four miles from Beechworth, soon became the

richest gold-producing area on the field. John Johnson, from Sydney, first worked the creek in 1853. He was soon joined by Duncan (Dan) Cameron, James Lonnie and others. It was Dan Cameron who, in 1856, when campaigning for his election as the first Member of Parliament for Beechworth, created a world-wide news phenomenon, when he rode into Beechworth on a circus-pony that was shod with 'golden' horseshoes.

May 1852 – Yackandandah, north-eastern Victoria

The diggings at Yackandandah were opened by a digger named Carrol.

In an article written to the Mines Department in Melbourne many years later (1905) David Reid explains how he had found gold in Yackandandah many years before Carrol in early 1846, in exactly the same way as gold had been found in California:

> In 1845, or the beginning of 1846, I commenced the flour-mill, long known as Reid's Mill. We were cutting a race to bring water to the wheel. One day we were examining the stuff being dug out, and I took up a bit, and said, 'This looks like gold'. Afterwards gold was discovered in California in a similar way, later on, the ground around Reid's Mill was worked for gold, so that I actually found gold before its discovery in California, by Sutter in his mill race.[11]

Autumn 1852 – Eaglehawk, Victoria

The rush to Eaglehawk began in the autumn of 1852. It was followed by further rushes to the Whipstick and the low scrubland of Myer's Flat later in winter. When the news reached the Beechworth diggings on the Ovens River, so many picked up their picks and shovels and struck out for Eaglehawk that Beechworth was almost deserted.

The dense scrubland known as the Whipstick was crisscrossed with the 'circuitous, detached and disconnected' tracks of the diggers. This was uninviting country, flat, hot, gravelly, and in places almost impenetrable, men easily became lost, and several died, unable to find their way out, but it held the nuggets that were the goal of every

The New Rush at Myers Creek
(6–7 miles from Sandhurst)
Wood engraving by A. C. Cooke, *Illustrated Australian News*, Ebenezer and David Syme, Melbourne, 20 August 1867
(La Trobe Picture Collection, State Library of Victoria)

Miners can be seen crowding around a wagon which has arrived on these scrubby diggings just to the north of Sandhurst (Bendigo).

Licences are being sold from the cart which bears a banner reading: 'MINER'S RIGHTS, W C O D.'

> The hills are crowded with tents, among which are stores, butchers' and blacksmiths' shops and places where the initiated may obtain spirits at about 1/- per nobbler.
> When the police discover a sly grog shop they set fire to the tent and burn it with all it contains; for this reason the grog is generally kept in a small tent adjoining the one in which the proprietor resides, who of course knows nothing about the tent with the grog.

– Diary of Edward Snell, 8 April 1852

Miners on Mt Dromedary, (Tilba Tilba)

(Rex Nan Kivell Collection, TT138 By Permission, National Library of Australia)

Mt Dromedary is a large granite boulder-strewn outcrop just off the coast near Narooma, on the central New South Wales coast.

The difficult terrain meant that miners employed some creative architectural style to keep their tents anchored to the hillside.

Winches, pulleys and flying foxes were used to bring gear up and down, as well as buckets of ore for crushing.

Miners' Camp on the South Australian Diggings

(Photograph Courtesy of the State Library of South Australia)

Wherever the diggers went they had to make do with the materials at hand to create some rudimentary shelter for themselves.

It was only in later years, after the first rushes had died away, that attempts at 'permanent' dwellings were made.

This crude hut made of packing cases, bush poles, bark and scrub is home and hearth to quite a large party of diggers.

digger. 'Old Harry' Moorehead and 'Old Dan' Stewart were just two of those who were rewarded with a 22 ounce nugget; others found nuggets weighing 63 and 372 ounces.

The scrub was so thick that, at a place called 'Drunken Scotchmen's', two 'tall, bushy-whiskered mates' were able to work away undetected, coming out every couple of weeks to sell their pockets full of gold. It was only when their pack-horses were followed back into the scrub that they had to share their discovery. The rush to their remote gully was then on.

1852 – Tilba Tilba, New South Wales

Traces of gold were first discovered in the streams flowing from Mt Dromedary in 1852 by a clerical geologist, the Rev. William B. Clarke. There was also a short rush to the mountain in 1860, but, even though this had died almost as quickly as it had started, the Dromedary was not forgotten.

October 1852 – Onkaparinga, South Australia

W. Chapman, a digger returned from Bendigo, washed out some gold in the Onkaparinga valley near the old Wheatsheaf Inn on the Echunga Road. The next day he was asked to do the same again, only this time he was watched by a crowd of over sixty, including the Colonial Secretary and several mounted police troopers. To guard against fraud, Chapman was

I have got it

Eug. v. Guérar
Melbourne

The diggings in the Barossa were set among hills and valleys similar to those around Bathurst and Mt Alexander.

Although almost all of the likely young men from South Australia had left and tried their luck, first in New South Wales and then in Victoria, it was after they returned home, their pockets filled with nuggets, that they looked for gold in terrain similar to the diggings they had left behind.

This digger celebrates his good fortune as he washes out a pan with a good show of nuggets. Von Guérard's painting records the bustling activity on the early alluvial goldfields, with pan, puddling tub, windlass and shaft in evidence.

ordered to take off his coat and roll up his shirtsleeves (any claim on the reward for such a discovery was closely investigated). He scooped up a dish full of dirt, washed it through, poured the dirt off – and showed nothing.

The crowd was easily disappointed, and soon became angry at the 'swindler' Chapman. At that point there were many who would have liked to hang him from the nearest tree. Just as well for Chapman, he performed 'a quick twist of the dish, the rest of the dirt was shot out, and gold was seen gleaming in the bottom of the pan'.[12]

The rush to the Onkaparinga was on. There was so much excitement that day that everybody rushed to get something to use for washing out gold, even hats were used to pan out the stream, and there was so much noise that 'the horses broke their fastenings and galloped away into the bush'.[13]

Some mines were soon worked in the Barossa, at Gawler and Mt Pleasant, and there were some that were very rich indeed. However, the most gold South Australia ever saw was that carried back to the South Australian Treasury by Alexander Tolmer's escorts or brought back in returning diggers' swags.

When describing the rush to Echunga in his report of 2 October 1852, the Assistant Gold Commissioner remarked that it was unlike any of the other three eastern colonial fields:

> since my last report sixty licences have been issued, making it a total of three hundred and fifty-six … many families of respectability have arrived, and are now living in commodious tents. The presence of well dressed women and children gives to the goldfields, apparently distinguished for decorum, security and respectability. From the feeling of greater security and comfort, combined with cheapness of living, all classes of diggers are unanimous in their preference of this place to Victoria. [Signed] A. J. Murray.[14]

Luck at Last
Engraving from *Cassell's Picturesque Australia, 1889*
After a painting by G. R. Ashton
(PRIVATE COLLECTION)

South Australia had never been a transportation colony, so its citizens appeared to be, or were assumed to be, a bit above the rougher society of Victoria and New South Wales, and most certainly above those of Van Diemen's land.

The *South Australian Register* of 7 February 1853 reported the early demise of the Adelaide diggings:

> *The Gold Fields.*– Although there is at the diggings everything to indicate gold in large quantities, none have succeeded in realising their hopes. The majority content themselves with what they can get on Chapman's Hill and Gully, knowing that, if a fresh place is discovered, they will stand as good a chance as those who have spent months in trying to find better ground. The quantity of gold taken to the Assay-office, during four consecutive weeks, amounting to less than four thousand ounces, the Governor has proclaimed that after the 17th of February the office is closed.[15]

February 1853, Stringer's Creek (Walhalla)

Ex-convict Edward Stringer, and mates, William Griffiths and McGregor, found the first gold that opened the Walhalla diggings.

June 1853 – Mt Tarrangower (Maldon), Central Victoria

Tarrangower had been a pastoral run since 1839 when squatter Lachlan McKinnon settled in the area now known as Maldon. Typically, McKinnon had followed in the footsteps of Major Mitchell, and like so many other Scottish gentlemen he had taken up a large tract of land on which to fatten his flocks.

For once the discovery of gold is not credited to a shepherd occupying his daylight hours washing a bit of stuff out in the creek and filling his pannikin with nuggets. At Tarrangower it was a Polish sea-captain turned prospector who had taken to the hills in search of gold. Captain John Mechosk found the first gold at Tarrangower in June 1853. This discovery saw the end of the pastoral era, as over 20,000 diggers rushed to the granite hills in search of alluvial gold.

A Lament for My Thirty Shillings
Dedicated to the Echunga Victims

My one pound ten! my one pound ten!
  I paid as licence Fee;
Ah! Cruel Bonney! pray return
  That one pound ten to me.

When to Echunga diggings first
  I hastened up from town,
Thy tent I sought with anxious care
  And paid the money down.

And though my folly ever since
  I bitterly deplore,
It soothes my mind to know there were
  Three scores of fools before.

Then, Bonney, listen to my lay,
  And if you wish to thrive,
Send back the money quick to me,
  To number sixty-five.

Who wants but little here below,
  Nor wants that little long,
Had better to Echunga go,
  And not to Mount Coorong.

But as for me I like a swag,
  At least a little more
Than we got there in a week –
  Eight pennyweights 'mongst four.

For that, of surface earth we washed
  Of dray loads half a score;
I'll swear that cradling never seemed
  Such tedious work before.[16]

This disgruntled poem was circulated in Adelaide, but never published in the newspapers, as they were keen to promote South Australia in preference to Victoria and New South Wales and not hear of any complaints from disappointed diggers on these short-lived fields.

Melbourne Morning Herald,
13 September 1852

Between Little Bendigo and Aberdeen's
Store, on Forest Creek, three working
men have realised between them during
the last Three months 700 pounds.
The poor fellows, to appearance, seem
actually puzzled as to what to do with
their accumulated hoard of wealth.

Melbourne Morning Herald,
27 September 1852

At Forest Creek this week a lucky digger
took out an Escort receipt for 1093 ozs.,
worth 4000 pounds, got in three months
digging.

Melbourne Morning Herald,
23 October 1852

A splendid nugget belonging to Bennett,
Potter and Hazlett's party, found by them
near the surface, is being shown at the
Gold Deposit Office, Castlemaine.
It weighs forty-six pounds five ounces;
a splendid crust of iron and quartz is
visible in places on this splendid lump.
The weather still keeps fine, and thousands keep pouring into the diggings
from town weekly.

Age, 13 May 1857

A Pony Shod With Gold.– There are
now on view at Messrs. Brush and
McDonnell's establishment a set of shoes
made of solid native gold, weighing 24
ounces, and worth about £100 pounds.
They were made for a favourite pony
of a gentleman now deceased, who resided
in the colony, and bear evidence of
considerable wear. The gold was found
on land where the pony used to graze.

July 1853 – Buckland River, north-eastern Victoria

An American, Pardoe (or Pardew), had been secreted on the lonely Buckland River 60 miles from the Spring Creek diggings for four months before the news of his discovery there finally reached the outside world in July 1853. Within ten days a rush of over 500 diggers a day invaded his profitable peace and quiet.

3 August 1853 – Waranga, central-eastern Victoria

The first discovery on the Waranga diggings was reported in the *Argus* of 3 August 1853. A sawyer searching for timber saw the similarity of the terrain to that of Bendigo, and was lucky enough to pan out some gold in the St Louis Creek.

October 1854 – 'Canton Lead', Ararat, Victoria

Joseph Pollard discovered the first gold in Ararat in north-western Victoria in 1854. This sheep-herding country had been opened up by H. S. Wills in 1839, and, as on almost all other goldfields, the squatter saw his run taken over by diggers.

Over 700 Chinese, travelling across country from Robe in South Australia scratched out some gold on 29 June 1857. They didn't make it onto the Bendigo diggings where they had been heading. The 'Canton Lead' was one of the richest alluvial leads in the colony and the rush that followed laid the foundations for the town of Ararat.

The Chinese suffered indignities wherever they went but it is on the Ararat diggings where they suffered, probably, the meanest of them all. Chinese miners had toiled diligently in their shafts for over six months; digging, timbering and driving further and further into the ground. Once the news of this goldfield was abroad thousands of Europeans rushed to Ararat. Seeing the advanced state of the mines on arrival, the diggers decided to take over. As a ploy, some suggested that the Chinese may not have the required residence tickets.

On 4 February 1858, a small party of European diggers demanded that the Chinese show their tickets. When the Chinese were unable to do so, the Europeans invaded their shafts and evicted them. Sixty to seventy claims, worth over £1000 each, were jumped. The Chinese had almost all reached the bedrock where the gold was to be found. An inquiry was held but the Chinese were not able to win any concession other than the option to sell the timbers and equipment they had already installed and the dirt that they had carted to the tailing dumps. The injustice was further compounded for the Europeans set the value on the equipment.

THE WORLD TURNED TOPSY-TURVY

ALTHOUGH there had been several reports of the discovery of gold in Victoria throughout 1850 and early 1851 it was the announcement of the find in the foothills around Mt Alexander that captured the imagination of the newly separated Colony of Victoria and then the rest of the world. The reward offered by Governor La Trobe for the discovery of payable gold in the Colony had borne fruit.

A fear of the law, and indignation at injustice, are implied in John Worley's announcement, printed in the *Argus* on 8 September 1851 (see page 44). It indicated the prevailing sentiment among the working class in Australia that, while they feared the law and recognised they were subject to the Crown and to the established order, they were also gaining confidence in their desire for universal suffrage.

Workers' rights were not yet recognised as a movement, or even acknowledged as such, although a group of English farm labourers, known as the Tolpuddle Martyrs, had already spent some years in Australia after they had been banished to the Antipodes for daring to request some form of civil justice for working people. Workers throughout the Western world were beginning to demand 'a fair go'.

The discovery of gold bought instant wealth to the new colony, through migration, capital investment, trade and royalties paid by the Crown. At the same time it freed the workers from servitude, creating an independent workforce that needed no master.

The government acted swiftly to curtail the independence of the labouring class. The imposition of a hefty licence fee on all diggers seemed the disincentive needed to keep the shepherds with their flocks, the sailors on their ships, the troopers at their posts. It was to no avail. All the Governor managed to achieve was to set the diggers against him and his licence, and to establish a system of corruption, discrimination and bureaucratic chicanery that was eventually to bring the goldfields to insurrection. From the very beginning, the rapacious government demanded compliance with its fees, capriciously imprisoning and punishing its subjects as it lined its own pockets.

Britain eagerly awaits the news

Almost six months had passed between the time of the news of the first discovery at Bathurst in New South Wales and the news of the discovery at Mt Alexander in Victoria. While the London press was desperate for further revelations of the great finds west of the Blue

A New Chum and a Dirty Man Having a Discussion
Pen drawing by Edward Charles Moore, c. 1854
(REX NAN KIVELL COLLECTION, T1762. BY PERMISSION, NATIONAL LIBRARY OF AUSTRALIA)

The diggings were a great leveller. This comic drawing by E. C. Moore has the caption:

'New Chum'. (to dirty looking man) I say my man, I'll give you have a crown to carry my box to an Hotel for me.–

Dirty Man – You see my boot don't you? – It's unlaced – Well I'll give you a five pound note to lace it – You look hard up.

(OPPOSITE)
Female Emigration
Hand-coloured lithograph by W. Newman
G. S. Tregear, London, October 1834
(REX NAN KIVELL COLLECTION, U2599. BY PERMISSION, NATIONAL LIBRARY OF AUSTRALIA)

Dedicated with all due respect to the fair sex of Great Britain & Ireland by their obedient servant W.N.

FEMALE EMIGRATION!

Dedicated with all Due respect to the Fair sex of Great Britain & Ireland - by their Obedient Servant - W.N.

The embarkation — all agog for Sydney — bidding good bye to the land of Plum-pudding Penny magazines Poverty & Poor laws — For one of Convicts & Kangaroos!!

"In the bay of Biscay O" "Where every 'wild wave drown the Moon" — the topmasts playing at touch with the clouds — the Emigrants being all seasick kick up a breeze which increases to a complete squall

Nocturnal accommodation — Swing Swong all night long — the Emigrants stow'd in a bed from 7 in the evening till 10 the next morning — N.B. under lock & Key !!

"Look on this picture and on this" — The emigrant's berth - & Captain's cabin — the emigrant's fed on "A mouldy biscuit & water each per day. With a Sermon from the Honble & Reverend Dr Ruby-snout — While the Superintendant Captain Chaplain &c Guzzle themselves with 3 courses & a desert

Disembarking in the land of Felons — troubled with the blue devils — Escorted (in the smithfield style) from the ship to their Destination by a Regiment of Liberated Convicts-commonly called "Police" — Thermometer at 90 !!

The Lumber room — or as the Government advertisement calls it "the comfortable apartments of N. S. W. which will be prepared for the Emigrants on their arrival" — an old broken down Shed — something worse than a "stable — raining cats & dogs & pitchforks! — (the wet season having set in) still under the Survileance of the "Unborty"

What with the rain by day & damp Straw at night the Lumber room by degrees gets cleared of its tenants — the Survivers having Exhausted their little Stock of Money-Wait upon the Agent -When they are treated as Shewn above!!

A Specimen of the comfortable situations in New South Wales — the emigrant being thrown upon their own Resources-go in search of Work —— Jane R— one of these poor creatures after Traversing the Country is obliged to support Life by acting a Dust yard & Sift Sinders at 5 d per week & her hot Water

Last Scene of all which ends this strange Eventful history — A view in St Martins le grand — Jane R — after selling some time in the Dust yard is brought to England by a Humane Captain — Being entirely destitute and on the point of Starvation — she commits Suicide by taking Poison!!!

W.Newman Invent & Lithog   Publish'd by G.S Tregear 90 Cheapside October 1834   Printed by R.Redman

Port Melbourne
Engraving from *Picturesque Atlas of Australasia*, Sydney and Melbourne, 1888, vol 12, p. 210
(PRIVATE COLLECTION)

The Melbourne ports filled with hundreds of tall ships unable to make their return journey after their crews had taken off for the goldfields.

Edwin Canton Booth wrote in 1873:

It was of course impossible to keep the news away from the sailors, and to restrain men who had 'signed articles' for forty shillings per month from rushing off to a spot less than a hundred miles away, where they could gain as many pounds a day as they could earn on board ship in a year, was simply impossible.

The law was powerless, for the guardians of the peace had joined in the general stampede, and gone away in their hundreds to the diggings. Masters of vessels, finding their utter powerlessness in the matter, adopted a very sensible plan of making the most of things. They entered into a alliance with their officers and men, moored their ships as safely as possible, left one man in charge, and started for the gold regions in a body ... the bargain made by the masters was faithfully carried out so far as seeking for and dividing the gold went.

The return to the ship was a different matter. The Captain was bound to go back, but in the great majority of instances the men remained behind, having parted from their old commanders in perfect friendliness, both the richer and more contented than when they started.

— Edwin Canton Booth, *Australia in the 1870's,* Virtue & Co., London, 1873–6, pp. 21–3.

Mountains, they had not expected similar news from the newly established colony of Victoria.

When ships arrived back in British ports carrying news of gold in the gullies at Buninyong, gold in the creeks of Creswick, gold beneath the surface of the gravel pits at Ballarat, and gold in the foothills of Mt Alexander, London was ablaze with excitement. The Californian fields no longer held the same fascination, yet the gold finds in the central highlands of Victoria – so recently described by the acclaimed explorer, Major Mitchell, as 'Australia Felix', where so many sons of Caledonia had recently taken up vast and profitable cattle and sheep-grazing runs – captured the imagination of the entire population.

Victoria had never been a penal colony, and the cessation of transportation in 1846 had placed heavy demand on labour for the building and development of colonial infrastructure in both New South Wales, Victoria and South Australia. Following the rushes to California, and then to Bathurst, there was also a severe shortage of rural workers, of maidservants, of hearty lads and wholesome lasses who were needed to keep the squatters profitable.

The popular press in Britain offered all kinds of encouragement to aspiring emigrants who wished to go to the diggings. Scores of books and pamphlets rolled off the English printing presses. One such work, published in 1852, was John Dunmore Lang's *The Australian Emigrant's Manual*, in which Lang counselled both for and against throwing caution to the wind in the rush for easy riches. Lang exhorted the migrants to do their best, reminding them

that they are going to that distant land to assist in laying the broad and deep foundations of what will ere long be one of the mightiest

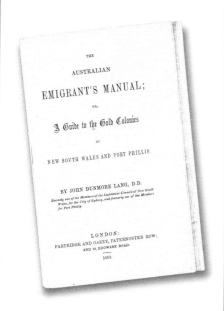

Immigrants line up for medical inspection, hoping to be declared fit for the journey to the colonies.

The diggings, with their tales of riches for the taking, exerted a powerful influence on the English public. War, disease and famine had cast a pall over Europe, and the new finds in the new colony were expected to blow it away – and hundreds of immigrants were ready to take the chance.

As John Dunmore Lang advised a young man in his *Australian Emigrant's Manual*, 'Go by all means; you can easily find your way back again, if unsuccessful.'

empires upon earth, I would simply say to all who possess the mental and moral qualities: 'Go where comfort and a moderate independence await the honest and perservering exertions of every prudent and industrious man'. Such persons are sure to rise in the social scale in the Australian colonies, as compared with their position and means of influence at home. For although we have had enough people in times past, under our wretched system of government in these colonies, who would gladly have raised themselves into the position of colonial aristocracy, with rank and titles to authorise them to keep down all classes around them, the prospects of these aspirants have been sadly blighted of late by the levelling and equalising tendencies of the gold discovery; and there is now no part of the world in which it is more true than it is at this moment in Australia, that … 'A man's a man for a' that' …[1]

Another comprehensive work was the *Emigrant's Guide to Australia* written by the enterprising John Capper, whose advice ranged far and wide. One chapter, entitled 'Who Should Emigrate and How, with a Few Words to Those Who Had Better Remain at Home', offered advice that seems based more on the need to encourage rural workers and domestic servants to choose Australia to replace those who had rushed to the diggings than to encourage the inexperienced to chance their arm on the 'glittering lottery':

Young unmarried women unacquainted with any form of farm or agricultural occupation would be of little use in the new colony. The drawing-room accomplishments of singing, dancing, painting, crochet would stand no shadow of a chance against the highly prized virtues of churning, baking, preserving, cheese-making and similar matters.[2]

The goldfields were the great leveller, where the notion of equality and liberty were tested. Jack did become as good as his master, no matter how hard the master worked at keeping him in his place. Just as the

British tried to dismiss the Californian discoveries in case Queen Victoria's subjects rushed off to enjoy the fruits of true freedom, so did the British government attempt, for pecuniary purposes, to keep a lid on migration. The great need was in the fields, not the gold-fields, in the milking sheds not milking the earth, in the kitchens not out under the stars.

Lang commented on the apparent mood among the elite who regarded the diggings with suspicion, and believed that gold had caused so many of the working class to eschew service:

> There are certain mawkish sentimentalists in this coun-try – certain people who pre-tend to be a great deal better than everybody else – who strongly encourage emigra-tion to Australia, but who endeavour to persuade the emigrant to in a sort of whin-ing tone by no means go to the diggings, as if there is something wrong in going there![3]

A City of Melbourne Solicitor

Topsy-turvey, or, Our Antipodes
Engraving by John Leech
Follies of the Year, London, c. 1860
*(REX NAN KIVELL COLLECTION, S2826.
BY PERMISSION, NATIONAL LIBRARY OF AUSTRALIA)*

The old order had little relevance to the reality of life on the goldfields, for on the goldfields even the lowliest could become wealthy overnight, and those used to giving orders could have no luck at all.

Here the recognised world has certainly been turned upside down, the scruffy diggers are being waited upon by 'learned' gentlemen and elegant ladies.

Newly-found riches changed everything.

A City of Melbourne Solicitor
Lithograph by S. T. Gill
De Gruchy & Leigh, Melbourne, 1866
*(LA TROBE PICTURE COLLECTION,
STATE LIBRARY OF VICTORIA)*

This down-at-heel character was well known on the streets of Melbourne at the time. He is seen here serenading a 'lady of the streets', who also looks a bit the worse for wear.

A Pair of Swells

(PRIVATE COLLECTION)

John Capper, in his work published in 1852, *Emigrant's Guide to Australia,* offered the following advice to gentlemen and women considering a trip to the new colony:

> Let men, for instance, avoid all sorts of fancy waistcoats, dandy boots, or costly cravats and ties; let women shun the idle vanities of silks and satins, of lace and ribbons, of many flounces and fashionable bonnets; and let both men and women forget that there are such things in the world as kid gloves, lavender water and toilet tables.[4]

Capper was obviously well aware of the reality of the life most would not be expecting to be living upon arrival at Hobson's Bay.

The streets of Melbourne did not resemble the elegance of Regent Street or the charm and bustle of Piccadilly in any way. The immigrant was set down in a dirty, dusty or muddy settlement of only a few hundred houses, and virtually no amenities.

His warnings may have gone unheeded, as there are many reports of auctions of unwanted goods carried all the way from England, which were of no use to those setting off for the diggings.

He also advised against investing in goods against the hope of high prices in the colony:

> I once advised an intending emigrant, who was going out to Australia with a capital of £1000 … not to expend one farthing of it in merchandise. But he preferred taking the advice of the captain … and he accordingly invested the whole of his fortune in goods. The result was, he lost upon everything, and was ruined.[5]

And another who had a good business of his own at home:

> Go, if you will; but you will probably be a great fool if you do.[6]

Yet, fuelled by reports in the press and fervour for adventure, excited emigrants soon filled scores of sailing ships. Entire villages packed up their tools – farm boys, working girls, clerks, lawyers, doctors, seamstresses; they came from all walks of life, from all classes, creeds and political persuasions – and headed for the diggings.

As one diarist wrote in his diaries, the diggings were

> a truly wonderful place … the Chinese is jostled by the Russian. The polite Frenchman is abused by the African negro. The people of our own country are called to order by its more precocious offspring the American … Men from all nations sit down at the same table and drink from the same bowl, they each talk and sing in their own tongue, get drunk according to their own fashion, quarrel, jangle, fight and embrace as their various natures dictate and … reel off to their own beds.[7]

The diggings became a great melting pot in the south that was to turn the whole world topsy turvy.

The Prospector
Oil on canvas by Julian Ashton, 1889

(ART GALLERY OF NEW SOUTH WALES COLLECTION)

THE LAST OF ENGLAND

THE POPULAR PRESS IN ENGLAND was caught up in the rush 'to the diggings'. The great colonial adventure captured the imagination of the entire population and spurred thousands to throw caution to the winds and sail for the other side of the world.

The press was filled with tales of life on board ship, the hardships encountered on arrival at Port Phillip, disease, shipwreck, the excitement of relationships developed over the long voyage. The diggings were celebrated in hundreds of popular songs, plays, books, editions of lithographs, watercolours and mementoes collected as souvenirs.

As Henry Kingsley wrote:

> the discovery of Australia … opened a career for young gentlemen possessed of every virtue, save those of continence, sobriety, and industry, who didn't choose to walk and couldn't afford to drive; and, viewed from this point its discovery ranks next in importance after the invention of soda-water – a sort of way of escaping cheaply from the consequences of debauchery for a time.[1]

While it may be imagined that the majority of immigrants to Australia were from the ranks of the 'respectable poor' who would have saved long and hard to put together the fare, it is surprising to

Emigrant Ship, Between Decks,
Wood engraving from *Illustrated News*,
London, *17 August 1850*
(REX NAN KIVELL COLLECTION, U5948.
BY PERMISSION, NATIONAL LIBRARY OF AUSTRALIA)

(OPPOSITE)

Coming South, 1886
Tom Roberts, born Great Britain 1856,
arrived Australia 1869, died 1931
Oil on canvas, 63.5 x 52.2 cm
Gift of Colonel Aubrey Gibson in memory
of John and Anne Gibson, settlers 1887, 1967
(NATIONAL GALLERY OF VICTORIA)

The 'buccaneering spirit' affected all kinds, as thousands set out for the Antipodes.

The migration of young, single women at this time was sponsored by philanthropist Caroline Chisholm. Most of these young ladies seen taking the air in their 'London frocks' were ill prepared for the unmade streets of Melbourne, and may have been seeking a more eligible suitor than the dirty shepherd or mud-caked digger who had little more to offer than a bark hut at the end of a dusty track.

Following the cessation of transportation of convicts, the poor and the homeless had their fares to the colonies paid for them. The government attempted both to provide for much-needed labour in the colonies and to clear the streets of the industrial cities of a burgeoning and undesirable underclass.

This sorrowful group bemoaning the leaving of the 'Old Country' are in sharp contrast to the scenes on Britain's docks after the discovery of gold in the Antipodes, when it was almost impossible to find enough ships to carry the eager throng.

realise the large number of the educated, well-connected, middle and upper classes who were also set for the diggings.

When dramatic changes to several laws to do with property, debt and estates brought about a reduction in legal business, a reduction in plaintiffs and court cases, a large number of practitioners of the legal profession, particularly graduates of Trinity College, Dublin, made the journey to Australia. They carved out distinguished careers for themselves far from the green fields of old Ireland, and often far away from the dusty goldfields. One Irish lawyer wrote in his application for a job at the Colonial Office in Melbourne in 1854 that 'the disgraceful state of the [English] bar… induced me to look to the colonies as a better field for my exertions.'[2]

As Kingsley wrote in the opening pages of his memoirs of life on the diggings:

> Yes, that's the land for me! A continent in itself, inhabited by only a few civilised beings and wild aborigines, while millions of acres of good land are waiting settlement by people of the right stamp, … a country possessing a genial climate and unlimited resources; while, more attractive than all, rumours are afloat that rich goldfields have been discovered in several parts of it. Who knows but that it may turn out to be a second California? Irrespective of gold, there is elbow room there … Under the Southern Cross there is room for all.[3]

The spirit of adventure struck deeply into the hearts of a group of distinguished English artists and writers. The poet Alfred Tennyson wished to go himself and try his hand at digging, but he restrained

(OPPOSITE)
Off to the Diggin's!
Or, London Schemes in 1852
(STATE LIBRARY OF SOUTH AUSTRALIA)

Poster for a popular play written by John Courtney, first performed at the Surrey Theatre, in London, on 1 November 1852.

This two-act play, with a cast list of a most Dickensian flavour, takes a humorous look at the fervour of emigration to the diggings contrasted with the reality of colonial life.

After which, EVERY EVENING, (7th, 8th, 9th, 10th, 11th, and 12th, Times) an Entirely New and Original High Pressure, Fast Train, Times Emblematic, New School Dramatic, Extravaganza, in Two Acts, teeming with Events and Doings of the Day and Year, typifying Prophecies to come, what we are, and where we may go, embracing Emigration and Australization, entitled

OFF TO THE DIGGINS!

Or, London Schemes in 1852.

The New Medley Overture Composed by Mr. Isaacson.   **The New Scenery by Mr. Dalby.**

George Gayland, (*a Young Gentleman who has not Bettered his Purse or Condition by Betting or Book-Making*) Mr. ELMORE,

Mr. Choker, { (*Proprietor of a Cheap Clothing Warehouse, not particular as to how he does the Purchaser so long as he can do himself*) } Mr. FENTON,

Tom Pickles, *alias* Alfred Sham Abram Montacute, Esq. (*Emigration Agent, Hooking and Booking all he can*) Mr. A. YOUNGE,

Achilles Stripe, (*His Co., Clerk and Director—Digging into all who wish to go to the Diggins*) Mr. SHEPHERD,

Julius Snivey, { (*With a Book for the Derby, any Quantity of Tips, and an Eye to Emigation— a Fast-Going Youth, and Cutter to Choker*) } Mr. H. WIDDICOMB,

Andrew Shock, (*a Yorkshire Tyke, Emigrant, and Agency Victim*) · Mr. W. ROBERTSON,

Patrick Macmur h, { (*an Emigrant from the Emerald Isle, Shillelah in Hand, ready for any Head, Friend or Foe's, another Victim of Agency*) } Mr. HARWOOD COOPER,

Sharp and Mull, (*Gentlemen of the Diggins*) Mr. BUTLER and Mr. PHELPS,

Monsieur Maladroit, (*Digging into the Diggers*) Mr. R. GREEN,   Kikogofatto, (*a Real Native*) Mr. YOUNG,
Natives, Diggers, Emigrants, &c., &c.

Mrs. Choker, (*rather inclined to choke Choker—Jealous and Clamorous*) Mrs. W. ROBERTSON,

Eliza Choker, { (*like many daughters besides Choker's, preferring her Lover to her Father, with an Elopement to follow*) } Miss BOWRING,

Isabella Such, { (*a Young Lady of the Needle, Regatta and Fancy Shirt Maker for Huff'em and Co., at Threepence Halfpenny each, fine-stitched*) } Miss CLARISSE DORIA,

Sarah Gull, { (*another Needle Victim, making Alpaca Paletots for Derby Gents and Sunday Swells, at Ninepence each, working for Sweat'em and Co.*) } Miss LEBATT,

Amina Squall, { (*First Contralto at the "Eagle and Baby Saloon—Admission Sixpence, with a Ticket for Refreshment included,"—the Jenny Lind of the East*) } Miss SOMERS.

ACT THE FIRST.—LONDON.
London Life.—London Schemes, & Emigration.

A LAPSE of TWELVE MONTHS is SUPPOSED to OCCUR BETWEEN the ACTS.

ACT THE SECOND.—AUSTRALIA.
LIFE AT THE DIGGINS.

Stage Manager, Mr. CRESWICK,   Acting Manager & Treasurer, Mr. W. S. EMDEN.
Composer and Leader of the Band, Mr. ISAACSON.

Boxes, 2s.; Half-price (at Half-past Eight), 1s.   Pit, 1s.   Gallery, 6d.
Doors Open at Six o'Clock, Performance to commence at Half-past.   Pass-Out Checks Not Transferable.
Children under Twelve Years of Age admitted to the Boxes at Half-Price.   Children in Arms Not Admitted under any Pretence whatever,

NO MONEY RETURNED.
Bill Inspector, Mr PECKHAM, to whom all Applications respecting Bills, &c., must be made
Season Tickets to be had of Mr. KERSOMNER at the Box Office, or at the Treasury of the Theatre.
John K. Chapman and Company, Steam Machine Printers, 5, Shoe Lane, and Peterborough Court, Fleet Street

The Last of England
Oil by Ford Maddox Brown, 1852–55
(BIRMINGHAM CITY MUSEUM & ART GALLERY)

This poignant image was painted soon after Brown and his companions, Dante Gabriel Rossetti and Holman Hunt, farewelled members of the Pre-Raphaelite Brotherhood who had responded to the call of 'the diggings'.

Ladies Cabin, Breadalbane
Pencil and wash by S. T. Gill, 1853
(LA TROBE PICTURE COLLECTION, STATE LIBRARY OF VICTORIA)

For most emigrants the trip to the colonies was not only the first time they had been on board ship, it was also the first time they had even been away from their birthplace.

Here S. T. Gill shows with some humour the 'joys' of transcontinental travel as couples attempt to navigate their way across the deck.

One poor fellow has his head over the side, demonstrating the meaning of the colonial expression 'chunder', a shortened version of the warning cry 'Watch under'.

*Thomas Woolner was to become one of Australia's foremost sculptors of the Victorian age.

himself at the request of his wife. The Pre-Raphaelite Brotherhood, a group of artists and writers in London, had hit a low patch in their fortunes and were considering migration as a body, in the hope of reversing that fortune, returning to England and being able to work unencumbered by the need of patronage. Their fortunes changed at home, and only three of the Brotherhood set out on the journey: sculptor Thomas Woolner,* and artists Bernhard Smith and E. La Trobe Bateman, sailed from Gravesend in July 1852. They were farewelled at the dock by Dante Gabriel Rossetti, Holman Hunt and Ford Maddox Brown, who was so moved by the emotional departure that he painted *The Last of England* soon after. The poignant narrative within this simple image was echoed time and again as thousands of others left their home in search of adventure or a new and better life.

Charles Dickens was another commentator who stood at the quayside watching a strange collection of his countrymen and women climb aboard one ship bound for Port Phillip. He shares his observation in *Household Words*, 17 July 1852:

Old men with grey hairs and faltering steps; young girls, pale from the factory or the garret; countrymen

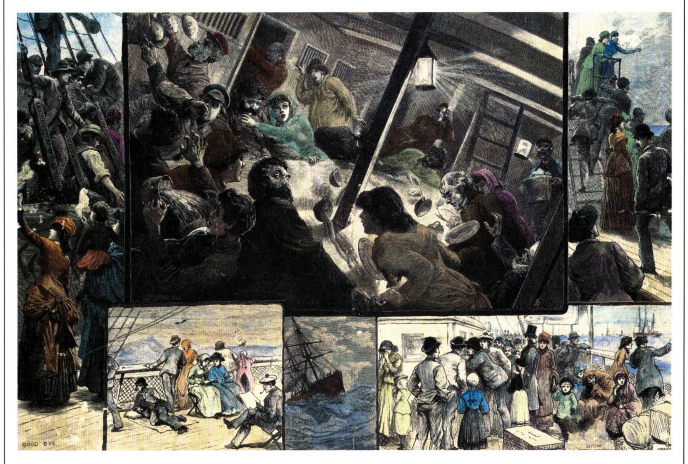

GOOD BYE

Emigrants Going to Australia
Hand-coloured wood engraving, c. 1880
From an illustrated English newspaper

*(Rex Nan Kivell Collection, S2829.
By Permission, National Library of Australia)*

The long sea voyage to the colonies must
have been arduous and boring.

The cramped quarters below deck
brought tensions and temperament to the
fore. This is illustrated in the centre panel
where high seas are shown making the
journey uncomfortable, in contrast to
the 'pleasures' to be taken on such a sea
voyage – of polite company, conversation
and leisure – rather like a holiday at the
seaside or weekend in the country.

Many travellers were shocked to find
that the spacious cabin, ship's doctor,
attendants and activities promised and paid
for, evaporated once aboard.

Although the day was long and the
cabins small, there was plenty of work
to be done. Passengers were expected to
assist in the galley and to clean the decks.
As sanitation was of paramount importance
and 'cleanliness next to godliness', they
were also expected to air their bedding
on deck every day.

in smock-frocks; lean-faced artisans; mothers with infants in arms; stout
servant girls …; two or three newly wedded couples …; a knot of oily-
headed, sleek-visaged shopmen, and city clerks; a few hale-looking country lads and lasses … I should have thought they were sailing to Botany
Bay, by the dismal misery written on the faces of those on deck!

Leaving home may have filled Dickens's Micawber with a 'bold buccaneering air', but it filled most others with mixed emotions of
expectation and fear. Embarking on a journey of four months or so
halfway round the globe in cramped and spartan conditions, through
calm and storm, disease and dismay, to step ashore at last – into what?

Ford Maddox Brown's melancholy image is an accurate one, contrasted with the buccaneering air affected by his friends who sailed
out 'armed to the teeth … stocked with corduroys, sou'westers, jer-
seys, fire-arms and belts of little bags to hold the expected nuggets'.[4]

On arrival at Port Phillip most were shocked at the state of the
fledgling settlement. Few had expected a frontier town of unmade
streets, mean and inadequate accommodation, rude inhabitants and
exorbitant prices.

So many ships arrived in such a short time that a tent city was established on the south bank of the Yarra River, affording reasonable
accommodation for the new arrivals before they rediscovered their
'land-legs' and began the march to the diggings.

Records show that, at times, there was an almost unbroken line of hopeful new chums making their way across the Keilor Plains out towards Diggers' Rest (the first day's resting place for most) on the Mt Alexander Road. And there was a similar line of the successful and not-so-successful on their way back again, either to spend up big in Melbourne or to look for employment in the town.

Good Business for Mrs Chisholm

Immigration was big business. The cessation of transportation in 1848 had put an end to cheap labour, and the discovery of gold in America in 1849 saw thousands of able-bodied Australians leave for the diggings there. The landed gentry in the colonies saw their livelihoods at a standstill, crops left unharvested, flocks untended, shops and factories without labour.

The rush to populate was pushed by several forces at once: the need to provide labour for the colonial enterprises – this generally meant rural, pastoral and domestic workers for the squatting classes; the need to provide for the dispossessed at home, the large number of homeless and unemployed from the outer reaches of the British Isles, the Irish, the Scottish and the English poor; the need to counter the depopulation following the American discoveries; the need to create a stable colonial community through the migration of women suitable for marriage to the large number of men who had come alone to the diggings.

The British Colonial Land & Emigration Commissioners had not always been able to meet the demands of the colonists before the gold

Emigrants Embarking from England

The rush to emigrate to the colonies became a social phenomenon where thousands of men women and children, old and young, able, and at times not so able, took up the challenge of making a new life in a new land.

Through the marketing skills of the Emigration Societies and the promotional tours conducted by the likes of Mrs Chisholm, ships set sail from the English ports loaded to the gunwales with expectant emigrants taking their last look at the shores of 'home'.

Some would not survive the rigours of the long sea voyage, others would succumb to the dangers of the Australian bush, while many never became rich enough to ever consider returning home.

Almost all left with the expectation that they would soon make their pile, and change their lives forever. One thing was certain, however, no matter what lay before them their lives would all be changed by the experience of life at 'the diggings'.

Portrait of Caroline Chisholm
Lithograph by Thomas Fairland,
M. I. Laidler, *Advance Australia*, London,
1 September 1852

(*REX NAN KIVELL COLLECTION, U6413.
BY PERMISSION, NATIONAL LIBRARY OF AUSTRALIA*)

Mrs Chisholm was at heart a philanthropic gentlewoman.

The desire to do her Christian duty and rescue fallen women, while at the same time transforming the male-dominated society in the early colonies into a community stabilised by the influence of 'home and hearth', led her to pack hundreds of destitute girls into sailing ships bound for Australia.

Although she assisted the girls to find a worthwhile place in the colonies, once ashore they either found employment, found a husband or 'fell' again.

She suffered criticism from many quarters, and was accused of transporting prostitutes to the colonies without regard to the type of society she was creating.

EMIGRATION
TO
SOUTH AUSTRALIA

Her Majesty's Colonization Commissioners having determined to dispatch in the course of a few weeks a large number of Emigrants, all eligible persons may obtain, by making an IMMEDIATE application, a

FREE PASSAGE!

The classes of persons now in requisition are
Agricultural Laborers,
SHEPHERDS, CARPENTERS
BLACKSMITHS
AND
STONE MASONS
And all Persons connected with Building.

discoveries, but in 1852 they were deluged by over 700 letters a day from hopefuls desperate to be granted permission to sail. By the middle of 1852, 18,000 had applied for assisted passage to Australia.

The following advertisement was typical of the enticements to encourage emigrants to Australia, not to dig for gold, but to join in the hard work necessary in the building of the new nation:

WANTED – An opportunity now offers itself to all married persons of useful occupations particularly to agricultural labourers, carpenters, builders, stone masons, shepherds and blacksmiths of obtaining a free passage to Port Adelaide in South Australia (SA).

A free colony where there are no convicts sent and where every person who immigrates is as free as he is in this country. Besides the classes of persons enumerated above, bakers, blacksmiths, braziers and tin men, smiths, shipwrights, boat builders, wheel wrights, sawyers, cabinet makers, coopers, couriers, farriers, mill wrights, harness makers, boot and shoe makers, tailors, tanners, brick makers, lime burners and all persons engaged in the erection of buildings are always in great request. The applicants must able to obtain a good character reference as honest, sober, industrious men. They must be real labourers going out to work in the colony, of sound body, not less than 15 and nor more than 30 years of age, and married. The rule as to age is occasionally departed from in favour of the parents of large families. As a general rule each child is considered as extended the age plus one year. Sisters of married applicants are allowed to go free if of good character.

The province of SA is a delightfully fertile and salubrious country, in every respect well adapted to the constitution of Englishmen and is one of the most flourishing in all our colonies. It is well watered and there have never been any complaints from the colonists of a want of this valuable element. On the contrary, the letters from Cornishmen who have written home are very satisfactory on this point. It should be borne in mind that complaints of a scarcity of water do not apply to Adelaide but to other settlements not connected to SA.

Immigrants wishing to obtain a free passage this year must now have that opportunity if they apply immediately to Mr. I. Latimer, Truro, who is employed by Her Majesty's colonisation commissioners to engage for that fine first class teak built ship, the 'Java' of 1200 tonnes.

The ship's accommodations are unusually spacious and lofty and are so arranged as to ensure the comfort of all passengers. She will carry 2 surgeons and 2 school masters, the latter of whom will be

New Chums, Refreshing Sleep. 10/ a night!

Hard up! compulsory sales. *Melbourne, Dec. 1852.*

New Chums, Refreshing Sleep
10/ a Night – Hard up! Compulsory sales –
Melbourne Dec. 1852
Watercolour by William Strutt, 1852
(STATE PARLIAMENTARY LIBRARY COLLECTION, VICTORIA)

This painting depicts the common
experience shared by new arrivals
at Port Phillip. Highly-priced accom-
odation, and expensive goods and
provisions meant that many who were
financially ill-prepared sold what they
could to help finance the next leg
of their expedition.

(OPPOSITE)

**Gold Diggers Receiving a Letter
From Home**
Oil attributed to William Strutt, c. 1860
(ART GALLERY OF NEW SOUTH WALES)

News of home was eagerly awaited
by the immigrants who no longer
classed themselves as new chums but
as 'diggers'.

Strutt's painting shows a pair of diggers
reading their way through a pile of mail
that has just arrived on one of the migrant
ships.

Mail was regularly carried to the
diggings, as the postal services were
always one of the first agencies to
be established on any of the goldfields.

regularly employed in teaching the immigrants and their children. The
vessel will call at Plymouth to take in Cornish passengers and on or
about the 16th of October but in order to ensure a passage application
should be made forthwith.[5]

The Highland and Island Emigration Society was established to
assist the inhabitants of the Isle of Skye and other islands on the west
coast of Scotland to look for passage to Australia. Potato disease and
a subsequent famine had all but destroyed the islands, and it was
remarked that, even after migration, the 'docility' of these folk made
them of little use to their employers. It appears that after so many
years eking out a pitiful existence on their windswept islands that it
took many years under the southern sun to rehabilitate them.

The English philanthropist, Caroline Chisholm, and the Family
Colonization Loan Society set out to attract a better, stronger, more
suitable class of prospective migrant. Caroline had accompanied her
husband, Captain H. Chisholm, from Madras to Australia in 1848. It
was in Sydney that she saw the poverty of the lives of destitute,
unemployed women, and was made aware of the bawdy, boozing lives
of unaccompanied men on the diggings. Caroline believed that the
introduction of family life to the diggers would do much to redress
the awfulness of their frontier lives. She believed that the influence of
her women, 'God's police' as she referred to them, on the lives of the
frontier men would do much more than would any moralising priest
or didactic schoolmaster.

She organised convoys of women, going from farm to farm seeking
employment for them as she went. Her expeditions were outstand-
ingly successful. Before long Chisholm had established the Family
Colonization Loan Society, which sponsored females to travel to the

colonies, where they contracted to repay their debt to the Society after they had secured a position or a marriage partner.

Mrs Ellen Clacy, who came to Australia in 1852, writes:

No one in England can fully appreciate the benefits her [Mrs Chisholm's] unwearied exertions have conferred upon the colonies. I have met many of the matrons of her ships, and not only do they themselves seem to have made their way in the world, but the young females who were under their care during the voyage appear to have done equally well. Perhaps one way of accounting for this, is the fact that many of those going out by the Chisholm Society are from Scotland, the inhabitants of which country are particularly fortunate in the colonies, their industry, frugality, and 'canniness' being the very qualities to make a fortune there.[6]

But there were many in the colonies at the time who disagreed with Chisholm's overactive promotion of the benefits of colonial life. Polish gold-digger Severyn Korzelinski who had been at the Forest Creek and Bendigo diggings, writes in his memoirs: 'Mrs. Chisholm, painting only the bright side of Australia, omitted its defects'. He felt that Mrs Chisholm, in effect, was carrying on 'what amounted to trafficking in women'.[7]

Caroline Chisholm's agent in Melbourne took females straight off the migrant ships as they docked. They were sorted and most sent straight up to the bush. Of course this suited most of the arrivals as they did not really know where to go or what to do, and it suited employers very well. Those who were not taken up could look forward to an extended period in one of Mrs Chisholm's 'emigrant houses', where food rationing was so carefully worked out that the

Emigrants Landing at the Queen's Wharf
Wood engraving by Fredrick Grosse, Melbourne, c. 1861
(REX NAN KIVELL COLLECTION, S2853. BY PERMISSION, NATIONAL LIBRARY OF AUSTRALIA)

Although those who arrived in the early days of the rush were landed on the muddy shore of Liardet's beach, over a mile or so from the town, it was not long before the docks of Port Phillip were made ready for the hundreds of ships to follow.

'An English Gold Field' and 'A Gold Field in the "Diggins"'
Punch Magazine, London

The popular papers in England were fascinated by the great exodus to the colonies. They profited by it, promoted it, and, in the style of most newspapers even today, took their turn at cynicism and outright condemnation.

The illustrations at right express a cynical yet comedic view of the goldfields. The one above shows a group of happy little English children safe in their bountiful homeland; the one below shows the debauchery of the living hell that was Australia.

For many, Australia did become a living hell. For those without luck, on whom Mother Fortune showed no favours, Australia was the farthest from the delights of a remembered home that they could possibly imagine.

The press supported the migration schemes, and promoted Caroline Chisholm in her work; Charles Dickens repeatedly referred to the goldfields or travel to Australia as a kind of panacea for defeated or disappointed Englishmen; and advertisers, inventors, and clever merchants found new ways and new schemes to part migrants from their money before leaving England's shores.

girls were given simply enough to keep them alive. They took any offer from any comer, simply to escape.

Korzelinski commented:

> they were prepared to grasp at every opportunity and agreed to go with a sailor, ex-convict, anyone ... nor was there any difficulty in obtaining a woman from the emigrant house. Whoever wished arrived, picked one out to his liking and carried her away with him after reimbursing the institution a few pounds which the government had spent on clothing, because usually the women had arrived in Australia in tatters.[8]

There are records of hundreds of women at a time being sent to the diggings to save the diggers the time and effort of travelling to Melbourne in search of a wife. At one time any man on the Castlemaine diggings who desired a wife simply had to prove that he

The poster indicated in this small engraving reads: 'Emigration of females to Sydney with Sanction of Government'.

had £10, and he could take a woman, a dowry of a similar amount, a tent and a pair of blankets. But what sort of future was that for a young girl who would be likely to be left in an empty tent after the money ran out, and seeing her digger 'husband' take his leave to repeat the 'marriage' somewhere else?

> Let them reflect well on the unpaved streets, and the dust blowing every few days in Melbourne until you cannot see your own hand; on the heat, the flies, the mud, and slush, the moment there is rain, before they quit the smooth pavements and the comforts that abound in England. Let them reflect too, on the rude, chaotic, and blackguard state of the lower society in this suddenly-thrown-together colony.[9]

So wrote Howitt in his book, *Land, Labour & Gold*, in 1853, in warning to young maid-servants whom a correspondent of his was seeking to send to the colony. It was a warning to all young girls who may have looked to the goldfields as a place for excitement and emancipation from service in England:

> As to girls marrying here – the great temptation – that is soon accomplished; for I fear that lots of diggers get married almost every time they go down to Melbourne to spend their gold. A lot of the vilest scoundrels are assembled from all the four winds of heaven. Nobody knows them; much less whether they have left wives behind them in their own countries; and they marry, and go off, and are never heard of again … the experiment, however, is so awfully hazardous, that I should carefully avoid in all cases promoting it.[10]

Marvellous Smellbourne!

One hundred days away from Britain's shores, the migrants who had travelled so eagerly to the other side of the world were rarely prepared for the frontier society they were to find at the end of their journey. Most formed into digging parties of half-a-dozen or so on board ship, and upon landing spent the first few weeks in the colony putting together supplies necessary for the journey north. This gave them some time to explore the township of Melbourne, whose streets at that time were a far cry from the leafy avenues and promenades of London, Liverpool or Dublin.

Most writers describe the disgusting scene on arriving at Port Phillip. Slaughterhouses lined the river — wooden buildings with fenced yards to one side, holding the wretched beasts standing among the decapitated heads of their kind. Pigs snuffled about in the filth,

(OPPOSITE)
Primrose from England
Oil on canvas by Edward Hopley, c. 1855
(COLLECTION – BENDIGO ART GALLERY)

This beautifully nostalgic painting was donated to the Bendigo Art Gallery in 1940 by George Lansell Jr, son of George Lansell Sr, the Quartz King of Bendigo.

The painting depicts the arrival of a potted primrose on the docks at Port Phillip. This lovely fantasy is based upon an actual event, and depicts the longing that migrants can feel for 'home', and the ease with which a simple reminder can transport them back to that long-since-departed place.

What a great collection of colonial characters there are in this painting — the beaming Dickensian gentleman in his topper, the merchant, the farmer and his child, a bold digger stands back in the shadows, a rustic Scot beams towards the artist in the foreground.

(CONTINUED)

Others crowd at the door, the housemaid, the trooper, in the distance the tall masts of a sailing ship at the dock, while a group of young women gaze longingly at the potted blooms.

An Aboriginal is seen partially hidden in the shadows on the right. This may well be an allusion by the artist to the condition that Aboriginals had found themselves in following the colonisation of their homeland by Europeans.

It may also be the softness of that flower that contrasts so greatly with the comparative harshness of Australian flora that has them longing so wistfully for home.

tearing the flesh from the bones. On the riverside entrails, blood, gore and the stripped carcasses of rotting animals trailed into the river, creating a filthy and malodorous welcome to the newly arrived immigrant. Crossing to the other side of the river offered little respite from this gory scene.

Rendering plants, tanneries, fellmongers and wool-washers spewed their filthy aroma into the fetid air while the river was both source and sewer of the malodorous brew being created on the river's edge, enshrining the title conferred on the port of 'Marvellous Smellbourne'.

Although Melbourne had tried to keep the river clean for domestic use up until the 1850s, and bathing in the stream above the fresh-water mark at Queen's Bridge had been banned for a long time, the sheer crush of humanity that flowed into Melbourne during the goldrush placed incredible demands on the town's services. Things may have been worse: floods in 1842, '44, '48 and '49 swept most of the foulness down the river, including over 2500 sheep penned by the riverside at Philpott's boiling-down plant.

The dusty, at times boggy, streets were littered with garbage, dead and decaying animals; for miles around the outskirts of town the bush glittered with the broken shards of discarded champagne bottles:

HOBSON'S BAY
From the Signal Staff Williamstown

The first land fall for emigrants to the Colony of Victoria was at Hobson's Bay (Williamstown) which was some distance from the new port of Melbourne.

Smaller craft, steamers and ferries were able to take the expectant new chums further up the river to land on the shores of Melbourne on the Yarra Yarra River.

I have scarcely seen a tree under which do not lie the remains of bottles which had been dashed against it, as they have been emptied. Nay, I see whole bottles lying thrown out all about the outskirts of the town, which not a soul thinks it worth his while to pick up …[11]

Howitt reflects that the bottles are a passable blight, but only showing 'a recklessness of expense; but the dead horses and bullocks are disgusting'.[12]

It seemed that the citizens regarded their worn-out animals as criminals, and preferred to execute them where they fell, which was often at crossroads. Howitt continues:

the other evening we saw a bullock's head, with a large pair of horns, lying on the road, as if the animal, according to Milton's description, were just created and rising out of the earth, having as yet only got its head free.[13]

Life under canvas may have seemed exciting and adventurous at first, but the flies, mosquitoes, heat and dust soon took their toll. So many had arrived that the young town could not accommodate them in the few hundred houses that had been constructed by the first settlers and merchants. A tent city was established south of the Yarra below Princes Bridge to accommodate the thousands of new arrivals who could find no other place to stay. The town charged the immigrants and others who had made their way into Melbourne before striking out for the diggings 5 shillings a week on each tent.

Among these tents a little city had been established, known as Little Adelaide, where a number of families from South Australia, who had been seduced by the prospect of the Victorian diggings, were camped out, as they could not afford the prices of accommodation in the town.

Advertisement for Castlemaine tent-maker H. Winks
Winks had a business in the Market Square, Castlemaine.

Although there was a roaring trade in tents and other diggers' paraphernalia in England, there was still plenty of opportunity for entrepreneurs in the colonies to make their own bit 'of hay while the sun shone'.

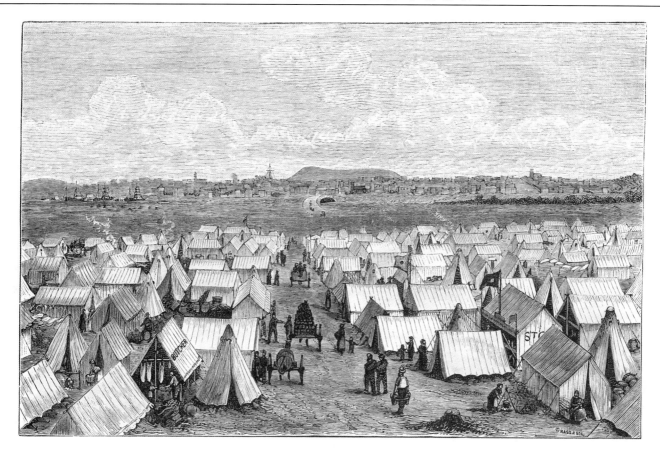

Canvas Town, South Melbourne
Hand coloured engraving from *Victoria and Its Metropolis: Past and Present*
(PRIVATE COLLECTION)

The new chums quickly took up all available accommodation in town before they kitted out and set off for the journey to the diggings.

Seen from the tent city that had been established on the south side of the river, Mt Macedon looms on the horizon, constantly reminding the tent dwellers of their goal, which lay a further 40 or 50 miles on from that brooding landmark.

For many the tent city gave them the opportunity to set up their gear and test their ability as 'campers' before they really put themselves to the test. Mrs Ellen Clacy took a stroll along the river one Sunday, in the company of her brother and a friend, along the river towards the Botanical Gardens. They came across two tents pitched on a slight rise beside the river:

> not far enough away from Melbourne to be inconvenient, but yet sufficiently removed from its mud and noise, were pitched two tents, evidently new, with crimson paint still gay upon the round nobs of the centre posts, and looking altogether more in trim for a gala day in Merry England than a trip to the diggings.[14]

What a jolly sight these tents must have made when they were eventually set up among the cacophony that was the diggings. The peacefully pleasant scene of canvas set among the gardens on the gently flowing river contrasts sharply with Clacy's description of her last night on the diggings some weeks later at the end of her colonial adventure:

> Imagine some hundreds of revolvers almost simultaneously fired – the sound reverberating through the mighty forests, and echoed far and near – again and again till the last faint echo died away in the distance. Then a hundred blazing fires burst upon the sight – around them gathered the rough miners themselves – their sun-burnt, hair-covered faces illumined by the ruddy glare. Wild songs, and still wilder burst of laughter are heard; gradually the flames sink and disappear, and an

oppressive stillness follows … broken only by some midnight carouser, as he vainly endeavours to find his tent.[15]

There were those who were never to experience the camaraderie that took over all life on the diggings. Life in Melbourne proved too distasteful, and they simply returned on the ships that had brought them out, having never even landed their sea-trunks. There were those who simply did not have the stamina to withstand the ravages of the new colony and succumbed to its excesses — excesses of heat, dust, flies, disease, alcohol, robbery or murder. It was a harsh new land that took away from many the pale-rose flush of England.

Howitt writes:

Hundreds have already gone back again, cursing those who sent such one-sided statements of the goldfields and of the climate. Thousands have been struck down, and many are still lying on their backs, from the effects of the change in climate … dysenteries, fevers, and rheumatism, which will cripple many for life, and have already carried many out of it. New as these diggings, there is a tolerably populous cemetery on a hill here; and some who crossed the sea with us are already sleeping there.[16]

Yet the discomforts endured in Melbourne did not deter most diggers from their quest: 'But for ourselves, we are no whit daunted. We shall dig, and we shall buy gold; and whether we shall get more or less, we shall be picking up information for an ultimate object'.[17]

That ultimate object was adventure, and the adventure was gold!

Advertisement from *The Emigrant in Australia*, 1852

Emigration was big business, the opportunities offered to the enterprising businessman catering to the needs and the fears of those embarking on the great adventure were limitless.

All kinds of products were created to assist in a successful voyage to the colonies and then in a successful venture on the diggings.

The fact that most merchants in London had little idea what the diggers would really find upon landing in the Antipodes did not deter them from making their pile at home.

Camping on the Road
Hand-coloured lithograph by Cyrus Mason, c. 1855

(REX NAN KIVELL COLLECTION, U2490. BY PERMISSION, NATIONAL LIBRARY OF AUSTRALIA)

– HARD TIMES & MRS CHISHOLM –

IN AUGUST 1847 Earl Grey had undertaken to send 5000 immigrants to Australia to relieve the chronic shortage of labour in the colonies. By September he had resolved to send not immigrants but exiles, convicts who had served part of their sentences in British gaols.

In December Caroline Chisholm published pamphlets attacking Grey's change of mind. She opposed the resumption of any form of transportation of convicts. The system had ceased seven years earlier following repeated protests by the wealthy citizens of the new society.

Instead she advocated a systematic form of assisted immigration, which helped hundreds of women make the journey to Australia to fulfil her aim of the civilisation of the men on the diggings.

What seemed to have begun as an altruistic effort to help the homeless, vagrant and unemployed women on the streets of Sydney to redemption through hard work became a profitable business for Chisholm. The Emigration Society that she eventually helped establish is reported to have returned her £3 per girl.

She did meet considerable criticism of her efforts to stabilise goldfields society through the benefits of 'hearth and home'. Many critics in the colonies accused her of 'trafficking in women', yet she continued to perform what she saw as her Christian duty, and was considered by others to have been worthy of the title of 'Australia's first saint'.

Chisholm and the Family Colonization Loan Society sought to send out a better class of future colonist than simply emptying Imperial gaols. She toured England extensively, promoting the colonies in the hope of filling 'her' ships – and, as some complained, her pockets.

The English novelist, commentator, journalist and philanthropist, Charles Dickens, shared a common interest

Caroline Chisholm
Lithograph by Thomas Fairland
M. I. Laidler, 1 February 1851, London

with Mrs Chisholm. His lifelong involvement in social, political and legal matters was central to his preoccupation with emigration.

Dickens wandered the foggy alleys and cobbled streets of London at night, where he encountered many young women who had taken to life 'on the game'. Through his 'Appeal for Fallen Women' Dickens was convinced that a new start was the only hope for the 'permanent reformation' of the fallen. His novels refer constantly to the promise offered by emigration, in the redeeming possibilities of life renewed in the colonies.

In 1847 Dickens opened Urania Cottage, a home for former prostitutes, in Shepherd's Bush, a working-class suburb to the west of London. He believed that only 'the prospect of marriage in a context free of past associations could be sufficient incentive for former prostitutes to give up their long-learned and enduring vices'. That

'these unfortunate creatures are to be tempted to virtue. They cannot be dragged, driven or frightened [into it]'.

He was interested in similar work by Chisholm and her Family Colonization Loan Society, as he had also supervised the sending of proposed residents to both Cape Town and Australia.

After he had visited Chisholm at her London home, apart from commenting on her bad housekeeping and her children's dirty faces, which 'haunted him' for some considerable time, Dickens created the character Mrs Jellyby and 'telescopic philanthropy' for his novel, *Bleak House*.

His characters, Little Em'ly and Martha Endell, were inspired by women he had met on the streets, and represented his belief that prostitution flourished in a male-dominated society, where class distinctions and sexual exploitation would ensure that a certain class of women was seduced into a state where the prospect of marriage was made impossible.

Dickens and Chisholm were actively promoting the same view. Their concerns for the well-being of the women they encountered, coupled with the demand for working-class emigration and the excitement of the gold discoveries in the colonies, ensured that the work of 'tempting' such girls to seek redemption through emigration was a very profitable outcome for all concerned.

Dickens could be satisfied that the outcome provided for 'the perfect penitence in these women – a kind of active repentance in their being faithful wives and the mothers of virtuous children'.

No matter that on arrival at Port Phillip they were most likely to be 'hitched up' to any old lag, any old hoary Vandemonian or lusty digger down on a spree, who was just as likely to leave them on the streets where they had found them and take off back to the diggings.

CHAPTER 5

THE ROAD TO THE DIGGINGS

ALMOST EVERY ONE OF US brought too much on our back and at every stage we lightened ourselves. At one camping place three pairs of trousers were thrown away, one of which were mine, and at our last camp in the valley, innumerable articles were left. Our company left our table cloths or oil cloths, two axes, 1 counterpane, prospecting pan, camp kettles, pannikin etc. Some left everything they had, determining never to camp out again: flannel drawers, shirts, blankets, kettles, rugs etc. were all scattered about.[1]

The road to the diggings took the newcomer across a landscape that had known no plough, and no roadmaking gang had ever toiled to ease their journey. The diggers trekked across windswept plains, forded rushing streams, climbed granite-strewn slopes and tramped into darkened forests of gnarled, black-trunked eucalypts.

With their gear strapped to their shoulders or pushed before them in hand-carts they cursed the heat, the flies, the mosquitoes, the cold, the damp, the sheer effort that was the 'rush to the diggings'.

It was a melancholy sight. Four hundred miles they had dragged along their carts, over gully, swamp, and mountain, leaving the richer diggings of the Turon and of Bathurst behind them to gather at the Ovens [Beechworth], as they had been assured, hundredweights of gold![2]

The Route to the Diggings
Liardet's Four-in-hand Coach, the 'Eclipse', making a trip to Ballarat
Watercolour by William Strutt, Melbourne, Victoria, 1851
(STATE PARLIAMENTARY LIBRARY COLLECTION, VICTORIA)

The adventurers make out for the diggings, on foot, bullock dray or pushing hand-carts before them as Wilbraham Liardet rides in comfort to take in the sights. Liardet was one of the earliest hotel-keepers in Sandridge, who began a coach service carrying 'tourists' on excursions to the diggings.

Shop clerks with carpetbag in hand, bushmen, sailors, and experienced old-hands are all on the road, with Melbourne and the masts of Flagstaff Hill not far behind.

The diggings were such an adventure that few could resist the call, even if it was for only a few days or just a jaunt with friends.

The New Rush
Colour lithograph by S. T. Gill, c. 1854
(COLLECTION – BENDIGO ART GALLERY)

A ragtag army of diggers makes its way to Bendigo.

Almost everything had to be carried on the diggers' backs. Few had horses, and only those newly arrived fresh from the old country with funds could afford the hire of a bullock dray.

Although there were many new chums who attempted to carry everything they thought they would need, the roads were soon littered with the trappings of polite society that were of no use at all in the bush, or were simply a burden best discarded.

In the towns and on every field the digger's auction was a common sight, as men sought to grab back a few shillings spent on non-essential goods they no longer wished to carry to the next rush.

The road through the forests was fraught with danger, and bushrangers and thieves seemed to wait at every turn.

One young fellow, who had spent a long time at Bendigo, had his horse stolen by a group of escaped convicts just out of Albury. It had pulled his cart from Bendigo to Sydney onto the Turon and back, to be taken by thieves half way back again. He had kept one nugget of seven or eight ounces as a remembrance of old times and feared that he would have to sell it to finance his way back to Bendigo.

Attack on the road was such a common occurrence that all who recorded their own stories of life on the diggings make reference to what they themselves had the mispleasure to experience:

Towards evening, a party of four, returning from the diggings, encamped a little distance from us. Some of our loiterers made their acquaintance. They had passed the previous night in the Black Forest, having wandered out of their way. To add to their misfortunes, they had been attacked by three well-armed bushrangers … two of the poor men had been wounded, one rather seriously. Hardly had they recovered from this shock, than they were horrified by the sudden discovery in a sequestered spot of some human bones, strewn upon the ground beside a broken-down cart. Whether accident or design had brought these

Gold Escort Attacked by Bushrangers
From *The History of Australia* by David Blair, McGready, Thompson and Niven, Glasgow, Melbourne & Dunedin, 1878
Lithograph by W. & A. K. Johnston, Edinburgh
(LA TROBE UNIVERSITY, BENDIGO, LIBRARY COLLECTION)

The roads teemed with hard men, ex-convicts, absconders, men brutalised by the system, backs scarred by the lash. These men took to the bush to take their fortune from the pockets of new chums or to prey upon the drays laden with nuggets under escort to the Treasury.

Here such hard men cared little for the lives of the troopers, or for the lives of those they robbed, tied to trees in the bush and left to the ants, the flies, dogs and crows.

The diggers demanded protection from the government, but little was given. The government found it difficult to discern between diggers of sound virtue and those without any at all. To most of the troopers and the police those on the goldfield were simply new chums ripe for exploitation.

Bushrangers on Rout [sic] **to the Goldfields**
Watercolour by S. T. Gill, 1852
(LA TROBE PICTURE COLLECTION, STATE LIBRARY OF VICTORIA)

There were many who also made the most of the opportunities offered to them by the great influx of migrants to the colony.

Hardened 'Vandemonians' often escaped from the prison colony of Van Diemen's Land to the mainland. There they plundered the new chum and the old hand alike, taking the hard-earned nuggets on a short cut to the city.

unfortunates to an untimely end, none know; but this ominous appearance seemed to have terrified them even more than the bushrangers themselves.[3]

To this report Ellen Clacy adds that her party doubled their watch on that night.

One young adventurer wrote to his mother back home in England with this request for a 'life-preserver':

I wish you had sent out one of Colt's revolvers, or a pair of good duelling pistols as I am more in want of them than anything I can mention. For Baker's revolvers they are asking £16 or £18 each, and for pistols that are 4/6 at home, 45/-. The town is in a dreadful state … This week ten bushrangers were taken. Their beat is on the road to the diggings, travelling in parties of 4 or 6. They stopped everyone they met, took them into the bush, stripped them naked, tied them to trees, and there left them until someone came by and released them.[4]

The roads were crowded with travellers all intent on one purpose:

In one week upwards of 2000 people were counted on the road to the Bathurst diggings, and only eleven coming down. Hundreds of men, of

***Melbourne 1855, as seen from the
north, near the road to Mt Alexander***
Lithograph by Henry Burn

*(LA TROBE PICTURE COLLECTION,
STATE LIBRARY OF VICTORIA)*

Crossing the open grassy plains to the
north of Melbourne took all of the first
day of any journey to the Mt Alexander
and Bendigo diggings.

After a single day of toil with a swag
over the shoulder, pick and shovel in
hand, the small settlement at 'Digger's
Rest' was a welcome sight.

This drawing shows a pair of diggers
resting by the side of the road as the
heavily guarded gold escort makes its way
back to the Treasury.

Melbourne's growing skyline can be
seen, not too far away, stretching across
the horizon.

all classes, threw up their situations, and leaving their wives and families behind them, started for the diggings. Whole crews ran away from
their ships, which were left to rot in our harbours ... the roads were
crowded with travellers, carriages, gigs, drays, carts and wheelbarrows:
mixed up in one confused assemblage might be seen magistrates,
lawyers, physicians, clerks, tradesmen, and labourers.[5]

As they tramped towards their El Dorado the new chums were
passed by others heading back to town, pockets filled ready for a
spree, and there were others who had had no such luck and were
already keen to give digging away; troopers crashed through the
bush, mounting guard over flatbed drays carrying boxes of gold ready
for the Treasury, and there was the ever-watchful villain lurking,
waiting for the unwary or the careless.

Apart from the bleached bones of a few unfortunate diggers, the
roads were also littered with the wrecks of expeditions gone wrong,
animals that would pull no more simply left to die by the side of the
road, goods piled high as merchants waited for relief, or discarded as
yet one more traveller sought to lighten his load. Bullock drays made
their painfully slow progress towards the diggings. It took a journey
of three, four or more weeks to get supplies up by wagon, the goods
carried this way arrived with a highly inflated retail value, but the
diggers on the fields had little choice but to pay the going rate or do
without.

Many an entrepreneur made a start in commerce by judiciously
investing in a drayload of goods that would bring a handsome profit
on the diggings. Diggers who had banded together often invested in

a pair of horses and a dray to carry the goods they thought essential on the diggings, but soon sold the beasts on arrival, as the cost of feeding and watering, combined with the difficulty keeping them corralled or safe from thieves, was prohibitive for most.

The end of the journey was near when a party became aware of a dull roar in the distance, a roar like slow-rolling thunder. The rocking of hundreds of cradles, the loading and discharging of hundreds of buckets set up a cacophony that grew louder as they approached, eager for the first sight of the diggings:

> **Our longing eyes at length obtained a view of El Dorado – Forest Creek. It was a sight! Mounds of earth lying beside holes presented the dismal appearance of a graveyard … the whole scene to a new chum was one of unspeakable squalor, surpassing all that his eye had seen or his fancy woven …[6]**

Another remarked as he topped the rise that led down to the Forest Creek diggings: 'its appearance was novel to us all, and the tents gave the impression that an immense army was in camp there'.

After several days on the road in an environment so unfamiliar and in many ways so hostile, the first sight of the diggings must have set many a stout heart a-flutter.

Martyrs of the Road
Watercolour by William Strutt, 1851
(STATE PARLIAMENTARY LIBRARY COLLECTION, VICTORIA)

All of the effort of struggle and defeat are drawn together in this powerful work by Strutt, as man and beast both strain to finish the journey, while some animals are finished by the journey itself.

Such a miserable sight was common to all who travelled to the diggings.

Whether summer or winter, the road made for a tortuous journey. In summer the heat, the dust and the flies made exertion intolerable, and in winter the sheer volume of traffic going both ways turned the earth into a quagmire.

And, all along the track, a never-ending line straining against the unfamiliar terrain, eager to reach their El Dorado.

– FREEMAN COBB & CO. –

TRAVELLING across the seas to Australia was the easy part. All a hopeful digger had to do was load his goods onto the boat, sit back for 100 days and there he was, landing all his gear at Hobson's Bay.

Getting up to the diggings took a bit more effort. Unlike the American diggings, which saw steamboats in service on the Sacramento River soon after the first rush, the trip to Mt Alexander was over almost-uncharted territory, over boggy plains in winter, a dust bowl in summer, through bushranger-ridden forest, and then another two days to go – on foot.

In July 1853 four enterprising young Americans who had gained some experience out West and on the Californian goldfields with Wells Fargo and the Adams Express Co., established their own coaching firm in Melbourne.

Up until this time passenger coaches in use were British imports, which had solid metal suspensions and steel-rimmed wheels totally unsuited to Australian conditions.

Freeman Cobb and his partners, James Swanton, John Peck and John Lamber, established the firm Cobb & Co., using light, leather-sprung American coaches built in Concord, Massachusetts. The first coaches ran between Melbourne and Castlemaine, the closest diggings to Port Phillip and the most popular at that time. They employed hundreds, kept countless horses, which were changed every ten miles on the run, scores of stablehands and drivers, hotelkeepers and changing-station attendants.

Cobb & Co. was famous for the quality of its service and for the skill and popularity of the drivers. One of the most famous of them all was Edward Devine, a great 'character', also known as Cabbage-tree Ned, who drove the Ballarat to Geelong run.

Ned had even convinced his passengers that he had trained a kangaroo to

Coach-Driver Ned Devine

(*LA TROBE PICTURE COLLECTION STATE LIBRARY OF VICTORIA*)

The legendary coach-driver, 'Cabbage-tree' Ned Devine, showing the grip on the reins that made him famous.

meet the coach, take delivery of the mail, and carry it away in its pouch for delivery. Just after he had told this improbable story, his coach rounded a corner, and there stood a kangaroo by the side of the road. 'Nothing for you today, Jack', shouted Ned as the coach rolled by. The kangaroo simply turned and hopped away, much to the astonishment of Ned's passengers.

In 1862 Ned was the driver of the 'Great Coach', which was pulled by twelve grey horses and carried 90 passengers, among them the first English cricket team to tour Australia.

The largest of Cobb's Australian-built coaches was the 'Leviathan'. This massive coach, pulled by 22 horses, ran between Castlemaine and Kyneton.

Cobb & Co. had established a reputation for safety, comfort and reliability, so the firm managed to continue operation long after competition from the ever-extending railways which were reaching all corners of the country by the 1860s.

As the railways pushed further and further across Victoria, linking most of the major gold-producing centres with Melbourne, and with the discovery of vast new deposits in northern and outback Queensland, Cobb & Co. moved the headquarters of the firm to the New South Wales goldfields town of Bathurst in 1862.

Freeman Cobb sold his interest in the firm in 1861 to James Rutherford and coaching agent Walter Hall, who along with his brother Thomas had gained a lot of experience, not all to do with coaching and carting, on the Victorian fields. With his partner, Walter Hall, Rutherford was to continue to provide the service that Cobb had made famous.

Even though Freeman Cobb no longer had any interest in the company, the name of Cobb & Co. was kept and has remained synonymous with the excitement and romance of coach travel in the 'roaring days'.

UNDER SOUTHERN SKIES

Hurrah for the free new land
  And hurrah for the diggers bold!
  And hurrah for the strong unfettered right
  To search in the hills for gold!
  Turn up the sods my strong free mates,
  And dig with a fearless hand;
  For there's not a castled lordling here,
  In all this glorious land!

Breathe for a moment, one glad breath,
  Throw up the shadeless brow;
  Where is the paid task-master's eye?
  We were never men 'till now!
  Men with a right to toil!
  Men with a right to speak!
  And a strength we will never use, please God,
  To trample down the weak!

Song of the Gold Diggers
by M.H.F., Kangaroo Diggings
Mount Alexander Mail, 14 December 1855
The second verse of this song finishes with the lines: 'But never a lingering look cast back to the land where we were as slaves!', whereas the third ends with: 'The love of our Father-land, oh true! But her homes are cursed with pride; and her cottage walls are trampled down to make the palace wide!'
  Such sentiments laid the foundation of a free and classless modern Australian society

LIFE UNDER SOUTHERN SKIES! While the English press was filled with both the excitement of the adventure and news of great nuggets, it also offered many cautionary tales, generally to no avail. The movement away from tired old Europe and out into the new world was too enticing, too seductive, too liberating, to deny. The notion of a new start to life where one could be free and make one's own way, with prospects undenied by position or accident of birth, seemed too attractive to ignore.

The diggings paid no heed to class or creed; there all men were equal. As J.W. Bull wrote of the men drawn together on the Forest Creek diggings in March 1852:

Take a picture perfectly true. Here are four men working in a claim; next claim on one side four Californians; on another side, four Tasmanians (coarse fellows) and not far off a party of Melbourne men. All these men are on an equality as to their pursuit.

Did the well-bred men descend to the general manners of their surroundings? As a rule no. Civil and sociable remarks pass. The roughest of the men see and adopt, as far as they can, the manners of the gentlemen, and begin to see themselves to be respectable.

– News From –
1851

London, November 24
Three ships arrived from the Australian colonies today, carrying over seven tons of gold between them.

The biggest consignment was in the Eagle *from Melbourne, which was carrying over six tons, with a value of £600,000. The others with gold from New South Wales, are the* Sapphire *and the* Pelham.

But greater consignments are due to come. The Dido *is due to arrive in a few days carrying over 10 tons.*

The Times *newspaper calculated that the August yield from the Victorian fields was close to 10 tons, and that was 'in a wet month'.*

Our Camp at Castlemaine
Watercolour by Cuthbert Clarke, 1854

(LA TROBE LIBRARY PICTURE COLLECTION,
STATE LIBRARY OF VICTORIA)

Diggers loll about an old tree stump, and fashionable young ladies take the air. The rough-and-ready diggings soon established an air of normalised society where, among the mud and dust, all the trappings of life 'at home' were to be had.

Unfortunately for those who had established quite 'permanent' huts near the Castlemaine Camp, they were forcibly removed in 1852 after the government decided to enlarge the area it required and erect more permanent buildings where diggers' huts were standing.

No compensation was given to those who had previously laid claim to the hillside. Their tents and slab huts were summarily removed or destroyed, and they had to start all over again.

Frank McKillop, editor of the *Mt Alexander Mail*, wrote of the population on the diggings in 1855:

> The population of the field! What a heterogeneous collection! Nearly every race on earth was represented, with British greatly dominating – all on an equality in the eager scramble for gold. There were French, German, Italian, American and Chinese settlements.
>
> The bulk of the diggers were a manly, hardy and intelligent class of men – Britain's best to open up a new country and to carry forward British institutions and British ideals. They were for the most part strangers to each other these blue-shirted, horny-handed, stout-hearted diggers, many having been delicately nurtured, but social distinctions were unknown on the goldfields in this new land.[1]

The diggings offered all the opportunity to begin afresh, to be at the beginning of the birth of a new kind of society, a community where all 'men' were truly equal, where prejudices of class and creed were superseded by cash. The gracious boulevards of London were left far behind, the verdant sward of the Emerald Isle a distant memory, the

(Opposite, Above)

General View of the Diggings, Ballarat
Watercolour by Henry Winkles, c. 1853

*(Rex Nan Kivell Collection, R4749.
By Permission, National Library of Australia)*

Once the diggers descended on a rush it
didn't take long before the earth was
turned upside down.

Wherever the miners went the landscape was left in ruins, open shafts pitted
the ground, gullies lay clogged with silt
and gravel, streams muddied, diverted,
dammed and often destroyed.

The diggers often left as quickly as they
had come, rushing from place to place.
The Australian bush seemed endless, space
to spare; once one gully lay ruined there
was another over the hill, fresh, in waiting
for the attentions of the rapacious, greedy
digger.

(Below)

Golden Point, Ballarat
Watercolour by David Tulloch, 1851

*(Rex Nan Kivell Collection, T2253.
By Permission, National Library of Australia)*

Chinaman's Gully, 17 November 1852
Drawing by Eugène von Guérard

*(Dixson Galleries, State Library
of New South Wales)*

It was not only flags that indicated
nationalities but also banners which
stated political affiliations or sympathies.

This tent proudly displays the 'Lone
Texas Star', indicating that the diggers
within did not wish to be considered
as 'Yankees'.

Like the Californians, Texans rarely sat
comfortably with the rest of the United
States. They seceded from the Union in
1861.

purple heath and misty-shrouded crags of the Highlands a fading
echo. On the diggings all was as new, here was land never tilled by
plough nor trod by the hard hooves of grazing cattle. No crowded
streets, or darkened alleyways, no tenement or chilling croft, the
diggers could stake their claim where they pleased, and set themselves to toil, or not, as the fancy took them.

However, it was not long before the gentle valleys looked as if they
had been the scene of a great battle.

Nature had been rudely disturbed and peace and purity had fled for
ever; Mount Alexander looked frowningly down on the desecration and
desolation of Nature's bower, the crystal stream had vanished and a
muddy, repulsive flow had appeared, the green carpet of Mother Earth
had been cruelly rent and soiled and unsightly heaps, etc. were offending the eye along the streams and slopes, trees had been felled, the birds
had hurried shrieking away, bearded, begrimed men were feverishly
burrowing like moles into the earth scarring the face of nature, the air
was filled with the discordant shouts of men, the noise of the cradle and
the reports of firearms.

At night as far as the eye can see the camp fires of the invading Goths
and Vandals were burning – two long, irregular strings of luminously,
iridescent beads. The beautiful had given way to the materialistic, peace
has departed, and pandemonium reigned – all in less than a month.[2]

The arrival of the Commissioners brought some kind of focus to
the encampments. They generally positioned their 'Camps' on
vantage points overlooking the main diggings. In Bendigo they set up
on a hill overlooking what is now
known as Rosalind Park, on a rise still
known as Camp Hill; on Forest Creek
they first established themselves at Red
Hill, Chewton, but later removed to
the junction of Forest and Barker's
Creeks, also on a slight rise that is still
known today as 'Camp Oval'. The well-
ordered Commissioners' Camp on the
Ballarat diggings *(see title-page)* was set
up once again looking across the diggings, while the diggers' tents followed
the line of the creek or were set with
their backs to the trees.

It was not long before the vastness of the diggings and the jumble of canvas and bark dwellings made it extremely difficult for the diggers to locate one another, or even to find their own way back to their own tents. Traversing the diggings at night was extremely hazardous, especially if one had been 'out on a spree'. Apart from the tents and ropes and fallen trees, the terrain was littered with open shafts and deep and abandoned holes. Many an unwary digger was located in the morning, floating at the bottom of an abandoned shaft, after putting a wrong foot forward in the dark.

Flags were flown to indicate whose tent was whose. A Union Jack here, a Scotch Thistle there, the Fleur-de-lys, the Texas Star, all indicated the nationality of the occupier, and often served to inform of the languages spoken within. At Campbell's Creek one hotel was named The Five Flags, as five languages were spoken behind the bar. Stores were identified by their flags or letters emblazoned on their roofs. Bryce Ross, the correspondent for the *Melbourne Morning Herald*, compiled a directory of important or established dwellings in which he listed each tent in the order it stood in the gullies or along the flats, this directory enabled newcomers or those seeking stores or old friends to locate one another among the sea of canvas. Ross compiled his directories for almost all of the diggings, including Ballarat,

Ross's Store, Bendigo Goldfield
Watercolour by John Carter Northcote,
c. 1852
(COLLECTION – BENDIGO ART GALLERY)

Ross's store is typical of the enterprise of hundreds who had come to the diggings prepared to capitalise on the demand for supplies.

Stores were identified by flags flown, in this case, on a freshly-cut bush pole.

Few stores could afford to specialise in the early days, as most attempted to make the most of every opportunity, trading in whatever was available and whatever they could bring up from Melbourne.

At times almost anything at all could be had on the diggings. As bullock drays toiled to bring all kinds of goods up from the port advertisements appeared on tree trunks announcing the arrival of crates of porter, champagne, lace, ribbons, books, mining equipment, clothing and all kinds of fancy goods.

The diggers had the gold, and the merchants took every opportunity to take it from them.

Advertisement for English tent-maker
Benjamin Edgington of Duke Street,
London Bridge, Southwark

*(Rex Nan Kivell Collection.
By Permission, National Library of Australia)*

Edgington's products, of obviously
inestimable quality, were endorsed by
Mrs Chisholm.

In this advertisement the simple testi-
monial reads at right: 'No one must
expect to get a house or lodgings at Port
Phillip – every one must be provided
with a tent'. This message is transcribed
from one of Caroline Chisholm's many
addresses to the potential emigrant on
behalf of the Emigration Society, as
reported in the *Times* on 23 July 1852.

William Howitt records coming across
one such tent on his way to the McIvor
diggings:

I saw a tent by the side of the road,
having, 'Edgington, tent-maker, London,'
upon it. I went up to it, and found it
occupied by a solitary new-chum,
evidently a gentleman.

He was at breakfast; his plate rested on
the end of a box; a good English stove
burning in the tent, the pipes ascending
outside, and a double-barrelled gun
leaning against the back of his chair.

Although he had been left by the side
of the track by his mates after their cart
had broken down and they had gone with
half their load, he was at least still able to
breakfast in comfort.

Bryce Ross's *Diggers' Directory*

(Private Collection)

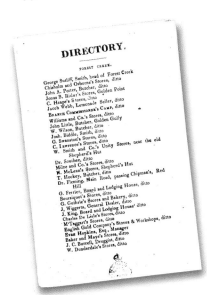

Bendigo, Forest Creek and the Ovens, and turned his knowledge into
a successful enterprise.

There were also numerous large trees left around the diggings that
were used as noticeboards; the trees served for a long time to display
messages from one party to another, to advertise goods or to carry
government notices: 'the Digger's Intelligencer, – a fine old gum on
whose weatherbeaten trunk was to be seen numerous postcards,
some pasted on, some wafered on, some nailed on' was an important
meeting point, and served to establish communication among the
hordes of itinerant diggers who passed back and forth from rush to
rush.

There were literally dozens of drays and heavily-laden carts arriving each week, followed by hundreds more on foot, who were intent
on the diggings:

The drays were laden with flour, corn, potatoes, sugar, tea, spirits, bot-
tled beer, and the like, as well, as spades, buckets, &c. On the roadsides
were stores displaying plentiful assortments of tin ware of all sizes, hanging in front – tea-kettles, bales of flannel, shoes, boots, ready-made
clothes, &c.; in fact, all such things as diggers are in constant want of.[4]

It was possible to buy goods on the diggings that were no longer
available on the streets of Melbourne, shipowners would unload their
cargo straight onto bullock-drays that headed out immediately for the
goldfields, such was the profit to be made from the newly-enriched
diggers.

Although it was illegal to sell any
alcoholic liquor on the diggings,
grog was in great demand, and the
carriers took great pains to keep
up the supply. Kegs of grog were
carried to the diggings hidden
among other goods loaded on the
drays:

We loaded in Elizabeth Street, at a
merchant's named Smithson. Our
loading was general stores and
grog. The grog was in 5-gallon kegs,
and addressed to different people,
for there was no spirits allowed to
be sold on the diggings. It was

placed in the middle of the dray, and the sugar, tea, etc., packed all round it and over the top, so the troopers could not see that we had any grog on board.[5]

John Chandler, who in his diaries stated that he had been on all the early diggings, continues:

> all spirits found in any tent or store, were seized, and carried to the Commissioner's camp and destroyed. But there never was a law so much evaded, for in nearly every instance, one tent in five was a sly grog shanty … had we been caught, we should have our horses, drays, and loads seized.

He concludes that, although the government tried to keep grog off the diggings, he had never seen so much drunkenness. In 1853, when the government gave up its prohibition, and granted licences to sell liquor, Chandler notes:

> they gave every little shanty with two or more rooms, a licence. They always go to extremes.[6]

As the canvas communities grew around the creeks, life there entered a familiar pattern. Digging parties divided themselves into working teams, which took shifts or turns in the pits and at the

Mount Alexander, Gold Diggings, Australia
Robert Shortreid Anderson, *Glasgow Examiner*, 30 October 1852
(*LA TROBE PICTURE COLLECTION, STATE LIBRARY OF VICTORIA*)

This very lively lithograph indicates the bustling activity that characterised the diggings.

Diggers seem like ants in their exertions, running from here to there and back again, seduced by the prospect of instant wealth.

A Good Day's Work
Hand-coloured lithograph
Cyrus Mason, Melbourne, 1855

(REX NAN KIVELL COLLECTION, U2493.
BY PERMISSION, NATIONAL LIBRARY OF AUSTRALIA)

A party of digger-mates examine their reward for a good day's work as they retire to their tent.

James Bonwick described the diggers domestic arrangements in a survey of Bendigo in the early 1850s:

[The diggers] live in canvas homes, or huts of bark and logs ... Our furniture is of a simple character. A box, a block of wood, or a bit of paling across a pail, serves as a table. Some luxurious ones positively have rough stools as seats: the majority recline upon their beds, or make use of a log, the ground, or a pail turned upside down ...

After a hard day's work one is not disposed to be too particular about the evening meal, and the mode in which it is prepared ... [some] will content themselves with dry or flat Johnny cakes, which are simply flour and water, with the addition of greasy accumulation of cookery, hastily prepared in the frying pan. Many lose health by inattention to meals ...

He remarks on the danger to health:

The sitting on the damp ground induces piles. Most attacks of sickness resolve themselves into fevers of the low typhoid type, as the powers of life are soon exhausted here ...[7]

However, most diggers believed that the rewards far outweighed the risks.

windlass, some even worked around the clock in an effort to make as much as possible in the shortest time and take the next steam packet home.

The day's work was hard for men who were largely unused to physical labour. Antoine Fauchery complained of the arduous labour, an aching back and blistered hands, but records in his diaries the pleasure of rest at the end of the working day:

the evenings are a delight at the end of the day's work, being both novel and picturesque. From every direction weary diggers are to be seen returning to their canvas homesteads, hundreds of fires are kindled and illuminate the scene, and at each tea is made and mutton roasted. The evening meal finished, the air is filled with the sound of firearms being fired, in order to be reloaded anew before the night.[8]

At every evening, and again in the dawn, the diggers fired their pistols into the air, ensuring that they had kept their powder dry and were prepared for any emergency. The noise was deafening as hundreds of firearms exploded simultaneously, shattering the peaceful twilight.

The cradles may have stopped and the digging ceased, but the evenings were still alive with the sounds of all creation as the songs of all nationalities were taken up on the cooling night air. Italians caroused at their operas, Germans had their 'oompah' bands trumpeting away, playing waltzes first heard by the Danube; and always the haunting strains of the lone Scottish piper stirred a thousand hearts far from the 'shores of Loch Lomond'.

Coffee tents and sly-grog shops were everywhere, the Chinese opened restaurants that catered for all tastes, little flocks of sheep were driven into butchers' pens ready for slaughter, as the demand for fresh meat was readily satisfied by the squatters upon whose runs the diggers had camped. Large tents were converted to theatres, where the leading performers of the day trod 'the boards', often rewarded with a shower of gold if they were any good, or hastened off stage in a shower of stones if no good at all. Circuses toured the diggings, and on Sundays, when by decree all digging ceased, tree stumps or drays were mounted by itinerant preachers who spread the word to the faithful.

The diggings quickly became a rough-and-ready parody of European society:

> Went to the consecration of the large tent which has been erected as a R.C. place of worship. There was such a crowd that it was almost impossible to get inside. Dr. Goold, R.C. Bishop of Melbourne, preached. Afterwards I walked to Canadian Gully, now pretty well the centre of the principal diggings. Found a great number of stores, eating houses, smithies, etc. had sprung up. Also to my surprise came upon Henri d'Orleans, who is now running a much decorated 'Lemonade tent'. He is doing a grand business during this hot season by selling all sorts of cooling drinks, and excellent havana cigars at 2/- a piece.[9]

Although there were those whose main aim was to get in, get rich and get out, there was also a large body of colonists who had no intention of returning to the country that had spurned them, and thousands more who were keen to make a new life far away from the gloomy streets of London – no matter how rough and tumble that life was in the beginning.

The diggings provided adventure that many had never really dreamed possible. The diggings offered freedom, they offered liberty, opportunity, camaraderie, excitement and cherished memories. As Ellen Clacy climbed aboard a slow-moving dray, ready for the return journey home, she gave the diggings a parting look. She recorded, somewhat wistfully, 'a slight turn in the road, and the last tent vanished from my sight. "Never," thought I, "shall I look on such a scene again".'[10]

Clacy, like so many thousands of others before and to come after, had enjoyed the great colonial adventure. She had seen the diggings, she had tucked away her memories of life lived under southern skies.

'Success at the diggings is like drawing lottery tickets – the blanks far outnumber the prizes.'
Mrs Charles [Ellen] Clacy[11]

The Diggers Take a Mid-day Meal
Illustrated Melbourne Post, 9 August 1862
(PRIVATE COLLECTION)

A trio of diggers take time to enjoy the adventure of living free.

Most were keen to re-create themselves in the new world, to leave behind their past, and to set themselves free from the class-ridden society back home.

A GLITTERING LOTTERY

THE NEW CHUMS' ARRIVAL ON A GOLD DIGGINGS.

*The New Chums' Arrival
on a Gold Diggings*
Hand-coloured lithograph, c. 1860
From *Sketches of Australian Life and
Scenery*, Paul Jerrard & Son, for Messrs
Newbold & Co., London

(LA TROBE PICTURE COLLECTION,
STATE LIBRARY OF VICTORIA)

Images of the diggings and diggers were
popular as keepsakes all around the world.

These lithographs form part of a series
depicting a wide variety of scenes and
events typical of life on the diggings, such
as a highway hold-up, a bush Christmas
and the arrival of the green new chum.

The arrival experience of all who
migrated was quickly put behind them as
they became diggers and 'wild colonial
boys'.

T HE DIGGINGS are a mere lottery. There is not above one out of
a hundred that do well here; and no one need go without £200 in
his pocket ... several of the *Great Britain*'s first-cabin passengers
are wheeling water for sale throughout the streets of Melbourne ...

So wrote the son of an Ayrshire gentleman who emigrated to the
colonies in May of 1852.[1]

One newspaper of 17 November 1852 reported that the rush to
Port Phillip was so great that, in just a few days seven ships had
arrived, adding a further 3600 souls to the fledgling township. Many
hopefuls had made the long voyage to find a crowded township, without adequate lodgings or adequate services, and with overpriced
goods and outrageously priced foods.

In the early days when the towns had emptied of their menfolk,
wages for any kind of position had skyrocketed; by 1852 oversupply
of labour had cut these wages right back.

There were also hundreds of disappointed diggers returning from the goldfields looking for just enough work to make the fare home, so that any chance of finding a position to tide the unwary traveller over until he got his land-legs was now almost impossible. For the hundreds who expected easy pickings, the diggings failed to live up to expectation. Only one year after the first discoveries the alluvial gold was all but gone, and then the real digging commenced. The days of the adventurer were rapidly coming to an end, yet the merchants' ships were still bringing hundreds at a time into an environment that was not about to satisfy them all.

> Of the 200 who came out in the Blackfriar, and went to the Diggings, nearly all have returned, and those remaining are earning only enough money to subsist on ... crime is very prevalent – in fact, the colony is getting bad altogether; and should the Diggings fail, I do not know what will be the consequence. The convicts shoot you in a moment ... in fact, it will be a complete California in a few months, if the Diggings keep failing as they have for the last two months.[2]

Yet still they came. The ships poured their eager human cargo onto the docks, and the roads to the diggings were filled with an almost endless stream of hopefuls who still believed that after a few weeks at the diggings they would fill their pockets, return to Melbourne,

Prospecting for Gold, or Rewarded at Last
Hand-coloured lithograph, c. 1860
From *Sketches of Australian Life and Scenery*, Paul Jerrard & Son, for Messrs Newbold & Co., London
(Rex Nan Kivell Collection, U2822. By Permission, National Library of Australia)

In this lithograph, diggers who had been on the field for some time are seen sharing their experience and good fortune with a new chum.

Their next move was to sell their claim, 'rich with nuggets', to the inexperienced gentleman and move on, to let him find out for himself how little they had left behind and ponder on how much it had cost him.

The Newly Arrived Inquiring
Lithograph by S. T. Gill, 1852

(REX NAN KIVELL COLLECTION, S183.
BY PERMISSION, NATIONAL LIBRARY OF AUSTRALIA)

Gold Panning, Ballarat Diggings, Victoria
Watercolour by William Strutt, 1851

(VICTORIAN STATE PARLIAMENTARY LIBRARY COLLECTION)

and then home again on the next steam packet available – rich, experienced, and set for life.

No matter where the expectant diggers went they were confronted with the same bustling scene:

The first sight of the … diggings, after passing through tents scattered here and there for nearly five miles, is that which you would imagine to be a citadel thrown to the ground, and some thousands of men running about like rabbits in burrows, all having an appearance of deep yellow earth – yellow clothes – yellow hands – yellow faces – yellow everything, and working in closely-compacted pieces of ground as thick as possible over the whole surface of the hill or mountain.[3]

Antoine Fauchery, the photographer who left behind a marvellous pictorial record of the diggings, wrote in his letters published in Paris in 1857, that 'the only resolve to take on the diggings is to make a fortune at one stroke and then get away, without even looking back'.[4]

Many believed they too would return to their mother country, but they simply 'spent, wasted, swallowed!' what they had won in the greatest lottery of them all, condemning themselves to exile forever in this very foreign landscape.

The diggings were regarded by many as a lottery, where some win, and win handsomely, and many others lose. And when the winnings do come, and the gains are spent at the bar in some grog shop or splashed around with largesse in the streets of Melbourne, all it would take is another trip to the diggings to start all over again. Many diggers could not resist the 'easy come, easy go' attitude of this magnificent lottery, and were trapped by its attractions.

> There is a great restlessness among the miners, a constant shifting of their position, and exchange of holes by purchase ... a man may gain but a small return, though he goes deeper than a neighbour almost adjoining him, who is literally gathering gold. The inequality of the distribution is remarkable, and gold-finding is a perfect lottery – at least with the present imperfect knowledge of the nature and cause of this inequality ... the whole work is one of hazard.[5]

Fauchery may have been right – to work hard, take the reward, and leave. But only a few took that advice. He remembers a sailor named

Diggers at Forest Creek
Photograph by Antoine Fauchery

(LA TROBE PICTURE COLLECTION, STATE LIBRARY OF VICTORIA)

Fauchery not only recorded life on the diggings as it was, he also created photographic tableaus that were artistic statements in much the same way that artists composed their canvases.

Here Fauchery has gathered a group of miners in a composition focused on the metal in the panning dish.

Only one man is gazing at the camera, the artistic foil to the obvious sentiment Fauchery has created in this photograph.

This is a dynamic composition flowing from right to left, the strong repetitive pattern of figures leaning towards the circular shape of the pan, the centre of the composition. The arched figure on the left counterbalances the dynamic of the movement and the shovel handles thrust the form back again.

A beautifully balanced, yet totally contrived 'moment in time'.

The Disappointed Digger
(*PRIVATE COLLECTION*)

The Disappointed Digger

– THE SARAH SANDS –

The monster nugget referred to here was later named the 'Sarah Sands' after the ship in which it was carried back to England.

The sailors who had discovered the nugget returned to England on the same ship that had brought them out – and after only two days at the diggings.

Both Eugène von Guérard and Fauchery have described seeing this nugget just after it was brought to the surface. In fact, it was around this time (January 1853) that Fauchery had joined up with von Guérard's company as mates on the Ballarat diggings.

Von Guérard's group was an unusual one, consisting of an eclectic group of European middle-class artists and intellectuals.

Both von Guérard and Fauchery had female companions, young women of good breeding and similar background, who had accompanied them from Europe. They are at times referred to as wives, at other times as *bonnées* or friends. In all accounts the young ladies were regarded as equals in the company, and took part in the business of gold digging as much as the men.

Antoine, a fellow-countryman, who had taken 126 lbs of gold from a claim on the Eureka line. Antoine had already 'dissipated the 50,000 francs' worth found at Bendigo' and was on his way to drink the remainder in whatever bar he could find. Fauchery met Antoine on his way to Ballarat a few months later, with nothing left but a pair of nugget earrings. He came across him again in Ballarat, where Antoine was found dead-drunk in the bottom of a 140-foot shaft. He had squandered over 156,000 francs in that short time, 'easy come, easy go'. In fact, it seems that Antoine had been a very lucky digger, believing that it was as simple of digging a hole to get his gold, then he would 'buy a brig and take to the sea again'. But in the meantime the adventure of it all was totally captivating.

Fauchery relates the story of some other sailors who had also made a fortune in a few days and then left again on the same ship that brought them to Port Phillip:

On the first voyage of the Great Britain, an immense steamship built in the Liverpool yards and sent out to Melbourne, the whole crew deserted within sight of the town, in Hobson's Bay. At that period no crew ever acted otherwise. Two of the steamer's passengers and three of the sailors formed a party and made for the mines.

The day after their arrival, armed with tools whose use they did not yet properly know, one of the partners, no doubt anxious to familiarise himself with the emotion that seizes every individual sent below the surface on a rope, wanted to be lowered into a shaft, an abandoned one, – the first encountered … his companions laughed as they let him scramble down to a depth of about fifty feet, and the neighbours laughed at his companions.

Our man, at the bottom of the hole where no one had even taken the trouble to pierce any galleries, was seized by a new fancy: while he was there, why not push his investigations further? … taking one bit of digging with another, it was as good here as anywhere … so he asked for a pick and declared that he would not come out of the hole without adding another foot to its depth.

Pick and shovel were sent down, and he started striking out in all directions; his companions hoisted up the excavated earth, grumbling a little about a joke whose prolongation would only be a waste of time; officious neighbours asked if the 'old hand was trying to get home by the shortest way,' … suddenly the sound of two metals meeting rang out from the point of the pick; he stooped down: a shining yellow spot had been laid bare!

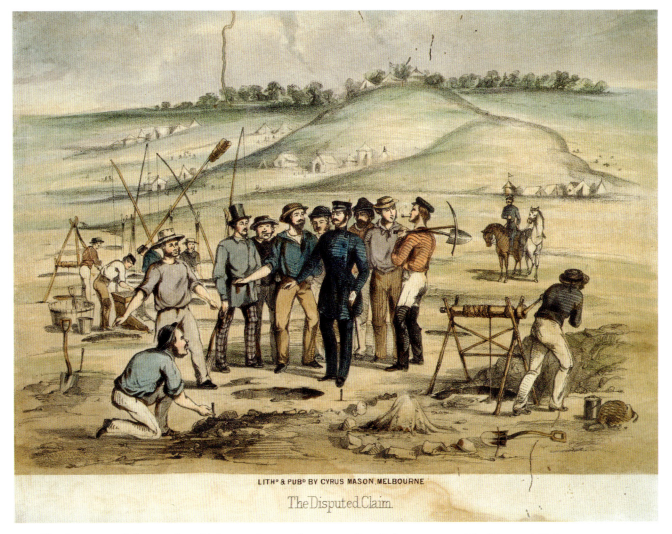

LITHº & PUBº BY CYRUS MASON, MELBOURNE

The Disputed Claim

He dug around the patch, which grew larger, he scraped and dug out more earth, looking for a break in the continuity of the patch, which still grew larger! … after unheard of efforts, for you can't imagine how patches like this are encrusted and cling to the soil, it was at last brought to light; then it proved not to be a patch, it was a mass the size of a paving stone, a piece of gold set right in the middle of the hole,– a piece of gold weighing 132 pounds!

I was not on the spot at the moment the man who made this wonderful discovery came up from the hole; I saw him only an hour later. He was a negro … he had hardly recovered from an excitement that was quite justifiable in such a case, his face still bore traces of that livid pallor peculiar to coloured people that makes the white lips stand out strangely from a grey mask. He was speaking very softly, like a man who has just committed a crime. His white partners were in little better case than he was; they were stunned by their success … one of them, however, came out of his torpor, shook the others, and the monster nugget, placed in the bottom of a bag slung on a long stick, was hoisted on to the shoulders of two of the fortunate proprietors and carried to the commissioner's …

The day after this memorable event the five partners, who had worked all night and collected another 150 ounces of gold in a very small piece

The Disputed Claim
Hand-coloured lithograph,
Cyrus Mason, Melbourne, 1855

*(REX NAN KIVELL COLLECTION, U2491.
BY PERMISSION, NATIONAL LIBRARY OF AUSTRALIA)*

Altercations between the diggers were not at all uncommon, sometimes a fight would break out or, as in this case, a trooper intervenes to settle the dispute.

The diggings were riddled with holes, shafts and underground tunnels. If the ground was thought to be good and nuggets ready to find, disputes over the legitimacy of the size and position of claims regularly flared up.

The prize was great, and every foot dug could make the difference between wealth or poverty.

Golden Point, Ballarat
Watercolour by William Strutt, 1851

(STATE PARLIAMENTARY LIBRARY COLLECTION, VICTORIA)

Strutt's drawings of Ballarat record a wealth of detail about the daily activity on that field. A dray carrying diggers' equipment arrives, the diggers follow behind, a butcher's shambles* with fresh carcasses hanging in the shade, a group of natives watch at the right, and across the creek the digging proceeds apace.

---

*Shambles – an old term for a butcher's shop or slaughterhouse. It derives from the name given to a table for selling meat, which was called a *shamble*.

of ground, handed over to some enthusiasts, for a sum of £500 (12,500 francs), the chance of making a fortune after them in a hole whose exploitation had hardly begun. Satisfied with the result of a few hours' work, they announced their intention of making it back for Europe immediately.

And actually, having gone back to town, they embarked on the same steamer that had bought them out, taking with them on one hand two hundred thousand francs' worth of gold, and on the other hand the memory of having been miners for two days.[6]

News of this discovery spread across the Ballarat diggings, and abandoned shafts in Canadian Gully became busy again near the site of the monster nugget. That week other discoveries were made, including one nugget weighing 94 lbs and another of 78 lbs.

Diggers who had worked these claims bottomed out at around 50 feet, but big nuggets were found below this false rocky bottom, as lines of ancient creek-beds ran at various depths further below.

At one elbow on the Regent's Gully lead a party of four Americans had taken 1,300 lbs of gold from a claim measuring only 24 square feet. Another on the Gravel Pit line had taken 900 lbs from an area 3 ft wide, 24 ft long and 8 ft deep.

Fauchery recalls: 'I once saw coming out of a hole at New Eureka a hatful of earth: this earth contained 17 pounds of fine gold'.[7]

The Ballarat leads took commitment and staying power, the shafts were deep, the work hard, and months would pass before any show of colour would repay tired diggers for their investment. Some never saw their reward. The week before Fauchery left the field seven diggers were killed in their shafts; some drowned, while others were crushed by a falling plank or bucket. In Fauchery's own claim one of his mates had his head 'horribly chipped' and his shoulder dislocated in an accident below ground.

There were some spectacular discoveries that left the world reeling at the sheer size of the nugget. John Deason and Richard Oates, two diggers from the island of Tresco, 31 miles from Land's End off the south-west coast of England, had followed the rush to Bendigo in 1854. They stayed for eight years before taking up a farm on the plains near Moliagul, about 37 miles to the west. They pegged out a claim, stripping the surface layer of the land and washing it in a puddling machine not far from where they made their historic discovery on the morning of 5 February 1869.

Deason was digging around a tree when he struck something solid at the base. 'Confound it! I've broken my pick', cursed Deason when his pick rebounded from beneath the roots. 'I wish I had broken it, if it had only been over some nugget.'

Deason, Oates, friends and family re-enact the discovery of the Welcome Stranger
Photographer unknown
(Private Collection)

The Welcome Stranger Nugget
Engraving from *Picturesque Atlas of Australasia*, vol. 40, p. 741
After the nugget had been placed in Deason's fireplace, small bits of quartz broke loose. Several of the gold encrusted crystals were given to favoured onlookers and friends as keepsakes.

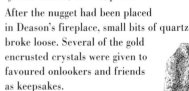

John Deason poses for a commemorative photograph with his pick and shovel, which we may assume were his authentic digging tools, but the 'nugget' is certainly not authentic. A lump of quartz of approximately the correct size and shape has been placed on a box, as the original nugget had long since been broken up.

    All drawings of the Welcome Stranger were done from memory much later.
(Private Collection)

Gold At Last!
Wood engraving, Ebenezer and David Syme, The *Illustrated Australian News*, 28 January 1874

(La Trobe Picture Collection, State Library of Victoria)

A minute afterwards he called out to Oates, who was ploughing in a nearby paddock, and told him to 'come and see what this was'.[8] Sticking several inches out of the ground, 'like a boulder on a hill', was a mass of gold.

They retrieved the nugget, which was almost 12 inches across and nearly the same in length. It was almost too heavy for them both to lift. They then covered it again, continuing to work as if nothing had happened. Later in the day they took it by dray to Deason's house, where they placed the nugget in the fireplace. The effect of heat on the gold forced it to expand, and quartz attached to it became brittle and broke loose. Even the quartz that broke away, after crushing and washing in Deason's puddling machine, yielded 10 lbs gold.

It was the weekend so the nugget was kept on the kitchen table, hidden under a cloth. Deason held a party for his friends, and later that night dramatically revealed the solid gold nugget. Once they had recovered from their shock at being the first to see the largest nugget ever found in all the world, he invited them to stay the night and help escort it to the bank the next day.

The following day the nugget was taken into Dunolly to the London Chartered Bank where it was cut down for smelting. It took Archie Walls, the local blacksmith, five hours to reduce the massive nugget of pure gold, 'as clean as well-cut Cheshire Cheese', into manageable pieces.

The Welcome Stranger weighed 210 lbs. Its value in 1869 was £9210; its estimated value in 2001, $3,000,000.

As to the success or unsuccess of the Diggers, it cannot be denied that, if a man work hard and persevere, notwithstanding first disappointments, he is sure, ultimately, to produce for himself, at least a renumerative amount of wages ... if a man, however, only but obtain his ordinary wages, or if he should not do this, he still has the chance of getting a prize in the great lottery of the auriferous field ... the whole is a lottery, and essentially the lottery of the working man; where, for the price of his license – thirty shillings a month – and strong exercise of his muscular powers, he may draw a prize ...[9]

NO PLACE FOR A LADY?

A SURPRISING NUMBER of women travelled to the early goldfields, and, contrary to contemporary opinion, not all were ladies of ill repute. While there were many who specialised in trade other than gold seeking, a large number had travelled to the diggings in the company of their husbands, and a number of well-educated ladies had simply come, captured by the spirit of adventure, just like their male counterparts.

One young lady from Dublin, possessing a good education, good birth and a handy sum left from her parents' estate, described her desire to join in the great adventure when she accompanied her brother and his mates on board ship headed for 'the diggings'. After committing £300 to outfit their expedition they set out for the experience of a lifetime:

> I was resolved to accompany my brother and his friends to the diggings and I felt that to do so in my own proper costume and character, would be to run unnecessary hazard. Hence my change. I cut my hair into a very masculine fashion; I purchased a broad felt hat, a sort of tunic or smock of coarse blue cloth, trousers to conform, boots of a miner and thus parting with my sex for a season ... behold me an accomplished candidate for mining operations and all the perils and inconveniences they might be supposed to bring.[1]

She seemed to enjoy herself immensely on the goldfields. She arranged a sort of 'supplementary canvas chamber' within the tent occupied by her brother and travelling party, in which she slept, cooked and washed her clothes, and took to keeping watch over the 'heaps of gold dust and nuggets' they had found:

> Of course, my sex is generally known. I am called 'Mr Harry' (an abbreviation of Harriet); but no one intrudes the more on that account. I have

The Girls the Diggers Left Behind and What They Had to Do!
Watercolour by William Strutt, 1852
(STATE PARLIAMENTARY LIBRARY COLLECTION, VICTORIA)

This watercolour shows the grass widows of Melbourne, the women left behind to do men's work, while the only male on the street that creates any interest is an old gent in his top hat as the young ladies crane their necks for a glimpse of 'a man! – a man!'

> To wander through Melbourne and its environs, no one would imagine that females were as one to four of the male population; for bonnets and parasols everywhere outnumber the wide-awakes [a diggers' broad hat].
>
> This is occasioned by the absence of so many 'lords of creation' in pursuit of what they value – many of them at least – more than all the women in the world – nuggets. The wives thus left in town to deplore their husband's infatuation are termed 'grass-widows' – a mining expression'.[2]

Digger's Wife in Full Dress
Watercolour by George Lacy, 1852

*(Rex Nan Kivell Collection, R4111.
By Permission, National Library of Australia)*

The women who promenaded as 'diggers'
wives' had no benefit of bridal party, but
assumed the role of wife to any digger
who provided the wherewithal to play
husband:

> She dressed sumptuously, and arrayed
> herself in the hues of the rainbow.
> Her satin dress, which always looked
> as if it had been made for somebody else,
> was overlaid with a massive gold chain,
> a brooch as big as a warming pan, and
> a lace collar more costly than clean.
> Her hands, which were as red as raw
> beef, and big enough to fell a bullock,
> were garnished gorgeously with rings,
> her movements were more energetic than
> graceful; her language more emphatic
> than precise, and she was surrounded
> by an atmosphere redolent of Eau de
> Cologne, onions and bran.

The wealth that gold had brought to
these once-poor working-class folks may
have bought their freedom but could not
buy them class.

become a sort of necessity, as I am always ready to do a good turn – the
great secret, after all, of social success … I never refuse to oblige a
'neighbour'.[3]

For being 'neighbourly', for the cooking of an occasional pudding
or the darning of a shirt, she was often repaid in small nuggets. After
a short time she had accumulated about 10 lbs of gold:

> Wild the life is, certainly, but full of excitement and hope; and strange it
> is, I almost fear to tell you, that I do not wish it to end![4]

She writes of the enjoyable evenings spent with the diggers at the
end of a day's labour in their shafts:

> You can hardly conceive what merry company gather in our tent every
> evening, or how pleasantly the hours pass … as to suitors, I have them
> in plenty, and not despicable ones either, I assure you.[5]

This letter contrasts with the picture generally painted of the
women on the diggings, but this independent, educated and forth-
right young lady may well contrast with most others who had made the
journey, not for the adventure but out of necessity.

Ellen Clacy told a similar story. She also travelled to the diggings
with a party of men, one her fiancé whom she married just before
their return to London. Clacy published a record of her

travels in 1853. Her party travelled far and wide; she describes the journey out, the arrival in Melbourne, then the long trek to Mt Alexander; from there they went on to Bendigo, the Ovens, and then back to the port. She encountered bushrangers, murderers and thieves, but it is the topic of 'sly grog' that captured much of Clacy's attention and disapproval.

A large number of 'crones' made their fortune in 'coffee tents' which were fronts for sly-grog establishments. Clacy wrote of one such establishment that it

> was situated at right angles with ours [tent] and our shipmates, so the annoyance was equally felt … whilst her husband was at work farther down the gully, she kept a sort of sly-grog shop, and passed the day in selling and drinking spirits, swearing, and smoking a short tobacco-pipe at the door of her tent. She was a most repulsive looking object. A dirty gaudy-coloured dress hung about her shoulders, coarse black hair unbrushed, uncombed, dangled about her face, over which her evil habits had spread a genuine bacchanalian glow, whilst in a loud masculine voice she uttered the most awful words that ever disgraced the mouth of a man – ten thousand times more awful when proceeding from a woman's lips.[6]

Clacy is probably describing a pair of Vandemonian ex-convicts whose background and aspirations would be dramatically different to that of an educated Englishwoman on a 'colonial adventure'. For them, survival, in the colonies that had spurned them and separated them from the mainstream that was always wary of their type, was a desperate struggle. The Vandemonians were despised, feared and outcast, set apart from and against polite society.

Clacy described the influence that the fairer sex generally had on the lives of the diggers. Just as Caroline Chisholm was convinced of the civilising effect of female companionship, Clacy also makes the same observation:

> the interior of the canvas habitation of the digger is desolate enough; a box of wood forms a table, and this is the only furniture; many dispense with that. The bedding, which is laid upon the ground, serves to sit upon.
>
> In some tents the soft influence of our sex is pleasingly apparent; the tins are as bright as silver, there are sheets as well as blankets on the beds, and perhaps a clean counterpane, with the addition of a dry sack or perhaps a piece of carpet.[7]

Oh! My goodness gracious I'll be off –
Hold on, Poll my girl, all right
Watercolour by George Lacy, c. 1860

(Rex Nan Kivell Collection, R3803.
By Permission, National Library of Australia)

There were plenty of young women who weren't prepared to stay away from the diggings while their men had all the fun.

Many travelled with friends or male companions, with a brother and his mates; acting as cook and housekeeper, bringing some degree of civilisation to their calico encampment.

There were also plenty of convict girls who seized upon the opportunity to escape the drudgery of skivvying for a squatter, taking their chances along with everybody else.

The first woman to arrive on the Forest Creek diggings had pushed her barrow from Melbourne, taking four days to make the journey. She had brought a washing tub, but she intended to do no laundry:

She was soon surrounded by diggers who quickly ran her a tent up, and she started in the grog line. She was a lady of colour, and the scenes witnessed about her place at night were something to be remembered. Twice in one week was her tent burned down by the police, but as quickly went up another, in about a couple of hours.

But night at the diggings is a characteristic time: murder here – murder there – revolvers cracking – blunderbusses bombing – rifles going off – balls whistling – one man groaning with a broken leg – another shouting because he could not find his hole, and a third because he had tumbled into one – this man swearing, another praying – a party of bacchanals chanting various ditties, to different time and tune, or rather minus both. Here is one man grumbling because he has brought his wife with him, another ditto because he has left his behind, or sold her for an ounce of gold or a bottle of rum.

Sometimes a wife is at first rather a nuisance; women get scared and frightened, then cross, and commence a 'blow up' with their husbands; but all their railing generally ends in their quietly settling down to this rough and primitive style of living, if not without a murmur, at least to all appearance with the determination to laugh and bear it. And although rough in their manners, and not over select in their address, the digger seldom wilfully injures a woman; in fact, a regular Vandemonian will in his way, play the gallant with as great a zest as a fashionable about town – at any rate, with more sincerity of heart.[8]

Any woman set among this society had to be either strong, accompanied and protected, or just plain tough, and it appears that there were plenty of tough 'sheilas' about, and there were boatloads of young women disembarking who were willing to take a chance in the marriage stakes in the colonies.

Looking for Ladies of Easy Virtue

Although prostitution operated on the diggings, the almost total lack of its description in most written records may indicate that it was either not all that remarkable, or that it was an activity best not recorded, after all what young man or long-departed husband would record in his diary a visit to a house of ill fame.

The *Hill End and Tambaroora Times* described in a report of a visit to the Chinese camp on the Turon in 26 May 1875 that

every hotel and place of entertainment was entered. Large numbers of Chinese were found in most of them, but, contrary to expectation, comparatively few women … a girl of about 18 years of age was seen in bed sipping tea preparatory to indulging in the pleasures of the pipe*… Occasionally in the street, a white object, seen indistinctly in the darkness that prevailed, was descried. A few paces would bring the visitor close enough to distinguish it was a woman 'out on her rounds'.

While the Chinese had no women of their own race with them on the diggings, they did use prostitutes for their own pleasure and for their own gain. It was quite common for European working girls to be engaged by the entrepreneurial Chinese, who saw no barrier to making a little out of every opportunity that presented itself.

Great Bourke Street, Melbourne
Engraving by W. Ralston
News Letter of Australasia
(*Private Collection*)

A pair of diggers can be seen taking the air and the sights in the streets of 'Marvellous Melbourne'.

So much wealth had been taken from the Victorian goldfields and invested in the growing capital of the Colony of Victoria that at the turn of the century it was the richest and fastest-growing city in the world.

It drew visitors from around the world – princes and poets, novelists, actors, artists, priests and paupers made the journey to 'marvel' at Melbourne.

---

*The pipe referred to here is opium. The same article in the *Hill End and Tambaroora Time*s describes a scene quite common in Chinese encampments:

In some cribs the dim lamps were enveloped in dense haloes of opium, the atmosphere was almost suffocating.

Alarming Prospect, the Single Ladies Take Off for the Diggings
Watercolour by John Leech, c. 1852

(REX NAN KIVELL COLLECTION, S2877. BY PERMISSION, NATIONAL LIBRARY OF AUSTRALIA)

Distraught suitors offer marriage settlements that would once have had any single young girl swooning with delight.

The lure of the diggings and the promise of an exciting match made in 'El Dorado' quickly abolished the image of a rose-covered cottage from the mind of those who had their heart set on gold.

John Chandler, whose carrier's dray was a familiar sight on the early diggings, recorded in his diaries that women would offer to travel with him. He remarked that they would go up with one man, stay on the diggings for a while, and then come back down with another:

> I have heard carriers boast of how many women they had taken up. As I was coming into Melbourne once I was met by a young woman, and she was good looking. She asked me for a ride, so I told her to get up. She invited me to go home with her. She soon let me know to what class she belonged.[9]

Chandler and the young woman pulled into the stables where he was to put up for the night; however, the thought of what he was about to do so filled him with dread that he panicked while taking the harness off his horses. When he returned to the dray she was gone. He thanked 'the dear Lord for delivering [him] from joining his body to a harlot'.[10]

While the intention of most who migrated was not to work on the streets but to find a good husband and make a respectable life, a lot of young ladies took the easy way out, making the most of their assets soon after they hit the streets of Melbourne. After all, they were a long way from home, and the intention was to find a partner who could keep them in the manner to which they had never before been accustomed. It was common for these women to 'marry' successful diggers. After they had had their fun, and emptied pockets of nuggets and dust, they left their 'husbands' and 'married' another, just down from the diggings.

The Castlemaine Police Court . Summons for Assault. Damages £19.19.11¾

Young working-class girls, domestic servants or rural labourers had little chance of improving their station in class-ridden English society, but were free to make their own place in the anonymity of the new world. Prostitution was endemic to the streets of London in Victorian times, as the upper classes took their pleasure at leisure among the working girls. Many of those who had been transported to the penal colonies were categorised as prostitutes, yet they may more likely have been convicted of theft than of living a life of easy virtue. However, many probably used their feminine wiles to break away from servitude on arriving in Sydney or Port Phillip.

One such lass, Alice Armstrong, transported to Sydney from Ireland in 1845, absconded soon after landing, and was found carousing with a sailor in Bathurst Street, Sydney. The 20-year-old had been listed as a vagrant sixteen times, her crime of the theft of a watch was at the time of the great potato famine, which caused so much misery in her native Enniskillen. Her transportation did little to ease her misery. She married after she had pretended to be a 'ticket-of-leave' convict, and had arranged to be stationed to a position in the country. Her husband of only three weeks took off for the diggings in Port Phillip, leaving her once again to look out for herself. What hope did such a girl have for redemption? What future lay in store for her? What could she do that would enable her to make her own way?

The diggings provided just the right opportunity for prostitution to flourish and prosper, yet there is little written evidence, apart from the descriptions of the many girls whose charms were noted by many

The Castlemaine Police Court
Drawing by George Rowe

(CASTLEMAINE ART GALLERY & HISTORICAL MUSEUM COLLECTION)

The prisoner, Catherine Crane, was brought before the Castlemaine Court charged with assault, against whom is not indicated in this drawing. What hope would this weary-looking crone have against the gentlemen arrayed against her?

Here stand the noblest legal minds, police magistrates, JPs and military personnel available for the dispensation of the best of British justice on the Mt Alexander goldfields.

She was fined almost £20, which was a huge sum at the time. Her offence must have been grave or else her trade highly illegal, and therefore profitable, for her to be able to sustain such a heavy impost.

It appears that on the diggings the court room was no place 'fit for this lady'.

The Great Social Evil
Cartoon by John Leech
London Punch, 1857

– PROSTITUTION –

In Victorian times prostitution was common on the streets of London. Many 'enlightened' men in the ruling and the upper classes held the view that 'Victorian morality' was a corruption of nature and repressive of natural, and no doubt some 'un-natural', proclivities. They saw working-girls as sexual innocents uncorrupted by Victorian repression: 'the fact that the girls had to open their legs to a succession of strange men was a matter of minor importance'.

Most prostitutes were single, domestic servants who had lost their virginity in the 'doggy world of working class sex'.

Their patrons were convinced that these women would enjoy the benefits of prostitution, giving those working in brothels clean living, food and good clothing.

The moral reformers were convinced that all were heading straight 'for hell in a handcart', and that redemption was only possible through marriage, family hearth and home.

For almost all working girls this was an unattainable prospect unless they were prepared to migrate. Thousands took the opportunity offered by the Family Colonization Loan Society, only to find that themselves in much the same situation in the colonies.

a journalist or artist. William Kelly described the audience in the dress-circle boxes of the Queen's Theatre, Melbourne, in 1853 attending a performance of *Hamlet*:

the dress circle was crammed beyond sitting posture with florid-looking women in too low satin dresses, some in their smeared hair, with their pinned bonnets dangling in front of the boxes; others crowned with tiaras like rose bushes in full bearing, and all hung around with chains, watches, collars, and bracelets of most ponderous manufacture.

He describes the diggers who accompanied them:

their lords-in-waiting were habited in tartan jumpers or red worsted shirts, smoking short pipes, and indulging in indelicate attentions, which frequently 'brought down the house'.[11]

The third act of this particular play developed into an exchange of views between 'Hamlet' and several diggers from Eaglehawk, who wondered aloud about the depth of the grave and the return to the tub. 'Hamlet' gave up his soliloquy, and joined in the jolly repartee. At the fall of the curtain the cast was showered with nuggets instead of bouquets. The diggers and their companions were out for fun, and had enough capital to ensure their place on the social scene.

Almost all records tell tales of diggers' 'weddings'. The gold and jewellery, fine gowns and large rings that were bestowed upon young 'brides' were astonishing to all well-bred folk. The streets of Melbourne were treated to parade after parade as diggers celebrated their good fortune by the taking of a bride – of sorts.

Hackney carriages were to be continually seen driving through the streets, filled with men and women of the most doubtful respectability – men with coarse blackguard-looking features, half finely and shabbily dressed, and some in their coarse working-clothes, and seated beside women tricked out in the most gaudy and expensive goods the shops of Melbourne could furnish.[12]

In fact, the diggers and their 'wives' had so commandeered the hackney cab that respectable, sober gentlefolk would not be seen in one – the diggers by their crude extravagance and boisterous behaviour debased the elegance of the carriage trade:

Gold-diggers think nothing of giving £50 or £60 for a couple of two-horse flies to drive a wedding party about the town for two or three hours. There are one or two of these weddings every day; the party driving up one street and down another half the day, showing themselves off, gradually getting drunk as the day advances. You would stare in London to see such a wedding; the whole party, excepting perhaps the bride and bridesmaids, smoking; and generally one, the drunkest of the lot, leaning half over the back of the fly, black bottle in hand, inviting the public to have a 'nobbler'. [13]

Plucking Mrs Chisholm's Chickens

Ellen Clacy suggests that the better class of eligible young men, the squatters and the provident diggers, who generally returned to Britain to marry, would not be satisfied with the immigrant lass, no matter how pretty, unless she was cultivated and of the right class, 'unless her manners are cultivated and her principles correct': [14]

Much is said and written in England about the scarcity of females in Australia, and the many good offers awaiting the acceptance of those who have the courage to travel so far. But the colonial bachelors, who are so ready to get married, and so very easy in their choice of a wife, are generally those the least calculated, in spite of their wealth, to make a respectable girl happy. [15]

Digger's Wedding in Melbourne
Lithograph by S. T. Gill, Macartney & Galbraith, Melbourne, 1852

(Rex Nan Kivell Collection, U999. By Permission, National Library of Australia)

Such weddings were popular with diggers who had come down to Melbourne eager and very willing to spend their gold. Champagne flowed freely, and the young ladies provided much sought-after female companionship – for the time being. The 'marriage' lasted as long as the gold; when that ran out so did they, and the diggers headed back to their claims.

The manner in which the successful diggers' weddings are conducted exhibits the reckless extravagance of these men and their doxies; the former we have no hesitation in stating to be 'old hands' in the colony, who do such things out of bravado to eclipse one another in vain show; as they formerly drank champagne out of buckets and latterly devoured five pound notes between slices of bread-and-butter.

– Samuel Mossman, *The Gold Regions of Australia: A descriptive account of New South Wales, Victoria, and South Australia. With particulars of the recent gold discoveries*, Orr, London, 1852.

Off to the Diggings
Hand-coloured lithograph
Cyrus Mason, Melbourne 1855

The young husband is about to leave for
the diggings. With a wagon packed high
with provisions, all that is left is to pack
the swags and to bid farewell to his wife
and child.

In the distance can be seen the
flagstaff that towered over Port Phillip.
(Today this rise on the northern side
of Melbourne's Yarra River is still known
as Flagstaff Hill.) At times when several
ships arrived in the port at the same
time, the grounds on this gentle rise
were literally covered with new chums
camped out for the night.

The class system that so many were seeking to escape was still
accepted and understood by those who sat at the top.

When Bill Armstrong, a digger from Ironbark Gully near Bendigo,
took a fancy to having a wife, he sold his half-claim, hopped aboard
the Cobb & Co. coach, and arrived in Melbourne determined to get
for himself one of 'Mrs Chisholm's Chickens'. He took a bath,
visited the barber and fitted himself with a new set of clothes, then at
midnight presented himself at the Women's Hostel. He had convinced the matron of the hostel that he had been so busy in preparation for his intended that he was unable to appear any earlier.

After some time a young girl appeared at the door, to his great
relief she was 'a winsome lass', who was nevertheless quite terrified
of what was to happen to her. Bill carried her away in a hansom cab
to a house he had just rented in Richmond. Within minutes they married themselves by 'jumping over the broom handle'– an old Scottish
custom that bound them in acceptable wedlock without the benefit
of clergy. Thus Harriet, one of 'Mrs Chisholm's Chickens', became
Mrs Bill Armstrong, a digger's wife. They partied until the money ran
out, then sold all and headed back to the diggings. In early 1854 Bill
and Harriet arrived at Jones's Gully, Campbell's Creek, near
Castlemaine, 'with nothing left of their "days-of-wine-and-roses" but
a tent, shovel and pick, and the spiritual gain from having been properly 'churched'.[16]

Bill and Harriet stayed together, working with a Danish digger, Claus Gronn, until Bill died from a chest complaint that had long troubled him. Gronn moved into Castlemaine, pitching his tent next to Dr Preshaw's, where Harriet found employment. She later married a prosperous brewer, and bore him many fine children – the diggings were no place for a respectable lady to be alone.

In November 1854 Caroline Chisholm visited the goldfields and was presented at a soiree held in the 'Hall of Castlemaine', a canvas-walled and roofed auction rooms built by William Hitchcock, a prominent figure in early Castlemaine society. Hitchcock introduced Mrs Chisholm with the homily that 'that lady had been staying with him for two days – would that she were to be his guest for two years', a comment which was greeted with much applause.

However, there was a degree of opposition to Mrs Chisholm's activities. Hitchcock referred to the fact that some 'persons were blaming her for bringing to the colony a class of persons not sufficiently good'.[17] Caroline Chisholm replied 'that so far from having sent out persons not sufficiently good, one man … had blamed her for conveying away the very cream of the English population'.[18] There were also those who accused her, a Roman Catholic, of 'endeavouring to spread the Roman Catholic religion'. Although Chisholm appeared to be the epitome of the Victorian philanthropist, and sincere in her belief that the 'gentle sex' could do much in the civilisation of the digger, there may be some truth in these remarks. Her promotion of the family as a haven for the digger, and his redemption being the hearth and home, may well have stemmed from her own strongly-held commitment to salvation.

In addressing the crowd gathered in the 'Hall of Castlemaine', Caroline remarked that:

Dr Preshaw's Tent at Campbell's Creek
*(CASTLEMAINE ART GALLERY,
& HISTORICAL MUSEUM COLLECTION)*

His flag can be seen flying from the pole at the front of his tent. Claus Gronn pitched his tent alongside Preshaw, but which one of these we cannot know.

A Woman! A Woman!

The sight of a woman on the diggings was quite rare in the early days, particularly a young woman, and especially one who had come to Australia without assistance from the Crown.

The following extract is from the diary of George Ogilvy Preshaw, son of Dr Preshaw, a Scottish surgeon who had migrated to Australia in 1852:

> In the month of December, 1852, my father paid us a flying visit (to our Melbourne quarters) and returned with my eldest sister, who was one of the first women on the Mount Alexander diggings. She drove up in a cart on the top of some loading, and was five days on the road. As they rode through Forest Creek the cry ran along the lead, 'A woman! a woman!' Men shouted out to their mates below, who hurried to the top, and hundreds of eyes were fixed on her the whole way from Golden Point till she reached her future home at Campbell's Creek.

George noted in his diary that about two weeks after this incident the entire family arrived at the Forest Creek diggings, where they set up their large tent – with the Scotch Thistle flag flying proudly out in front.

From thousands of miles away even Charles Dickens noted Preshaw's presence on the field when he wrote in *Household Words*:

> we note Dr. Preshaw, of Edinburgh. He begs to intimate that he has pitched his tent at Moonlight Flat, Forest Creek … his tent will be distinguished by his name across an ensign flying, and a Scotch thistle on end …

Such was the worldwide interest in the diggings.

Sly Grog on the Diggings
The Discovery of Gold – 1851, engraving
from Victoria and Its Metropolis, from a
sketch by S. T. Gill
(*PRIVATE COLLECTION*)

Grog was the bane of many diggers and
the delight of 'the traps' (the police).

A large number of 'Coffee Tents'
were established by women who called
themselves purveyors of 'cool drinks'.

However, it was illegal to sell grog on
the diggings, and the troopers took great
delight in destroying the property of any
who transgressed.

Claus Gronn recalled an incident on
Winter's Flat near Castlemaine when his
mate, who had been playing reckless
tricks on the troopers, was horrified to
see, on emerging from his shaft, that his
hut was on fire:

> I arrived at his bark and canvas hut just
> as he was cornered by six troopers …
> There was a brief scuffle and Jack was in
> irons. Soon, with his legs tied, he was on a
> wagon that was there ready and waiting.
> Though men converged from all quarters,
> not a soul lifted a hand to put out the fire,
> save any of the contents or even offer any
> comfort to his wailing wife and children.
> Jack and his wife had been trading in
> illicit rum and cognac to those 'in the
> know', but had not taken the precaution
> to 'splash liberal "palm oil" around to
> various "upholders of the sacred law" '.

They suffered the consequences. As Jack
was trundled away he cried:

> G'bye Charlie! Think of me when you
> make your fortune – And look after me
> wife 'n' kids! Certain – You will never see
> me again!

Gronn adds that he never did.[19]

the husbands who have left their wives at home, will find that I shall follow them. There are many of them about the diggings. The other day, as I was passing along, a digger whom I approached gave a sudden start and said, 'That's Mrs Chisholm!' I acknowledged my identity. 'Oh,' he said, 'I never thought of sending for my wife until I saw you'. Now for two years that man had been digging at Castlemaine – dig, dig, digging, and yet, as he assured me, he had never thought of sending for his wife until he saw me.[20]

The diggers were eager to press their grievances upon Mrs Chisholm in the hope that she would have influence upon the Governor, but she would not act in this manner on their behalf:

> I do not feel sympathy for any body of men who pay so little respect to their own sex as to live without wives when they can well afford to pay for them … what a cheer the diggers would give if the houses they go to at night were something better than the blankets which they had to creep like dogs …
>
> If I had the power to do so, I would relieve of taxes all the married men and give a bounty on all the women and children introduced into the diggers' districts. The diggers have great grievances, but they are not competent to decide on the remedy. It is impossible for them to act with discretion and judgement, huddled together as they are, in fifties listening to the evil agitator. It will be when they are really at home with their wives and families, when they live in peace and quietness, that they will best be able to tell what they want.[21]

These remarks were made only days before the battle at the Eureka stockade. It is curious to reflect that it was primarily the Irish Catholics, many accompanied by their wives, who knew very well what they wanted from the British, and that was the freedom that they had sought for centuries.

Chisholm seemed to accept the British class structure and its implementation in Australia, and aided in the maintenance of the established social order by seeking to keep the working class happy, content and quiet in their family units, while the landholders, the aristocrats, those of good quality and noble birth, were free to get on

with the business of running things properly. She may have been a true 'Victorian' Christian imbued with the desire to do good deeds, as many of her class did seek their own redemption through adherence to the Bible teachings ('as much as ye do for the least of these my brethren, ye do unto me'), but it was really too late. The diggings changed the way in which the working people felt about themselves; the class struggle had begun long before; and Eureka was one more battle to be fought as men, and women, fought to take their place in the new world, regardless of birth or station.

Caroline Chisholm said that:

I know many girls get into difficulties through being discharged from one place before they have another to go to. They seek temporary lodgings, are exposed to temptations, and generally the more innocent the girl the sooner she falls.[22]

She proposed the establishment of a series of houses along the road from Melbourne to the diggings, built to protect such young ladies who were in danger of 'falling', yet she may just as well have sought to influence those who were responsible for the way in which such girls were employed and discharged so readily.

One young lady appeared before the magistrate in Bendigo with a complaint against her employer, the owner of a restaurant and

Breaking the News
Oil on canvas by Sir John Longstaff, 1887
(ART GALLERY OF WESTERN AUSTRALIA COLLECTION)

Longstaff was born in the central Victorian goldmining town of Clunes on 10 March 1861.

Most scholars consider that this painting depicts the great mining disaster of 1882 in which 22 miners lost their lives trapped underground in the rapidly flooding New Australasian Mine at nearby Creswick. However, a note from Sir John himself pinned to the wall in the Clunes Historical Museum explains that this is not necessarily so.

This painting represents childhood memories of a scene he had observed played out so many times on those early diggings. There has been a fatal accident, and the young wife fears, yet knows, what news her husband's mate is bringing.

This typically sentimental image, of the kind popular in the Victorian age, won for Longstaff the first travelling scholarship from the National Gallery School of Victoria.

A Digger's Wife, a Spanish Woman
Watercolour by George Lacy, c. 1852

(REX NAN KIVELL COLLECTION, R4456.
BY PERMISSION, NATIONAL LIBRARY OF AUSTRALIA)

The 'wives' of the diggers were spared no expense, the diggers lavished on them fine silks, and velvets, parasols, and plenty of champagne.

Lord Robert Cecil, who for health reasons travelled to Australia and on to the goldfields in 1852, described a digger and his female companion as they strolled around the diggings:

we saw a digger in his jumper and working dress walking arm in arm with a woman dressed in the most exaggerated finery, with a parasol of blue damask silk that would have seemed gorgeous in Hyde Park ...23

Lord Cecil adds that the woman was an Adelaide 'notoriety, known as Lavinia', who had agreed to be the wife of the digger for a few days. No doubt she would relieve him of his gold dust while he was in an enamoured state.

A digger had told Cecil that a woman at Bendigo had offered to be his wife for the moderate charge of 1s 6d.

But more often than not, once they had had their fun, the diggers went back to the goldfield, leaving the ladies on the streets to go back to work.

accommodation house for diggers. Having just arrived in the colony, she had been engaged in Melbourne for a position in Bendigo at 30 shillings a week and her keep. Upon arrival she discovered that she was to occupy the same room as the owner and his wife. She

didn't like it – hasn't been used to that sort of thing, was told she would be made comfortable, and have a nice room all to herself. [That] things have been grossly misrepresented, and she wishes to return to Melbourne, but the defendant refuses to pay her unless she gives him a month's notice.24

The young lady, described as an 'attractive female assistant' was demanding £12 for her troubles. Magistrate McLachlan, known locally as 'Bendigo Mac', railed at the defendant: 'And this thing to have occurred in the nineteenth century, and in a British community! Verdict for the plaintiff for the full amount!' Now in complete control of the situation, she eyed the judge, and, whimpering, remarked that she had left behind a good situation following glowing reports of Bendigo, and asked 'if something for damages cannot be added to the compensation awarded [already] for breach of agreement'.

The magistrate surveyed the lass, first with a 'searching scrutiny', then with 'wonder', followed by 'sympathetic gravity', and finally 'an unmistakable look of admiration [was] discernible in his features'. Her 'musical voice, comely appearance, lithesome figure, and tidy apparel' had done their work. 'Damages!' he exclaims, as if astounded at so moderate a request. 'Most decidedly! £10 damages!' and, turning to the police attendant, 'You will make a careful examination at once of all restaurants, and report if any are without proper sleeping accommodation for young female assistants'.25

While such young ladies were often at the mercy of the unscrupulous, this one had little to learn about survival. On leaving the court she received a proposal of marriage from the proprietor of a rival restaurant, and the couple were married a week later. They went on to draw to their establishment most of the customers from her previous employer.

It appears that such working-class girls were keen to make a match and free themselves from servitude as they eagerly entered into the service of their 'husbands' and their families. The topsy-turvy world of the diggings offered them the opportunity to make a way for themselves.

– THE DARLING OF THE DIGGERS –

BORN IN LIMERICK, Ireland, in 1818, Maria Delores Elisa Gilbert took the stage name Lola Montes (Montez), and captivated audiences around the world with her exotic performances.

Her marriage to an English Army officer stationed in India was no deterrent to this fiery young Irish lass who seemed intent on leaving her mark on the world.

Convinced of her ability to perform and to entertain, Lola left her husband and took to the European stage. She became the friend of the famous, the confidante of politicians, and the lover of not just a few of the great men of her time, including Alexander Dumas, Franz Liszt and Ludwig, the King of Bavaria.

Lola once stripped to the waist and thrust her breasts into the King's face in order to prove that her charms were all her own (after which she was granted a generous engagement to the Munich Theatre).

After Ludwig had fallen from favour and was exiled, she sailed to New York in 1851, and then on to San Francisco and the goldfields, where she found a devoted and adoring audience.

Lola became known as 'the darling of the diggers', on both the Californian and Australian goldfields.

The notorious 'spider dance' became the hallmark of her exotic performances. It was this dance that ensured her popularity with the Australian diggers, yet at one time she had been booed off the stage with the same show in California. Maybe the Californian diggers had witnessed the earlier performances given by La Petite Susan in the Coloma 'theatres', who did her own 'spider dance' and 'Highland fling' to great acclaim.

Portrait of Lola Montes
Hand-coloured photograph, c. 1855

(REX NAN KIVELL COLLECTION, R10777.
BY PERMISSION, NATIONAL LIBRARY OF AUSTRALIA)

Lola (a.k.a. Maria Gilbert) left her native Ireland to dance and strut her way across the world stage. She was one of the first superstars. She took countless lovers, including Franz Liszt, Alexander Dumas and Ludwig I of Bavaria, and kicked up her heels and showed her shapely legs to diggers from California to Castlemaine.

VICTORIA THEATRE, BALLARAT.

This New and Elegant Theatre WILL OPEN

On SATURDAY, Feb. 16,

1856, under the Management of

MR. JAMES CROSBY,

Late Manager of the Victoria Theatre, Sydney,
On which occasion that world-renowned Artist, MADAME

LOLA MONTES

And Troupe, will have the honor of making their first appearance, supported by the

Best Company ever assembled on Ballarat!
Aided by New Scenery, Dresses, and Appointments.

Although Lola scandalised proper citizens wherever she appeared, and there was always criticism of her abilities as a performer, the diggers on the goldfields went wild with excitement every time the curtains opened.

After her home at Grass Valley, California, was burnt to the ground in 1855, Lola travelled to the Australian goldfields.

The *Melbourne Argus* reported her arrival in Port Phillip on 22 August 1855:

Captain Gilmore of the Wonga Wonga, which arrived from Sydney today, informed our shipping reporter that Lola Montez had arrived in the city under the name of Madame Landsfeld Heald.

Lola travelled from diggings to diggings. Her performance at the Hall of Castlemaine on 17 July 1855 opened the newly refurbished auction rooms with yet another stirring performance of the 'spider dance'. The *Castlemaine Mail* reported that she caused 'a near riot'. She so enchanted her audience that at each performance the stage was showered with lumps of gold.

The hall was later renamed the Theatre Royal. Although it is unlikely that it was named in her honour, it is certain that Lola was the closest to 'royalty' of any who had performed on that stage.

William Craig, a digger on Bendigo describes a performance by Lola at a Theatre there:

We hear the 'town crier' ringing his bell. 'Oh yes – oh yes! – oh yes! This is to give notice to all and sundry that Lolar Montes, the late queen of Bavary, will appear in a bran' new startlin' tragedy to-night at the theatre – to be follered by a side-splittin' comedy ... Roll up! – roll up! – roll up! God save the Queen!'[26]

When Craig took his place in the crowded theatre, he remarked on the

Lola Montes
Engraving from a contemporary
illustrated newspaper

*(La Trobe Picture Collection,
State Library of Victoria)*

beauty and presence of the 'star' the moment she walked on stage:

> there is no mistaking the leading 'star' when she makes her appearance. She has evidently inherited the best points of her aristocratic Irish father and her handsome Creole mother. One has only to look at her magnificent dark flashing eyes, her willowy form, the traces of former beauty, and her lithe, active movements to see that one is in the presence of a very remarkable woman, and it is not hard to believe that she should have been able to bewitch a king and cost him his throne.[27]

Craig was not, however, without criticism of her abilities as a thespian, but was enamoured of her self-control and iron nerve, especially after she was almost struck by a bolt of forked lightning that flashed through the canvas roof of the theatre, destroying part of the scenery only a few feet from where she was performing. Lola, ever the trouper, announced to the audience:

> 'There is to be a little thunder and lightning in the latter part of the play ...'

The crowd loved her, rejoining with remarks such as 'Isn't she a stunner', 'Bravo Lola!', 'Oh, but you're a darlint Loly!' 'Tis a pity yez aren't some dacent man's wife!'[28]

In her spider dance Lola wore a highly-coloured costume of many petticoats, among which several black 'decorations' had been sewn. Throughout her dance, she would flail about provocatively in an attempt to free herself of the 'spiders'. This excited her rough-and-ready audiences, hungry for the sight of female form, but also bought her reputation as an artiste into dispute.

It was her lack of any real ability to adequately perform the other advertised items on her programme that often drew more-than-appropriate criticism from the colonial press. On 19 February 1856 Henry Seekamp, the editor of the *Ballarat Times,* printed a

criticism of her illustrious past in his editorial, ignoring her performance as an actress. This incensed Lola, who had suffered criticism of her performances from the press for a long time. She took her revenge with a riding crop on Seekamp, who was in the bar of the United States Hotel, next door to the

Victoria Theatre where Lola was performing. He was attacked by Lola as she descended the stairs to the bar. He retaliated with his own whip, and they flailed at one another for several minutes before they were dragged apart.

Lola set out to destroy Seekamp's livelihood. First, she charged him with criminal libel. He was committed for trial, but he paid his own bail of £300, with a further £300 surety, and in turn summonsed Lola for assault. She retaliated, and had him charged with publication of an unregistered newspaper. As Lola was very popular with the diggers and a good many of the judiciary, nobody was prepared to fight for Seekamp. This action destroyed the *Times.*

Seekamp was one of the few gaoled after the riot at Eureka; he was probably the only one never missed.

Lola retired from performance shortly after, and went on the lecture circuit, touring America and England. Although Lola had suffered criticism of her ability over and over again, from the Munich Theatre to the bar of the United States Hotel in Ballarat, and had suffered at the pens of her critics, she remained convinced of her innate ability to entertain, and, more curiously, her ability to influence political events.

It is believed that dementia, brought on by syphilis, contributed to her early demise. She died of a stroke, penniless, and alone in a New York boarding house on 17 January 1861. Letters found after she died, showed that she had been preparing a plot to capture California from the United States and to install herself as Queen of 'Lolaland'.

Neither of her two children made the effort to claim her body. Lola, who had captured the hearts of so many was neglected by her own. At the age of only 41 'La Belle Horizontale' was laid to rest in a pauper's grave.

'SHOW US YER LICENCE!'

Diggers Licensing, Forrest Creek [sic]
Lithograph by S. T. Gill, Macartney
& Galbraith, Melbourne, 1852
*(REX NAN KIVELL COLLECTION, U990.
BY PERMISSION, NATIONAL LIBRARY OF AUSTRALIA)*

Diggers waiting in line to purchase
licences complained of the time wasted,
sometimes for two days or more
as they waited on the pleasure of the
commissioners.

The License [sic] ***Inspected***
Watercolour by S. T. Gill, 1852,
Macartney & Galbraith, Melbourne, 1852
*(REX NAN KIVELL COLLECTION, U1006.
BY PERMISSION, NATIONAL LIBRARY OF AUSTRALIA)*

This painting shows a familiar scene:
the trooper checks the fortunate digger's
licence (fortunate that he had one),
while in the background others are seen
scurrying away.

The licence fee was indiscriminate –
it did not matter whether a person on
the field was a successful digger or not,
merchant, baker or blacksmith,
companion or friend, all were forced
to pay the same fee.

It was the overzealous enforcement
of this law, always to the financial better-
ment of the troopers, that caused so
much dissent, and so many attempts at
non-compliance.

T HERE WAS NO MORE DESPISED BODY of officials on
the goldfields than the 'traps' (the police). There was no more
hated piece of paper than the gold licence. There was
no quicker way of firing resentment among the diggers than the
dreaded 'licence hunt', and no surer way of sending diggers running
for their holes than the cry of 'Joe! Joe! Joe!'

All men on the diggings were required to hold a licence and had to
have the licence on them at all times. The traps raided the diggings
with military precision; they stretched out across the gullies and
worked their way from one end to the other. A digger caught
between the shaft and his tent without his licence in his pocket would
be immediately chained like a dog to other unfortunate fellows, and
driven back to the Commissioner's Camp to be 'chained to the logs'
until a magistrate could be found. Diggers were sent to be chained to
logs or the trunks of trees, with the excuse, real or pretext, that the
lock-ups were full, and often left outside all night and in all weathers.

From there, it was off to the roads for seven days. The government
used errant diggers as labour to level the roads to the diggings and
were always keen to have an endless supply of labourers for this
important task. The diggers rightly believed that the licence fees
would give the administration adequate funds to provide both protection and services. The roads to the diggings were in a shocking
state, and the diggers demanded that something be done. The irony

*The First Commissioner Hardy
Collecting Licences and Diggers
Evading*
Pen and wash drawing by George Lacy,
c. 1852

Diggers can be seen heading for the hills,
while others hide beneath a cleft in a
rock, hoping to avoid scrutiny by the
traps.

Any digger found without a licence on
his person was immediately marched away
to be chained to the logs, fined heavily, or
imprisoned and set to work on the roads.

For the digger out of luck it was either
a quick sprint into the trees or a week's
work for the government.

was that many of them would be the very labourers providing the
muscle for that service.

The government attitude was, in the first place, to levy such a heavy
licence fee that labouring classes would be deterred from leaving
their employment and taking off for the diggings. This ruse failed
completely. But the licence remained as a vital source of revenue to
support both La Trobe's and later Hotham's inept bureaucracy. The
diggers were the most heavily-taxed group in the colony, the most
efficient producers of any commodity, the largest consumers, and yet
aggrieved that they were totally unrepresented in the legislative body.
William Howitt states:

> there is a strong feeling against the arbitrary treatment of the diggers by
> the Commissioners and police, and for an elective franchise – the prin-
> ciple of the British Constitution being grossly violated in the persons of
> the diggers, who are heavily taxed and totally unrepresented.[1]

Police were dispatched to any new rush almost as quickly as the diggers had opened it. While the government did little to enhance the
amenity of the diggings with the funds they gathered, they certainly
invested heavily in providing their own manpower to collect the
taxes. The majority of troopers and magistrates treated the diggers
with little regard for the intention of British law. One police magistrate fined a digger brought before him on a charge with contempt of

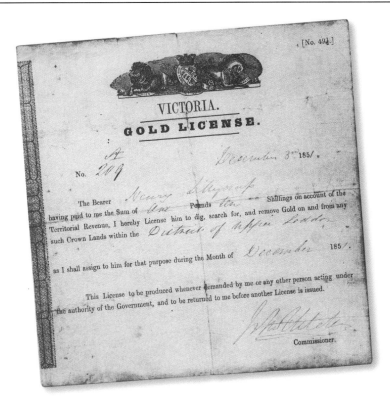

Gold License [sic] No. 209, issued to
Henry Lillecrap, 3 December 1851,
at the District of Upper Loddon

(CASTLEMAINE PIONEERS & OLD RESIDENTS ASSOCIATION
COLLECTION)

court simply for answering when questioned. At a subscription ball where all classes were admitted, a magistrate seized a well-dressed digger and his wife. The digger had been brought up before him earlier on 'some charge', so the magistrate had the man sent to the lock-up, and refused him bail.

The troopers' eagerness was no doubt encouraged by a commission paid on all fines meted out to the diggers. Many are known to have retired from the diggings with considerable savings in their bank accounts. One fellow at Bendigo, Hermsprong by name, retired from the diggings with £15,000, a sum he had collected in only two years; over that time his salary was set at £400 a year. Hermsprong was recognised, not only for the amount he had taken but for his riding whip, which had a brass knob on its end the size of an apple. He used 'green apples' to devilish effect as he rapped the skulls of any who displeased him. He was dedicated to the destruction of the sly-grog trade, that is, any sly-grog seller who was not one of his 'supporters'. His penchant for a bribe was legendary, and he took great delight in the destruction of the property of those who were not his friends. Countless sly-grog tents operated with trooper Hermsprong's full knowledge, but they took the precaution to grease his palm well beforehand.

Hermsprong assailed one poor Irishwoman whose husband had died in a mining accident; she was left with several small children, the youngest only a few days old. Several fellow-countrymen had advised her to engage in a bit of sly-grog to support her family, promising they would give her their custom, and, knowing the power of the legendary Irish thirst, she and her children would have been well

The morning was fine,
The sun did brightly shine;
The diggers were working away –
When the inspector of traps
Said, 'now my fine chaps,
We'll go license hunting today'.
Some went this way; some that.
Some to Bendigo Flat;
And a lot to the White Hills did
  tramp –
Whilst a lot more did bear
Towards Golden Square;
And the rest of them kept round the
  camp.

Each turned his eye
To the holes he went by –
Expecting down on them to drop;
But not one could they nail,
For they'd given leg bail,
Diggers ain't often caught on the
  hop.
The little word 'Joe'
Which all of you know,
Is a signal that the traps are quite
  near;
Made them all cut their sticks,
And they hooked it like bricks;
'I believe you my boy no fear'.

Now a tall ugly trap,
Espied a young chap,
Up the gully cutting like fun;
So he quickly gave chase,
But 'twas a hard race –
I assure you the digger could run.
Down a hole he went pop,
Whilst the bobby up top,
Says, 'just come up', shaking the
  staff:
'Young man of the crown,
If you want me come down;
For I'm not to be caught with such
  chaff'.
– from 'License-Hunting',
by Charles Thatcher.

– THE DIGGERS' MINSTREL –

Charles Robert Thatcher was born in Brighton, England in 1831.

Having been taught the flute as a child, sixteen-year-old Thatcher set off for London to try his luck on the stage. He began playing in various theatre orchestras, for dramatic performances and vaudeville acts, and it was on the London stage that Thatcher was introduced to the style of popular entertainment known as 'The Music Hall'.

Like so many others he was seduced by the promise of easy pickings in the gold-fields, and in 1853 he joined the throng and sailed for Port Phillip.

Having little luck at gold-digging Thatcher decided to polish up his flute and fall back on his old trade. He first found a job with the orchestra at the Royal Victoria in Bendigo, and it was here, between performances, that he filled in by singing new words to popular tunes. He soon became the most popular satirical performer on the goldfields stage.

Although he was thought the cleverest of all the contemporary song writers, not everybody found him amusing. The Bendigo newspaper considered his 'clever sarcastic songs' to be 'really good', yet Thatcher was in and out of battle as those he lampooned often took issue with him.

He performed widely over all the diggings, including those in New Zealand, then retired to London in 1867. He established himself in the West End as an importer of curios, scouring Europe, Japan and China for goods and souvenirs. He died, from cholera, on one such trip to Shanghai in September 1873.

provided for. Hermsprong charged her with the sale of grog, which she did not deny, exclaiming to her accuser, 'What your honour, was I to do?'

Hermsprong answered by ordering the police accompanying him to 'Fire that tent!' All of the children were asleep in the tent at the time, and the police refused to act on his command. Hermsprong swore at them for their 'damned nicety', leapt down from his horse, took a flaming brand from a fire in front of the tent and set it ablaze. The terrified woman had just time to rescue her baby and her other children before everything she owned was consumed. Hermsprong rode away satisfied.

He was forced to leave the diggings following this incident, but it was simply one of hundreds of occasions when petulant troopers regarded the letter of the law as their excuse for 'sport'. The often arbitrary, and then rigid, nature of apprehension and fine grated upon the diggers:

> **Any one found without the licence in his pocket – though he have it in his tent – is, without excuse or explanation allowed, marched to the camp, and there summarily fined £3 to £5; and if he show any reluctance or indignation at this treatment, he is, without ceremony, handcuffed and dragged off.**[2]

Many recorded that, upon arriving at the diggings, they were fined before they had even started to dig for gold, before they had even had an opportunity to look for and purchase a licence. One group of Americans just out from California had spent over £150 getting their goods up by bullock wagon, and each was arrested and fined before they had even had an opportunity to set themselves up. They were

125

taken before the commissioner, who, on hearing their complaints and deciding they were honest men, paid for their licences from his own pocket. The American diggers were able to repay him within a week from the nuggets they found. This same group was dismayed to discover that they were unable to purchase land on the diggings; they had come to the colony prepared to stay and make their future there, but turned back for California soon after.

It was not long before demands were made on the government to open up the land for purchase, as well as to repeal the onerous licence fees. However, the government was not at all interested in encouraging the working classes to take over the land once held by squatters, in fact the licence fee had been levied with exactly the opposite in mind. But the pressure of dissent and active opposition to the position taken by the government did lead to an eventual resolution.

John Chandler writes:

> There was now a very large number arriving on the diggings, and the government made a charge of 30s per month for a licence to dig. This was very hard as there were hundreds now on the diggings who could not get the colour, in fact not more than one in five was successful, as all the best ground had been worked. The government was very harsh. They sent out four to six constables in a company with muskets and bayonets fixed, and every man that had not got a licence, even if he had not had time to get to the commissioners, which was a place now called Castlemaine, and many poor fellows had spent every shilling to get there, for provisions were very dear, but they were all driven off the ground before these hirelings who consisted mostly of old hands, in other words, old convicts from Van Diemen's Land. They were fined 40s or locked up for seven days if they did not have the money.[3]

The cry of 'Joe' preceded the entry of any squad of traps who came onto the diggings with 'licence hunting' in mind. The cry spread quickly from one end of a gully to the other, and unlicensed diggers would disappear down their holes like rabbits. Any left above ground without their licences would be marched away, a bayonet at their back. The troopers were well aware that unlicensed men were hiding below ground, but were also aware that any trooper who climbed down into a shaft could well meet with a 'mining accident'.

However:

> The zeal with which the collection of the thirty shilling gold licence was proceeded with, made up at once for all accruing deficiencies. Every

– WILLIAM STRUTT –

Colonial artist William Strutt arrived in Hobson's Bay on the *Culloden* in July 1850.

He was descended from a long line of accomplished artists – his father, William Thomas Strutt, was a noted miniaturist, and his grandfather, Joseph Strutt, an artist and author who had illustrated his own works, *Dresses and Habits of the English People* (1796–99) and *The Sports and Pastimes of the People of England* (1801).

Strutt had studied in Paris, but the stress of his early occupation as an engraver had caused him severe eyestrain and near-breakdown. He travelled to the colonies hoping that the outdoor life would improve his health.

At the time of Strutt's arrival, the established publisher and engraver, Thomas Ham, was under contract to the Victorian government. Ham Bros had engraved Melbourne's corporate seal, the first postage stamps, various maps and currency notes for various banks.

Before Strutt's arrival there were no illustrated newspapers in Australia, but his arrival in July coincided with the first issue of the *Illustrated Australian Magazine*. Ham Bros had announced their intention to publish an illustrated magazine, and Strutt's abilities and experience gained him a position as illustrator soon after he stepped on to colonial soil.

Strutt's legacy of superbly drafted images of early Melbourne, his portraits of important figures and his drawings of the diggings, seem as fresh today as they must have been 150 years ago.

Aboriginal Black Troopers
Watercolour by William Strutt, 1851

Captain Dana parades with his squad of finely presented troopers, resplendent in their green and black uniforms, with opossum skin facings and red stripes, short carbines, bayonets and swords.

At first the black troopers were the only mounted police at Ballarat. Strutt thought it a bad move to employ the Aborigines for the collection or examination of licences because 'they could not discriminate between one piece of paper and another'.

Following Dana's death in 1852, the black squad was disbanded, with many of the troops themselves setting off to the diggings.

The native police were replaced by squads comprised of pensioned soldiers and ex-convicts from Tasmania, who were generally disliked by the diggers, 'not only for their brutality and excessively coarse demeanour, but also for their incompetence and corruption'.

young man, having the requisite qualifications of incompetence and a letter of introduction, was straightaway encased in a suit of blue and silver, furnished with sword and pistol, mounted on a horse, and forthwith constituted a trooper. as a practical foil to the shortcomings of the mounted men – most of whom were exceedingly decent fellows – such as old ticket-of-leave holders from New South Wales and Tasmania as were too lazy to work, and too cowardly to steal, were enrolled as foot-police-men – 'traps' as they were called by the diggers, and the name was by no means unsuitable to them. Horse and foot alike, they were despatched in hundreds on the one errand 'digger-hunting.'[4]

This system of policing was termed 'Man hunting', and the police 'Man-catchers' or 'Bloodhounds'. The diggers grew to resent the actions of the traps, and considered them guilty of 'cold-blooded, un-English, un-Christian despotism'.

Howitt commented:

No voice, however powerful or piercing, could touch the tympanum of Government; and official injustice and insolence became gigantic in their proportions, and peculation and bribery walked hand in hand.[5]

The government seemed determined to persist in feeding the flames of the revolution it was at most pains to avoid.

To His Excellency Charles Joseph La Trobe
Esquire Lieutenant Governor of the Colony of Victoria &c

The Humble Petition of the Undersigned Gold Diggers
and other residents on the Gold Fields of the Colony

Sheweth

That Your Petitioners are the Loyal and Devoted Subjects of Her Most Gracious Majesty Queen Victoria the Sovereign Ruler of this Colony &c &c

That in the present impoverished condition of the Gold Fields the impost of Thirty Shillings a Month is more than Your Petitioners can pay as the fruit of labor at the Mines scarcely affords to a large proportion of the Gold Miners the common necessaries of life

That in consequence of the few Officials appointed to issue Licenses the Diggers Storekeepers and other residents lose much time at each Monthly issue in procuring their Licenses

That the laborious occupation of Gold digging and the privations attendant on a residence on the Gold fields entail much sickness and its consequent expenses on Your Petitioners

That in consequence of the Squatter Land Monopoly a large proportion of Successful Diggers who desire to invest their earnings in a portion of land are debarred from so doing

That newly arrived Diggers must lose much time and money before they become acquainted with the process of Gold Mining

That in consequence of Armed Men (many of whom are notoriously bad in character) being employed to enforce the impost of Thirty Shillings a Month there is much ill feeling engendered amongst the Diggers against the Government

That in consequence of the non possession by some of the Miners of a Gold Diggers License some of the Commissioners appointed to administer the Law on the Gold Fields have on various occasions Chained non-possessors to Trees and Condemned them to hard labor on the Public Roads of the Colony — A proceeding Your Petitioners maintain to be contrary to the spirit of the British Law which does not recognize the principle of the Subject being a Criminal because he is indebted to the State

That the impost of Thirty Shillings a Month is unjust because the successful and unsuccessful Digger are assessed in the same ratio

For these reasons and others which could be enumerated Your Petitioners pray Your Excellency to Grant the following Petition

First. To direct that the License Fee be reduced to Ten Shillings a Month

Secondly. To direct that Monthly or Quarterly Licenses be issued at the option of the Applicants

Thirdly. To direct that new arrivals or invalids be allowed on registering their names at the Commissioners Office fifteen clear days residence on the Gold Fields before the License is enforced

Fourthly. To afford greater facility to Diggers and others resident on the Gold Fields who wish to engage in Agricultural Pursuits for investing their earnings in small allotments of land

Fifthly. To direct that the Penalty of Five Pounds for non possession of License be reduced to One Pound

Sixthly. To direct that (as the Diggers and other residents on the Gold Fields of the Colony have uniformly developed a love of law and order) the sending of an Armed Force to enforce the License Tax be discontinued

'RED-RIBBON' REBELLION

Governor Charles Joseph La Trobe
Engraving from the *Picturesque Atlas
of Australasia*, edited by Andrew Garran,
1888

(PRIVATE COLLECTION)

La Trobe was an old-fashioned, establishment figure. Through his petulance and
greed he set the scene for the rebellion
that overtook the Victorian diggings.

(OPPOSITE)

The Bendigo Petition, 3 August 1853

(LA TROBE PICTURE COLLECTION,
STATE LIBRARY OF VICTORIA)

The petition, which contained over 5000
signatures, was presented to Governor
La Trobe following the great meetings
held in Bendigo in the middle of 1853.

The petition called for changes to the
licence fees demanded by the government
from all who were on the diggings.

It was the first truly organised protest
to the Governor, but was to no avail.

La Trobe responded by sending a
further consignment of troops to Bendigo.

The full text of the petition is reproduced on page 134.

WHEN EARL GREY, British Secretary of State for the
Colonies, warned: 'There is spirit abroad which must be
carefully watched and promptly brought under control if
this colony is not to parallel California in crime and disorder,'[1] he
was reacting to the rumours of discontent and open dissent reported from the colonies. The majority of diggers were disenchanted
with rule by a despotic military, and sought justice and fair repre-
sentation of their grievances from Governor La Trobe.

The issue of taxation on the goldfields was at the core of most of
the dissent. Governor La Trobe had set a licence fee of 30 shillings
per month on all male persons on the goldfields, whether they were
engaged in digging or not.

The licence fee was considered as excessive by most, but it was the
corruption, the oppression, and the disregard for the rights of the
ordinary citizen that brought dissent to a head.

Not all diggers on the Australian goldfields were natural-born subjects of Her Majesty Queen Victoria; and many who were had little
desire to remain so. There were thousands of Irish Catholics who
cared little for the niceties of English law, and saw no need to tug
their forelocks to the British so far away from 'that sceptred isle'.

The diggings fast became home for adventurers from across the
world – French, Italians, Greeks, Hungarians, Austrians, Germans,
Jews, Russians, Balts, Americans, West Indians and Chinese had all
come to Victoria looking for excitement. Very few of these had any
real regard for 'Mother England', or any reason to wish to return to
their own corner of a war-torn Europe ravaged by revolution. Few
had any desire to live under the yoke of a dissolute military, harassed
by thugs in uniform, often gaoled, frequently abused, driven in
chains for glancing sideways at an officer.

There were shiploads of free Americans who, for well over a century, had been free of British rule; they were well versed in matters
political, having been free to stand, free to oppose, free to dissent,
and used to the exercise of their hard-fought suffrage. It was the
influence of these Americans, the 'Yankee-style Red Republicans',
that was most disturbing to Earl Grey.

The spark of rebellion was fanned easily in such a climate; the
uprising that eventually engulfed the Ballarat goldfields was kindled
by La Trobe and fuelled by his own fears of such a revolution. As in
California, where the discovery of gold had saved America from
financial disaster, it was the toil of the diggers that La Trobe was to
tax so heavily in order to save the Colony of Victoria from ruin.

On 15 December 1851 over 10,000 diggers responded to this notice pinned to trees across the Mt Alexander goldfield, which read:

FELLOW DIGGERS!

The intelligence has just arrived of the resolution of the Government to double the license fee. Will you tamely submit to the imposition or assert your rights as men? You are called upon to pay a tax originated and concocted by the most heartless selfishness, a tax imposed by Legislators for the purpose of detaining you in their workshops, in their stable yards, and by their flocks and herds.

They have conferred to effect this; they would increase this seven-fold but they are afraid! Fie upon such pusillanimity! and shame upon the men, who save a few paltry pounds for their own pockets, would tax the poor man's hands!

It will be in vain for one or two individuals to tell the Commissioner, or his emissaries, that they have been unsuccessful and that they can't pay the license fee. But remember that union is strength, that though a single twig may be bent or broken, a bundle of them tied together yields not nor breaks. Ye are Britons! Will you submit to oppression or injustice! Meet – agitate – be unanimous – and if there is injustice in the land, they will, they must, abolish the imposition.
Yours faithfully, A Digger.

A report published in the *Argus* on 18 December 1851 records the spirit of the meeting as a Mr Potts addressed the large crowd:

I see before me some 10,000 or 12,000 men which any country in the world might be proud to own as her sons. The very cream of Victoria, and the sinews of her strength … let it be seen this day whether you intend to be slaves or Britons, whether you will basely bow down your neck to the yoke, or whether like true men you will support your rights … the 30 shillings charged by the government is an illegal taxation, and that His Excellency has no power to tax us … because a few men think proper to say, you shall pay, that is no reason why a body of men such as I now address, should accede to such extortion.

Following the 'Great Meeting of Diggers', held at the Old Shepherd's Hut on the outskirts of Dr Barker's run near Chewton, the miners resolved to refuse to pay any licence fee at all. Delegates – Captain Harrison, Dr Richmond and Mr Plaistow – were sent to Melbourne to press the diggers' claims to Governor La Trobe. La Trobe's response was to send a further 130 troops to Forest Creek.

Captain John Harrison, RN

(LA TROBE PICTURE COLLECTION, STATE LIBRARY OF VICTORIA)

He took a deputation from Bendigo to present the diggers' claims to the Governor.

The Great Meeting of Diggers
15 December 1851 – from Ham's *Five Views of the Gold Fields of Mount Alexander and Ballarat, in the colony of Victoria*
Thomas Ham, Melbourne, 1852

(COLLECTION, ALLPORT LIBRARY AND MUSEUM OF FINE ARTS, HOBART)

This was the first of the many meetings that were held across the goldfields in protest at the licence fee that was proving a hardship for many diggers, and also in protest at the behaviour of the police and troopers who benefited from the fines levied on the diggers.

One police inspector, a former black-smith turned law-enforcer, whose arm once 'used to smite iron, now smote men', was forced to retire from the Bendigo diggings after two years of protest at his overzealous force in upholding the law.

The behaviour of the police who profited from the arrest of the diggers, who were free of constraint by the government, were a law unto themselves, creating more unrest than they seemed prepared to prevent.

The diggers' protest may have caused the government to rethink the issue of the licence fee, but until military rule was abolished the goldfields remained a hot-bed of sedition.

On arrival on the goldfield the 99th Regiment (made up of army pensioners) found themselves outnumbered 200 to 1. They were met with derision, and were unable to take control by their show of arms. La Trobe was eventually forced to capitulate, and the licence fee remained unchanged.

William Howitt writes:

the most glaring sign of the fatuity of a Government, is its unconscious-ness of its own weakness, or the power of those whom it seeks to control … but the most fatal error which a Government can commit, is to teach its subjects its utter inability to compel them, if they choose to resist; except it be of setting them an example of injustice and rapacity.

If La Trobe was unable to learn from his mistakes of 1851, his successor, Charles Hotham, was determined to repeat his errors of judgement three years later. The consequences were to change the colony forever.

The diggers were not, as a body, a lawless lot; they simply felt that they were being treated unfairly, and that the troopers, who received a commission on all the fines extracted by the arrest of the diggers, were overzealous in their prosecution of the law.

William Howitt complained of this on his arrival in Bendigo:

once there, with weary limbs, and empty pockets, before we could dig up a grain of gold the police were down on us for £1/10 shillings each for licences. We did not object to the licence, that was quite just and fair;

but we thought it hard to be dragged off to the camp at a moment's notice, and expected to pay before we had had a single day allowed to get the means.[2]

David Tulloch writes:

While jealous of their rights, and prepared to withstand oppression, they [the diggers] were not desirous to evade any just claim of the Government; they were willing to submit to *equitable* taxation.[3]

But the government could only see the 'milch cow' that the diggings had become. Mrs Gilbert, wife of the Gold Commissioner at Bendigo, told Howitt (who recalled it in his letter of 25 September 1852) that diggers had been arriving in Bendigo at the rate of 5000 to 6000 a week, with issues of licences increasing in equal proportion. She said that 'at that Digging [Bendigo], a few months ago, the monthly licences were 6000, then 8000, then 10,000, and now they are 20,000'.[4]

George Edward Thompson
Thompson was one of the leaders of the Anti-Gold-Licence Association that had formed in Bendigo on 3 June 1853.

The deposits in the coffers for the benefit of the bureaucracy were enormous, and all the government of the day had to do was to sit back and watch the money pour in. Or so they thought. Those making the deposits were increasingly demanding that the government put something back into the colony at large.

Little was done to make safe or even slightly comfortable access to the diggings, police oppressed rather than protected, diggers were unable to purchase land and invest in their future in the colony. The government and the squatters held control of the land and did their best to keep the workers without opportunity. However, the diggers began to sense a power of their own – the power of common rights, of unity, of equality, of suffrage – and they soon demanded their rights.

Dissent grew apace. The Anti-Gold-Licence Association was formed in Bendigo in June 1853. The leaders of that Association, George Thompson, Dr Jones, and an Irish-born American, 'Captain' Edward Brown, sought to represent the concerns of the 23,000 diggers and their families on that goldfield to the government.

By 3 August a petition of more than 5000 signatures, and 30 metres in length, was signed by the diggers and taken to Melbourne to be presented to Governor La Trobe. The diggers must have moved pretty sharply among the men to collect so many signatures in only four weeks.

On 13 August 1853 over 10,000 diggers (although Howitt suggests a figure closer to 4000) assembled at View Point, a central point close

W. D. C. Denovan
(BENDIGO ART GALLERY COLLECTION)
He led the Bendigo rebels agitating for removal of La Trobe's hated licence fee.

THE GOLD DIGGERS' ADVOCATE

AND COMMERCIAL ADVERTISER

"Labour founds Empires; knowledge and virtue exalt and perpetuate them."

No. 28.—Vol. I.   MELBOURNE, VICTORIA, SATURDAY, JULY 22, 1854.

**Masthead of the *Gold Diggers'
Advocate and Commercial Advertiser***
22 July 1854

(LA TROBE PICTURE COLLECTION,
STATE LIBRARY OF VICTORIA)

The *Advocate*, published in Melbourne in
the early days of the goldrush, was filled
with advertisements for tents, tools and
tucker. In fact, everything the digging
party would need for a successful expedition to the goldfields.

The *Advocate* was a vocal supporter
of the movement for diggers' rights; this
empathy is expressed best in the design
of the shield shown supported by a pair
of diggers. The shield is divided into
quarters showing the pick and shovel,
the cradle, and the pan, representing
labour; as on the diggers' flag – a purse
for nuggets is displayed in place of the
bundle of faggots.

Here individual success is celebrated
rather than unity, yet the whole is
crowned with the kangaroo and a rather
oddly-shaped emu, celebrating Australia.

The motto of the newspaper reads
'Labour founds Empires; knowledge
and virtue exalt and perpetuate them'.
It would appear that such noble senti-
ments never reached the ears of the
Governor.

Bendigo, looking from View Point
Artist unknown, c. 1852

(BENDIGO REGIONAL LIBRARY COLLECTION)

View Point, Sandhurst (Bendigo), is at
the heart of the now-bustling city. On
the diggings it had been known by various names: Charing Cross (a boulevard
with the name Pall Mall runs from this
point), as Jackson's Corner (after a shop-
keeper who was the first to set up there),
and finally as View Point.

to the camp at Bendigo, to greet the delegates on their return from
Melbourne. The meeting was excited, and at times agitated; those
gathered represented the great number of nations on the field at that
time.

A fife and tambourine had led the parade from the White Hills to
View Point. First were the Irish behind a green and gauzy banner of
great length, then came the Scots, the Union Jack, and the revolutionary flags of France and Germany, the Germans carried the
schwarz-roth-und-gold (black, red and gold) flag of the German revolution, then came the American Stars and Stripes, followed by flags
of various smaller countries, some with original designs.

William Howitt followed the procession to View Point, where a
tent and bunting awaited the speakers. In the centre of the clearing
flew the diggers' flag:

> The flag showed the pick, the shovel, and the cradle, – that repres-
> ented labour. There were the scales, – that meant justice. There was the
> Roman bundle of sticks, – that meant union: altogether, – all up at
> once. There were the the kangaroo and emu, – that meant Australia.[5]

–THE BENDIGO PETITION–

Governor Charles Joseph La Trobe
Engraving from the
Picturesque Atlas of Australasia, 1888
(PRIVATE COLLECTION)

His Excellency Charles Joseph
La Trobe Esquire
Lieutenant Governor of the
Colony of Victoria &c.

The Humble Petition of the
Undersigned Gold Diggers and
other residents on the Gold Fields of
the Colony
Sheweth That your petitioners are
the loyal and Devoted Subjects of
Her Most Gracious Majesty Queen
Victoria the Sovereign Ruler of this
Colony one of the dependencies of
the British Crown
    That in the present impoverished
conditions of the goldfields the
impost of Thirty Shillings a Month
is more than Your Petitioners can
pay as the fruit of labor at the
Mines scarcely affords to a large
proportion of the Gold Miners the
common necessaries of life
    That in consequence of the few
Officials appointed to issue Licenses
the Diggers Storekeepers and other
residents lose much time at each
Monthly issues in procuring their
Licenses
    That the laborious occupation of
Gold digging and the privation
attendant on a residence on the
Gold Fields entail much sickness
and its consequent expenses on Your
Petitioners
    That in consequence of the
Squatter Land Monopoly a large
proportion of Successful Diggers
who desire to invest their earnings
in a portion of land are debarred
from so doing
    That newly arrived Diggers must
lose much time and money before
they become acquainted with the
process of Gold Mining
    That in consequence of Armed
Men (many of whom are notoriously
bad in character) being employed to

enforce the impost of Thirty
Shillings a Month there is much ill
feeling engendered amongst the
Diggers against the Government
    That in consequence of the non-
possession by some of the Miners of
a Gold Diggers License some of the
Commissioners appointed to administer the Law on the Gold Fields
have on various occasions Chained
non-possessors to Trees and
Condemned them to hard labor on
the Public Roads of the Colony –
A proceeding your Petitioners
maintain to be contrary to the spirit
of the British Law which does not
recognize the principle of the
Subject being a Criminal because he
is indebted to the State.
    That the impost of Thirty
Shillings a Month is unjust because
the successful and unsuccessful
Digger are assessed in the same
ratio
    For these reasons and others
which could be enumerated Your
Petitioners pray your Excellency to
Grant the following Petition
First. To direct that the License Fee
be reduced to Ten Shillings a Month
Secondly. To direct that Monthly or

Quarterly Licenses be issued at the
option of the Applicants
Thirdly. To direct that new arrivals
or invalids be allowed on registering
their names at the Commissioners
Office fifteen clear days residence
on the Gold Fields before the
License be enforced
Fourthly. To afford greater facility
to Diggers and others resident on
the Gold Fields who wish to engage
in Agricultural Pursuits for investing their earnings in small allotments of land
Fifthly. To direct that the Penalty of
Five Pounds for non-possession of
License be reduced to One Pound
Sixthly. To direct that (as the
Diggers and other residents on the
Gold Fields of the Colony have
uniformly developed a love of law
and order) the sending of an Armed
Force to enforce the License Tax be
discontinued
    Your Petitioners would respect-
fully submit to Your Excellency's
consideration in favour of the
reduction of the License Fee that
many Diggers and other residents
on the Gold Fields who are
debarred from taking a License
under the present system would if
the Tax were reduced to Ten
Shillings a Month cheerfully comply
with the Law so that the License
Fund instead of being diminished
would be increased.
    Your Petitioners would also
remind your Excellency that a
Petition is the only mode by which
they can submit their wants to your
Excellency's consideration as
although they contribute more to
the Exchequer than half of the
Colony they are the largest class of
Her Majesty's Subjects in the
Colony unrepresented.
    And your Petitioners as in duty
bound will ever pray etc.[6]

**Post Office, Sandhurst, Victoria,
in the 1850's, c. 1855**
Watercolour, artist unknown

*(Rex Nan Kivell Collection, R3642.
By Permission, National Library of Australia*

The Post Office stands beside the creek
which runs through the heart of
Sandhurst (Bendigo). It was along this
muddy boulevard that a procession of
irate diggers carried their flag from the
White Hills to View Point.

**Advertisement for Jackson's Gold
Office at View Point**
Henry Jackson gave his name to the
point where View Street met the
Bendigo Creek. It was known for many
years by the diggers simply as Jackson's
Corner.

The diggers' flag had been designed by a Mr Dexter, a china
painter from Devon, who as it appeared had learnt much from his
time spent among the French 'Red Republicans', and deemed it a
great honour to have given his talent to the meeting.

There were those who decried the Union Jack and supported the
cause of revolution, but they were countered by the loyal response
of most of the crowd, who called for three cheers for the British
flag. The diggers may have had a grievance with their Governor, but
they were not prepared to stand by as others attempted to revile the
very 'bosom of the grand old mother-country which had suckled
and raised him to man's estate'.[7]

George Thompson, one of the delegates to the Governor, leapt to
his feet and cheered the British ensign, 'which had led the way to the
pre-eminence of England all over the world, and to the liberty they
were that day enjoying'.[8]

Despite the diggers' enthusiasm, the petition fell on deaf ears. The
diggers resolved once again to resist the Governor. They agreed to
offer no more than ten shillings when licences next fell due.

About this time it was reported that Sir Charles Fitzroy, the
Governor of New South Wales, had decided to abolish the licence
fee in that colony. La Trobe wrote a letter to Fitzroy, which was published in the newspapers, strongly advising against such action.
Fitzroy ignored La Trobe's entreaty.

This brought the situation to a head. On 27 August another meeting was held at View Point. This time a much larger procession, led
by two pipers, gathered. The diggers at this meeting again agreed to
pay no more than ten shillings a month, to present themselves to the

3 Cheers for THE ARGUS &c.
Pen and ink drawing, unknown artist
(REX NAN KIVELL COLLECTION, T2249.
BY PERMISSION, NATIONAL LIBRARY OF AUSTRALIA

This rather primitive sketch records the great meeting of diggers on 11 December 1851.

The note states:

The 'Diggers' after giving 3 cheers for the *ARGUS* 3 for the *DAILY NEWS* and three groans for the *HERALD* – then separated – the great meeting at the diggings against Governt Licences.

authorities on the appropriate day and, if the 10 shillings were refused, to offer themselves to be taken into custody.

As a symbol of this defiance they took to wearing a red ribbon in their hats, to show that those who wore the ribbon would no longer tender the old fee. The so-called 'Red-ribbon Rebellion' was born. The wearing of the ribbon became so common that supplies of red flannel, a popular material used in the making of diggers' shirts, all but dried up.

La Trobe was indecisive in quieting the dispute. A number of soldiers and cannons were dispatched to Bendigo, yet the diggers remained steadfast: 'firm and resolved, … used no idle threats, or military parade'.[9] They carefully stayed within all other aspects of the law.

At Waranga the Commissioners foolishly arrested several men for refusing to pay the full licence. The fully-armed diggers marched in a body upon the Camp, and forced the release of their mates.

Following this news the Governor hurried to the Legislative Council, and 'in a speech replete with indications of terror, proposed at once to abandon the license-fee altogether'.[10] Then he placarded the goldfields with conflicting messages. Two placards bearing the same date, 1 September, bore different messages, the first from the Governor who told the diggers the new laws were before the legislature and that fees due for that month were waived, the second from Chief Commissioner Wright, who stated that, although laws were before the Legislative Council, the last law was still in force, and that diggers should pay as usual.

The diggers' representatives once again sought clarification from the government, which then acquiesced, reducing the fee to £1 a month, £2 for two months or £8 a year, adding a registration fee on all businesses and a gold export duty. The diggers had won some concession from government, but not all were happy with the result.

After continued public protest against the Governor, La Trobe was recalled to England in May 1854. He sailed away from a colony in

1853

– London Times –
'The Government is humbled in the dust before a lawless mob'.[12]

Governor Charles Hotham
(PRIVATE COLLECTION)

Hotham unfortunately mistook the diggers' delight in welcoming him as the new Governor as unquestioning patriotism to the Crown. He seemed to understand little of the diggers' real feelings.

> When he paid a visit to the goldfields he saw a woman helping her husband at the windlas [*sic*], and when he got back to Melbourne he recommended that women should pay a licence-fee as well as the men! ... [a] cry of execration ... arose amongst the diggers; – they would not have it.
>
> – William Ottey, 25 March 1887.[12]

Gold licence instructions:

> The Bearer, ..., having paid to me the Sum of One Pound, Ten Shillings, on account of the Territorial Revenue, I hereby Licence him to dig, search for, and remove Gold on and from any such Crown Land within the .... District, as I shall assign to him for that purpose during the month of .... 18..., not within half-a-mile of any Head station.
>
> This Licence is not transferable, and to be produced whenever demanded by me or any other person acting under the Authority of the Government, and to be returned when another Licence is issued.

The following regulations were printed on the back of the licence:

> Regulations to be observed by the Persons digging for Gold, or otherwise employed at the Gold Fields.
> 1. Every person must always have his Licence with him, ready to be produced whenever demanded by a Commissioner, or Person acting under his instructions, otherwise he is liable to be proceeded against as an Unlicensed person.
> 2. Every Person digging for Gold, or occupying land, without a Licence, is liable by Law to be fined, for the first offence, not exceeding £5; for a second offence, not exceeding £15; and a subsequent offence, not exceeding £30.
> 3. Digging for Gold is not allowed within Ten feet of any Public Road, nor are the roads to be undermined.
> 4. Tents or buildings are not to be erected within Twenty feet of each other, or within Twenty feet of any creek.
> 5. It is enjoined that all Persons at the Gold Fields maintain and assist in maintaining a due and proper observance of Sundays.

debt, a bureaucracy in decay and a citizenry in revolt. La Trobe left Victoria indebted to the British banks for £1,000,000, and more than one-quarter of that sum could not be accounted for. There was a glaring discrepancy between the amount received from gold licences and what should have been in the coffers if all diggers had paid the fees or if all fees had been properly accounted for. La Trobe's administration had seen hundreds of petty officials enriched at the expense of the citizens, the taxes extracted from the diggers diverted into the pockets of the police.

His successor, Charles Hotham, was received enthusiastically by the diggers at first. They feted Hotham and his wife on his early visit to the goldfields; at Castlemaine the diggers met his carriage some miles from the camp, removed the horses, and pulled the entourage with jubilant manpower towards Forest Creek. They were overjoyed that the new Governor was keen to see at first hand the state of the diggings, and they were anxious to impress upon him their hard work, their enterprise and the richness of the field. They may have overplayed their hand a little when Hotham was amply rewarded with nuggets in his dish after they had led him to try his hand at prospecting – from a 'salted' shaft.

Hotham was to return to Melbourne with the impression that the diggings were occupied by a most enthusiastic population, industrious, cheerful, and above all patriotic. Uppermost in his mind was the crippling debt left to his colony by the excesses of the La Trobe administration. He mistakenly looked to the diggers for the funds to bankroll his bureaucracy. The licence fee remained the easiest method of raising funds; rule by military the surest way of enforcing compliance.

La Trobe's legacy to Hotham was the unrest that simmered throughout his years in office, and the conflagration that was shortly to engulf the entire colony.

CHAPTER 11

THE BATTLE AT BALLARAT

Swearing Allegiance to the 'Southern Cross', December 1st 1854
Watercolour by Charles Doudiet
(BALLARAT FINE ART GALLERY COLLECTION)

(OPPOSITE)

The Eureka Flag

(BALLARAT FINE ART GALLERY COLLECTION)

Following the battle at Ballarat, John King, one of the troopers, volunteered to tear down the ensign, which by this time was riddled with bullet holes. King cut it away with his bayonet and trampled it into the dust, where he bayoneted it again.

This original flag has hung in the Ballarat Gallery for over 100 years. For a long time the flag was viewed with some suspicion, not venerated but treated as a curiosity. Snippets were taken from time to time and given as mementoes to various visiting dignitaries or curious celebrities.

'We swear by the Southern Cross to stand truly by each other, and defend our rights and our liberties'

– Diggers' Oath, Eureka Stockade, 1854

KARL MARX wrote of the diggers' agitation as a 'revolutionary movement of the workers', but it must be remembered that Marx wrote his observations from afar and that such an interpretation suited his political ideology. A body of men rising together to overthrow the ruling class, if successful, would have been a major fillip to the cause of universal class struggle and revolution.

The diggers at Ballarat did not play by standard revolutionary rules. While there certainly were many disaffected diggers who did harbour truly revolutionary ideals, for most their resistance was rooted in economic reality and a distaste for arbitrary and perverse 'justice'.

John Basson Humffray

A report to Governor Hotham found that 'foreigners formed a larger proportion among the disaffected than among the miners generally'. This simply supported his belief that most loyal diggers would not do such an 'un-British' thing as to seriously consider revolt.

Nursed in intrigue, the foreigners, who had been members of secret societies in Europe, were conspiring with the worst class of the Irish on the gold-fields, and no vile art was wanting among the desperadoes whom Italy, Germany, and France had yielded to the Australian mines.[1]

There was a persistent belief that the 'rebellious element of Ireland, who thought to fright the British Isles from their propriety in 1848* were represented in some strength', and it was probably justified.

The goldfields did have all of the elements of serious social unrest, if not actual revolution, thrown together in a unique environment. There was little diversion to hold the interest of such a large body of energetic, excited and politically aware young men, other than hard labour and hard drinking. The constant calls to take control of their own destinies fell on eager ears.

Prelude to Battle

For months dissent and resistance had been growing across all the Victorian goldfields. The story was the same everywhere; protest meetings were being held from Waranga to Bendigo, Forest Creek to Ballarat. Resistance to licence fees, revulsion at the random and oppressive digger hunts, objection to the privilege assumed by the capricious and dissolute troopers on 'the Sacred Camps', were common on all the diggings.

However, it was the failure of deep mining on the Eureka field, where no lead had 'bottomed out' for over five weeks, that put increased pressure on the diggers around Ballarat. Meetings and protests had been held across the diggings from the first 'Great Meeting of Diggers' in December 1851 to the Bendigo petition in 1853, but it was the brutal murder of a Scottish digger, James Scobie, and the subsequent fire that destroyed the Eureka Hotel at Ballarat on 17 October 1854, that changed the diggers' mood from petition and deputation to direct action and revolution.

A Diggers' Reform League had been proposed to represent all of the diggings, but by 11 November the anger that followed Scobie's murder, and the ineptitude of the justice system to deal adequately

* The Young Ireland Movement, formed in 1842, was a movement that echoed European romantic nationalism and a collective consciousness for Ireland.

The movement believed in 'physical force politics' to free the Irish from the bondage of English landlords, but the movement disintegrated after the failed insurrection of 1848, and several leaders were transported to Van Diemen's Land.

William Craig, who had travelled to Australia with Peter Lalor, later recalled in his work, *My Adventures on the Australian Goldfields,* that Lalor

> never tired of descanting upon the wrongs of Ireland ... was a strong believer in the use of physical force for redressing her wrongs.

DOWN WITH THE LICENSE FEE!
DOWN WITH DESPOTISM!
"WHO SO BASE AS BE A SLAVE?"
ON
WEDNESDAY NEXT
The 29th Instant, at Two o'clock.
A MEETING
Of all the DIGGERS, STOREKEEPERS, and Inhabitants of Ballarat generally, will be held
ON BAKERY HILL

For the immediate Abolition of the License Fee, and the speedy attainment of the other objects of the Ballarat Reform League. The report of the Deputations which have gone to the Lieutenant-Governor to demand the release of the prisoners lately convicted, and to Crewick and Forest Creeks, Bendigo, &c., will also be submitted at the same time.

All who claim the right to a voice in the framing of the Laws under which they should live, are solemnly bound to attend the Meeting and further its objects to the utmost extent of their power.

N.B. Bring your Licenses, they may be wanted.

Down with the License Fee!
November 1854
(PUBLIC RECORD OFFICE COLLECTION LAVERTON)

This poster was placarded across the Ballarat diggings, calling all those on the field to meet on Bakery Hill at two o'clock on 29 November.

The meeting was to greet the delegates Humffray, Kennedy and Black on their return from Melbourne, and to press once again for the abolition of the licence fee and the release of the three prisoners who had been convicted for the destruction of the Eureka Hotel.

**Moral persuasion is
all a humbug
Nothing convinces
like a lick in
'the lug'.**

Chartist couplet, quoted by
Tom Kennedy, a prominent
Scotsman who had little desire for
the moderation shown by others in
the Ballarat Reform League.

with his killer, forced the Ballarat Reform League into being.

Its main proponents were Henry Holyoake, a London chartist; George Black, a well-educated Englishman who published the *Diggers' Advocate;* and the more moderate moral-force exponent, Welshman J. B. Humffray. There were present at these early meetings those who favoured a more energetic form of protest. The German, Frederick Vern, promoted 'red republicanism' and Tom Kennedy, the Scottish chartist, was in favour of direct and physical action.

The Ballarat Reform League adopted a platform far more extreme than that proposed at earlier meetings. Black, Humffray and Kennedy were sent to Melbourne to put the demands that the Gold Commission be disbanded, the licence fee abolished, manhood suffrage introduced, and a raft of other matters to put before the Governor.

On 16 November 1854 Governor Hotham established a Royal Commission to inquire into concerns on the goldfields, but just one week later, and before the Reform League delegates had even reached Melbourne, he dispatched all available troops to Ballarat. On Monday, 27 November, the Governor agreed to receive the deputation from Ballarat. The Ballarat diggings were placarded with posters calling for a meeting on the 29th to hear the report of their delegation. However, it appears that the diggers were already resolved to burn their licences. The Ballarat Commissioners' Camp was barricaded with bales of hay and bags of oats, and the military seemed none too confident about the outcome of the next few days.

Governor Hotham believed, as did his Commissioners on the field, that the rebels were 'foreigners and Irish'. This may well have been true of this little corner of the vast Victorian diggings, but the troubles had been brewing for over three years.

Troops despatched by Hotham entered the Ballarat diggings on Tuesday, the 28th. They marched in with bayonets fixed. And were met with hoots of derision. As they passed through the Eureka lead they were pelted with stones, carts were overturned, and a drummer

boy inadvertently shot; he later died from the wounds sustained in that frivolous skirmish. In revenge, the troopers drew their swords and flailed into the fray in an attempt to recover both government property and their dignity.

This action of the hotheads at Eureka angered the Reform League delegates who were, by this time, in Melbourne, as it had simply moved the Camp into battle mode and whetted an appetite for revenge. They returned to Ballarat on 29 November, only to find the situation had deteriorated after the debacle of the previous day. At a mass meeting, held on Bakery Hill, the Eureka flag was raised for the first time. The meeting was addressed by Peter Lalor, one of the founders of the Reform League, and licences were consigned to a great bonfire set by Frederick Vern.

On 30 November Commissioner Robert Rede ordered one more licence hunt as he attempted to show the diggers who was in command. Rede believed that the government must crush the movement at Ballarat if it were to control this and other goldfields. Rede had told a digger that morning that 'we will stand no more of this nonsense' as the troopers rode out. They were again pelted with stones, hooted and abused. They fired a volley over the heads of the diggers,

Burning of the Eureka Hotel
17 October 1854

Watercolour by Charles Doudiet
(Ballarat Fine Art Gallery Collection)

Doudiet's eyewitness accounts have only resurfaced since 1966. Unknown for over one hundred years, they were discovered in a collection of papers in Canada and brought back to Ballarat by public subscription.

His primitive, yet remarkably detailed, style prove the best account of the fateful events that changed the course of governance for ever in the Colony of Victoria.

– RAFFAELLO CARBONI –

The flamboyant Italian writer and chron-
icler was a keen observer who played a significant role in the Eureka uprising. His
book, *The Eureka Stockade*, published after
his acquittal from treason, remains the one
comprehensive eyewitness account of that
fateful day.

Blessed with blazing red hair and prominent beard, the Italian revolutionary
placed himself at the centre of the debate
over the diggers' resistance to the licence
fee. He was, however, at pains to ensure
that he was not considered a red republican
and that it was the licence issue that was at
the centre of his and the diggers' dissent.

Yet it was Carboni who stood with Peter
Lalor and Frederick Vern when the call for
all men on Ballarat to stand together
beneath the blue flag in defiance of the government was first heard.

Although he had not been in the stockade at the time of the attack, he was arrested later in the morning at the London
Hotel where he had been attending to the
wounds of his injured comrades. He was
sent for trial with all the other diggers'
leaders. After their acquittal he was one of
nine diggers elected to the local Ballarat
Court to adjudicate on mining affairs.

Disappointed by the act of a government
rising up against its own people, Carboni,
who was at heart an Italian patriot,
returned to his homeland after only four
years in Australia. There, ever the one to
put himself at the centre of great causes, he
worked with the Garibaldi forces for the
liberation and unification of Italy until he
died in 1875.

Peter Lalor
From *Picturesque Atlas of Australasia*
(PRIVATE COLLECTION)

and received several shots in
reply. Half a dozen prisoners
were taken.

The action of the troops this
day bought the immediate future
into sharp focus. Just before
noon on the 30th Rede arrived at
the Gravel Pits, where he called
on the diggers there to present
their licences. Lalor, Raffaello Carboni and their mates had gone to
their shafts earlier in the morning. The flamboyant Italian digger
Carboni was thinking of calling it quits for the day when he heard the
cry go up of 'The traps'.

Lalor later recalled :

I was working in a shaft at Eureka 140 ft deep, Timothy Hayes at the
windlass, when suddenly the news spread that the diggers were being
fired on at the gravel pits.[2]

Lalor was quickly hauled to the surface, and he rushed to the pits.
When Rede saw the Eureka mob hurrying up the gully, he read the
Riot Act and called for reinforcements from the Camp. The angry
crowd dispersed.

Later in the afternoon, as if by some unheard signal, crowds began
to assemble at Bakery Hill, where, in the absence of the Melbourne
delegates, Lalor again addressed the meeting. He recalled:

I looked around me; I saw brave and honest men, who had come thousands of miles to labour for independence. I knew that hundreds were
in great poverty, who would possess wealth and happiness if allowed to
cultivate the wilderness which surrounded us. The grievances under
which we had long suffered, and the brutal attack of the day, flashed
across my mind; and with the burning feelings of an injured man, I
mounted the stump and proclaimed 'Liberty'.

I called for volunteers to come forward and enroll themselves in companies. Hundreds responded to the call ... I then called to the volunteers
to kneel down. They did so, and with their heads uncovered, and hands
raised to Heaven, they solemnly swore at all hazards to defend their
rights and liberties.[3]

As G. W. Rusden had remarked, on all the diggings there were a
large number of men filled with revolutionary zeal, and countless
others had a particular axe to grind with the British Crown. One

- THE DEATH OF SCOBIE -

13 September 1854: The decision to instigate twice-weekly licence checks to bring order to the goldfields may well mark the date where the determined struggle for liberty really began.

Tension had been building between the troops and the diggers for some time, the licence fee and the 'diggers' hunts' were openly detested by the men, and this action to step up military activity simply added to the unrest.

It was the brutish murder of one of the diggers by James Bentley, the publican of the Eureka Hotel, an ex-convict with close connections to the corrupt magistrate's court, and the subsequent acquittal of the guilty party that inflamed the diggings. The obvious conspiracy, cronyism, ineptitude and sheer corruption of the goldfields administration was plain for all to see.

The Scottish digger, James Scobie, had been celebrating the arrival of a friend, Peter Martin, on the goldfield on 7 October 1854. Making their way home to Scobie's tent they came upon the Eureka Hotel. Scobie tried to gain entry to the hotel by banging on the door, waking up the owner, Bentley. They were told to go away, whereupon the already inebriated Scobie began to kick the door in.

A brief altercation followed, and Scobie made some unfortunate remarks concerning the reputation of the owner's wife, who by this time had joined her husband in the darkened bar.

Scobie and Martin quickly turned away from the hotel. Only fifty or so yards from the Eureka they were attacked by Bentley, his wife, and cronies John Farrell, Tom Mooney and Hervey Hance.

Martin, although beaten, was able to scurry into the darkness, but Scobie was surrounded, knocked to the ground and kicked to death.

It was not long before the news of this fracas spread across the diggings.

9 October: An inquest was held into the death of Scobie, but, much to the disgust of the diggers, an open verdict was returned.

10 October: Johann Gregorious, the Armenian servant of the Catholic priest, Father Smyth, was abused and arrested by police for not being in possession of a licence. Gregorious, who was crippled, protested that, as the servant of the priest, he was not in need of a digging licence, but the troopers were not interested. He was forced to march to the Camp by Officer Lord.

Gregorious was fined £5, but not for the original charge of being without a licence. Commissioner Johnstone changed the charge to assaulting a trooper in the execution of his duty, as he feared he could not justify the original in the face of the prevailing sentiment on the goldfield. The effect was much the same.

17 October: A meeting was held near the spot where Scobie died, to try to find a way to have the case of Scobie's death and the subsequent acquittal of Bentley brought before 'other and more competent authorities'. After this meeting several of Commissioner Rede's troopers, who had been watching the protest, moved across to the front of the Eureka Hotel, as Bentley feared some form of retribution by the diggers. The sight of the troopers, who appeared to be guarding the very source of their current discontent, brought the situation to the boil.

A young lad threw a stone at the lamp in front of the hotel, and before long the agitated assembly began to tear the Eureka apart. A fire, lit in an adjoining bowling saloon, quickly spread until both buildings were engulfed in flames.

The police lent Bentley a horse, on which he galloped away to the protection of the Camp – more of the same apparent collusion with the Camp that had created this uprising.

Governor Hotham believed that those who took part in the events of 17 October were preparing to 'overawe' him, and that he must show them 'that they could not take the law into their own hands'.

Hotham, however, responded to the diggers' demands with the arrest of Bentley, Farrell and Hance, and he

ordered an investigation into the affair by Sturt and two other magistrates.

Although James Bentley had served time on both Norfolk Island and in Van Diemen's Land, he had support from John O'Shanassy and F. P. Stevens; from the manager of the Bank of New South Wales, Alex Willis; from the Superintendent of Her Majesty's Hulks in Port Phillip; and from two auctioneers in Geelong: all of whom agreed to his fitness to hold a publican's licence. He was also supported by John D'Ewes, Senior Magistrate and Chairman of the Licensing Bench in Ballarat, from whom he had obtained the licence for the Eureka.

Bentley had a notorious reputation for the running of 'a slaughterhouse', as the hotel was known among the diggers. It was the biggest hotel on the Ballarat field at the time, and was well known for its strong-armed men who were not afraid to use their muscle if the occasion arose.

John Farrell was also an ex-convict, and had made his mark as a Crown Prosecutor in the Court of Petty Sessions in Ballarat and as a Chief Constable in Castlemaine.

Tom Mooney worked as roustabout and nightwatchman at the hotel, and Hervey Hance was in charge of the till.

The complicity between felons and enforcers is amazing to us today. The only barrier between them seemed to be the Bench, and people seemed to move freely from one side to the other. The game of law seemed to be the same for all players, the colour of the uniform and the braid on the shoulders, or lack of it, was the only thing separating the felon from the law.

25 October: A number of Father Smyth's parishioners met at the Roman Catholic chapel on Bakery Hill. They were of the opinion that the attack on Gregorious was an attack on Father Smyth (who was very popular among the diggers), and obviously an attack on the Irish community. Peter Lalor, who had previously held a claim next to Scobie, was now coming to the forefront of these agitations.

However, the digging fraternity were not altogether without blame. The Irish Catholics had largely hijacked the argu-

Troops' Arrival from Melbourne
(LA TROBE PICTURE COLLECTION,
STATE LIBRARY OF VICTORIA)

ment for reform that had begun with the birth of the Red-ribbon Movement at Bendigo and Castlemaine three years earlier. At Ballarat the 'Hibernian element' was eager to avenge centuries of mistreatment by the British Crown. Scobie's death was simply the catalyst for the revolutionary zeal that had been smouldering on the diggings since 1851. Hotham seriously believed that 'foreigners' were largely to blame for the agitation; however, the bodies at Eureka on 3 December were to prove otherwise.

17 November: A report of the inquiry into the Bentley affair was released, and it recommended that D'Ewes be dismissed from his position. It found that he was closely connected with, and indebted to, publicans on the field and had given false evidence.

18 November: Bentley, Farrell and Hance were convicted of manslaughter and sentenced to three years' imprisonment, with hard labour on the roads. It was on the evidence of Bentley's man, Tom Mooney, who had responded to a reward of £500 offered for information on Scobie's death, that the case was proved.

In the face of this evidence Hotham still despatched a further 450 troopers to Ballarat, with the instructions to Rede to 'use force whenever legally called upon to

Just as La Trobe had done at Bendigo three years earlier, Hotham replied to the diggers' petition by sending more troops onto the offending goldfield. This action, as at Bendigo, proved to be counter-productive, achieving the exact opposite to what was desired.

do so, without regard to the consequences that might ensue'. He demanded from Rede the arrest of those responsible for the burning of the Eureka Hotel.

23 November: Several diggers were arrested for this offence, but after the dismissal by Magistrate Sturt of the diggers Balderstone, Stuart, MacIntosh and Van der Byl, three unfortunate others, Andrew McIntyre, Thomas Fletcher and Henry Westerby, were the only men brought to trial.

The case against them was proved; even though admittedly they were present at the fracas, they were not solely responsible for the fire. A fourth man, Carey, was selected for trial but never brought before the magistrate (curiously, the fact that he was an American appears to have given him exemption from colonial justice).

The Ballarat Reform League immediately voted to demand the release of the 'three martyrs to British injustice'.

The League's demands were again refused by the Governor. It was the word 'demand' that so incensed Hotham, he advised Humffray, Kennedy and Black that 'I must take my stand on the word demand'. They reminded him of the royal prerogative of pardon that he, as the representative of the Crown, was empowered to give. They also referred to the pardon allowed an American citizen, but were to learn that it was a petition by the American Consul that had secured Carey's release.

The League's delegates, while imploring Hotham to show leniency in the case of the three diggers, and thereby diffuse the situation on Ballarat, were unaware that reinforcements for the 12th Regiment were already on their way.

such man was Peter Lalor, once a student at Trinity College, Dublin, a decent man who preferred to take the world as he found it. Yet his pedigree would not be denied; he rose to prominence at this time when his self-respect and indignation would not allow him to stand by any longer.

He was well versed in the art of dissent and political activism, and well practised in political debate; to take charge was grist to his mill. His father had been a member of the House of Commons, being elected in 1832 following his organisation of a campaign of resistance to the paying of tithes to the Church of Ireland, and had also organised a system of 'defensive resistance' using pitch-forks and pikes to defend local farmers against eviction until tithes were abolished in 1838.

His brother, James Fintan Lalor, had featured prominently in the failed 1848 rebellion, and was planning an armed uprising up until his death in 1849. He had devised a design of 'fortified circular encampments', whose design may have influenced the construction at Eureka. It was with this background that Lalor made his principled stand against the government.

At the meeting at 4 pm on 30 November 1854 Peter Lalor stepped up on a tree stump beneath the billowing Southern Cross flag, and into his place in Australian history. The diggers knelt, as one, on the dusty ground, placed their hands over their hearts and chanted together the diggers' oath: 'We swear by the Southern Cross to stand truly by each other, and defend our rights and our liberties'.

Over the next two days a thousand diggers began the construction of a stockade on the Eureka field. The roughly circular encampment was about an acre in area, and barricaded on three sides by a rude construction of pit logs thrown together in a higgledy-piggledy manner. There were also several tents within the enclosure.

At dawn on the morning of 3 December 1854 government troops attacked the stockade. It was a Sunday morning. As work on the shafts was prohibited on Sundays, it is fair to surmise that most diggers had taken some relaxation the previous evening and were well asleep at that early hour; a dawn raid was the last thing they would have

Commissioner Robert Rede ordered one final licence hunt, which so inflamed the diggers that revolution was the ultimate result.

– CHARTISM –

Chartism was a working-class movement begun in England whose principal aim was to gain political franchise and better working conditions for the ordinary worker.

The following six-point People's Charter was drafted in 1838:
- Universal Suffrage
- Secret Ballot
- Annual Elections
- Payment of Members
- No Property Qualification for MPs
- Equal Electoral Districts.

Three petitions presented to the English parliament in 1839, 1842 and 1848 made no impact whatsoever.

Australia had seen many transported for attempts to improve the lives of the workers. In 1834 Sydneysiders had turned out to witness the arrival of George and John Loveless, Thomas and John Standfield and James Harriett, a small group of agricultural labourers from Dorset who had had the nerve to try to establish a farm labourers' union.

George Loveless wrote:

We are uniting to preserve ourselves, our wives and our children from utter degradation and starvation, we have injured no man's reputation, character, person or property.

However, their attempt was an affront to the establishment, who were perfectly content to run the country as a personal fiefdom, so they were arrested, convicted and transported to New South Wales.

'The Tolpuddle Martyrs', as they were known, were another link in the chain of discontent that ultimately led to Eureka.

Notice placarded across the diggings, 2 December 1854

(Public Record Office Collection, Laverton)

This notice, dated one day before the battle at Eureka, indicates the paranoia of the government at that time.

Continued agitation and apparent dissent were to assume a cataclysmic importance for Hotham and his commissioners at Ballarat. They felt they were forced to act to bring the diggings to order, to show who was really in charge. What a pity for them that the action proved exactly the opposite.

P. Lalor.

Peter Lalor

Although Lalor's family history had instilled in him a resolve in defiance of the English Crown, on Australian soil he was determined to leave the old battles behind. But once he climbed up on that stump beneath the fluttering blue and white flag and took the diggers' oath he, somewhat reluctantly, embraced his destiny.

expected. In fact, very few were actually at the stockade, and those who were, were in little condition for battle. The attack was a complete surprise. The battle was short and bloody, leaving 22 diggers and six government soldiers dead or dying. The action of some troopers after the battle had ceased was barbaric; bleeding diggers were bayoneted where they fell. Tents were set alight without any attempt made by the troopers to remove the wounded within.

Lalor's left arm was shattered by a musket ball, and he lay wounded in a shallow shaft beneath a pile of logs. After the dust had settled, he was smuggled away by Father Smyth to the Presbytery, where his arm was amputated. Anastasia Hayes, wife of one of the 'rebel' leaders, was at the Presbytery and assisted in the operation.

Commissioner Rede issued the following proclamation from the Government Camp at Ballarat on the afternoon after the battle:

> Her Majesty's forces were this morning fired upon by a large body of evil-disposed persons of various nations, who had entrenched themselves in a stockade in the Eureka, and some officers and men were killed. Several of the rioters have paid the penalty of their crime and a large number are in custody. All well-disposed persons are earnestly requested to return to their ordinary occupations, and to abstain from assembling in large groups, and every protection will be afforded them by the authorities.[4]

Funerals for the dead were held all the following day. On the night of 4 December soldiers fired into several tents where 'illegal' lights were showing, with the loss of three more lives. It seems that Rede's promise of protection counted for nothing.

Poster offering a reward for information leading to the apprehension of the diggers' leaders, 18 December 1854
(BALLARAT FINE ART GALLERY COLLECTION)

This poster calling for information that may lead to the arrest of Lalor and Black, uses remarks made by them on or about 13 November as the 'treasonable' trigger from which charges could be laid.

Lalor and Black avoided capture at Eureka, and were sheltered by sympathisers and wellwishers until well after those sent to trial were acquitted. Following the trials the mood of the public versus the government crystallised. The government had to accede to the demands of the majority. The miners of Eureka, though defeated on the day, won the battle in the end.

(OPPOSITE)
The Storming of Eureka Stockade
3 December 1854 (detail)
Watercolour by J. B. Henderson
(DIXSON GALLERIES, STATE LIBRARY OF NEW SOUTH WALES)

This was painted soon after the battle at Eureka, and Henderson shows the battle from the perspective of sympathetic diggers.

The diggers are shown as a loosely disciplined motley of amateur soldiers, who are falling before the onslaught of an organised, practised and fearless military force – suffering is shown here, not glorious or heroic deaths, but simply wasted lives.

From the *Argus*, 4 December (obviously typeset and 'put to bed' before news of the previous day was broadcast):

> it is reported that a very active part is taken in the present disturbance by natives of other countries … if we are doomed to engage in a sad and serious struggle, let us at all events fight it out amongst ourselves!
>
> This is still an English colony, with English laws, English habits, and English sympathies! If we do fight, let the encounter be an English one, conducted upon English principles, and in an English spirit! … we trust that rumours of their identification with the movement may be unfounded; and that the leading men of their several nations will exert themselves to the utmost to retain them in their proper position of neutrality. Let them dig our gold and welcome, but they should abstain from interfering in our national disputes.

On 5 December martial law was declared in Ballarat, with Major General Sir Robert Nickle in command.

NOTICE
TO
SPECIAL
CONSTABLES.

All those who have been sworn in as such are repuested to
Attend Immediately
at the POLICE OFFICE, Swanston-st., when they will receive Instructions and Badges of Office.

J. T. SMITH,

Swanston-street Police Office, Melbourne,
6th December, 1854.

Mayor of Melbourne.

BY AUTHORITY JOHN FERRES, GOVERNMENT PRINTER, MELBOURNE

Poster, 6 December 1854
(LA TROBE PICTURE COLLECTION, STATE LIBRARY OF VICTORIA)

The government printer must have been kept busy running out copies of the large number of posters for Hotham.

Here he calls upon the volunteer constabulary to get into uniform and be ready for any sustained insurrection following the events of the previous day.

The *Argus* of 6 December reported that:

No further intelligence arrived last night from Ballarat. Up to one o'clock yesterday all was quiet in that locality, but an opinion prevailed among many people, well able to judge, that the calm was the result not of defeat but of a cool determination to attain a certain object.

Aftermath

William Denovan, one of the main agitators on the Bendigo gold-field, was on his way to Ballarat with Henry Holyoake, a Ballarat representative who had been in Bendigo giving an eyewitness account to his compatriots there. They got as far as the Guildford Arms Hotel near Castlemaine, where they stopped for the night. It was here that they received news of the battle and defeat of the diggers' stockade at Eureka.

On 9 December a large meeting at Castlemaine condemned military rule, and refused to pay the licence fee any more. Red ribbons, accompanied by mourning ribbons, were worn by many diggers at that meeting. Hotham's resolve to defeat Eureka had only hardened the resolve of the diggers right across Victoria.

As Denovan made his way back to Bendigo, a trooper followed him. Denovan strode into Bendigo in red shirt and white trousers, a scarlet scarf given to him by an admirer at Castlemaine flying at his neck. He was immediately recognised, and cheered all the way into the centre of the camp. However, the Bendigo diggings remained calm. The popularity of the Assistant Commissioner, Joseph Panton, was in stark contrast to the high emotion at Ballarat. Although feelings towards the government were high on all of the diggings, Forest

Anastasia Hayes
(LA TROBE PICTURE COLLECTION, STATE LIBRARY OF VICTORIA)

Irish-born Anastasia was the wife of Timothy Hayes, Chairman of the Ballarat Reform League at the meetings on Bakery Hill.

When Timothy was arrested following the battle, she confronted Lt Richards with the defiant outburst: 'If I had been a man I would not have allowed myself to be taken by the likes of you'.

The Eureka Stockade
From *Picturesque Atlas of Australasia*
(PRIVATE COLLECTION)

This engraving is in stark contrast
to the watercolour on page 149.
While Henderson's painting reflects
the battle from within the stockade,
where diggers stand to fight and fall
before the onslaught of the troops, this
image has all the hallmarks of classic
English army 'heroic' painting, such
as *The Charge of the Light Brigade* or *The
Battle at Rork's Drift*.

Here the diggers are shooting from
the safety of the stockade walls, and it
is the troopers who fall 'heroically'
before the lead onslaught. This engraving
indicates an orderly military engagement
between equals, one barricaded beneath
a 'foreign ensign', the other advancing
in the face of danger to carry out the rule
of law.

Creek, McIvor and other diggings more closely allied with Bendigo
were not all that eager to broadcast their support for the Irish at
Ballarat.

Although the movement was inclusive of all the nationalities who
came together under the Southern Cross, the predominance of the
Irish among those who defended the stockade led contemporary
commentators to conclude that it was a purely Irish, or Catholic,
protest, whose main aim was to win independence from British
rule.

Hotham began to justify his actions, and in his request to the
Secretary of State for a grant of secret service money he insisted:

**secret societies everywhere exist … the French Red Republican, the
German political metaphysician, the American Lone Star Member and
the British Chartist here meet not to dig gold but to agitate, overturn
the government and seize the land.**[5]

If the British had been more inclusive of the dispossessed and less
inclined to the promotion of established social orders to the exclu-
sion of almost all else, they may not have felt the need to rule with
military force. The Americans certainly had little love for England,
but were in no mind to attempt to overthrow the government. The
Irish Americans may have held Britain to blame for the potato

famine and the loss of 1,000,000 to the shores of America, but with that immigration they were free of the landlord class. Neither group had any reason to continue the struggle in Australia. However, few were prepared to be treated as 'base as slaves'.

Hotham certainly regarded the foreigners on the goldfield as more than influential, but it is difficult to guess whether he thought of the Irish as foreign. Certainly, adherence to the creed of Catholicism would have been regarded by him as foreign enough, if not downright seditious.

Several of the leaders of the Reform League had stepped back when they had felt that the agitation was veering away from 'moral force', and entering a 'forceful action' phase. Humffrays had withdrawn, as did other 'moral force' leaders, and Lalor stepped in and filled the vacuum.

The passwords, 'Vinegar Hill',* instigated by Lalor at the stockade represented a partisan political view commensurate with the 'lick in the lug' philosophy.

Commissioner Rede was to remark just before 3 December: 'the licence is a mere watchword of the day … a mere cloak to cover a democratic revolution'. The British-dominated bureaucracy was ever fearful of rebellion by those they sought to subdue; they had expressed the same views when it seemed that the Californian rush was about to cost them control over Oregon.

It was not only the citizens of Ballarat who showed concern after the events of 3 December. The following petition from the citizens of Geelong was sent to Hotham – it would appear that the threat of military rule and continued agitation against such rule would do more to destabilise the wider community than to serve it:

> To His worship the Mayor of Geelong, – Sir, – we, the undersigned inhabitants of Geelong request that you will convene a public meeting, to petition His Excellency Sir Charles Hotham at once to set aside the present licensing system of the diggings; convinced as we are that all the troubles and bloodshed that menace this colony originate in the manner in which such system is carried out. We publicly profess our loyalty to the throne, and our intention is to support the law; but our hearts bleed for the sufferings of our fellow-colonists at the diggings.

The *Mount Alexander Mail* of Monday, 11 December, carried a report of the 'greatest meeting that ever was held in Castlemaine' which 'took place on Saturday last'.

By and by there was a result; and I think it may be called the finest thing in Australian history. It was a revolution – small in size, but great politically; it was a strike for liberty, a struggle for principle, a stand against oppression.

It was the Barons and John, over again; it was Hampden and Ship-Money, it was Concord and Lexington, small beginnings, all of them, but all of them great in political results, all of them epoch making.

It is another instance of a victory won by a lost battle. It adds an honourable page to history; the people know it and are proud of it. They keep green the memory of the men who fell at the Eureka Stockade.
– Mark Twain, 1897

Twain visited the goldfields in 1895. Twain and his family are shown above departing Victoria B.C on 22 August 1895 on board the SS *Warrimoo*.

*Vinegar Hill referred to an incident in the uprising in Ireland of 1798, following the decimation of the English military by a body of armed peasants at Oulont Hill, near Wexford. The peasants were subsequently routed at Vinegar Hill. The main protagonists were arrested, convicted, and transported to Van Diemen's Land.

Gravel Pits XI

Gravelpits Ballarat

Dry Diggings, Gravel Pits, Ballarat
Watercolour by Charles Doudiet
(BALLARAT FINE ART GALLERY COLLECTION)

The Stars and Stripes flag of the United States of America is flown over one tent at the gravel pits at Ballarat.

> I think the practical miner, who had been hard at work, night after day, for the last four or six months, and, after all, had just bottomed a shicer, objected to the tax itself, because he could not possibly afford to pay it.
> And was it not atrocious to confine this man in the lousy lock-up at the camp, because he had no luck?

– Raffaello Carboni

Carboni had been working his shaft at the Gravel Pits next to Peter Lalor when following yet another of Rede's licence-hunts, he, Lalor, stepped up onto a tree-stump and rallied the diggers together under the Southern Cross flag for the first time.

Following this meeting, held only a few days after the fall of the Eureka stockade, the *Mount Alexander Mail* reported:

> That as the legislature have taken no satisfactory steps to redress the grievances of the residents on the Goldfields, this meeting protests against the injury done them, and resolves to take out no more licenses for gold digging, and to quietly abide the consequences; and as it is necessary that the diggers know their friends every miner agrees to wear as a pledge of good faith, and in support of the cause, a piece of red ribbon on his hat, not to be removed until the License-tax is abolished.

Denovan also addressed this meeting, wishing to encourage Castlemaine to unite with Ballarat and Bendigo and the Reform League, and to continue the fight against Hotham. The spark of rebellion that had begun in 1851 at Forest Creek, had seen the signing of the Bendigo Petition of 1853, and the destruction of the Eureka Stockade on 4 December 1854, was not going to be allowed to be extinguished. The 'Red-ribbon' Rebellion was about to join with the spirit of Eureka, and set its course to deny the Governor his taxes.

Of the 120 diggers arrested, the courts brought only thirteen to trial. The charge of treason was fearful, yet the jury set each man free. The American negro, John Joseph, was tried first and acquitted; he was carried from the court on the shoulders of the crowd. Carboni

Miner's Right issued to John Davis at Castlemaine in 1888.
(PRIVATE COLLECTION)

After the dust had settled on the battle-ground, and after the miners were tried and freed, the licence fee was abolished and replaced with a Miner's Right, with an annual fee of £1. Quite a saving.

The Trial on 22 February 1855
(LA TROBE PICTURE COLLECTION, STATE LIBRARY OF VICTORIA)

120 men were arrested following the defeat of the diggers at the stockade. Only thirteen were brought to trial in Melbourne, charged with treason.

Of these, Thomas Dignum, Timothy Hayes, John Manning, William Molloy, John Phelan and Michael Tuhey were of Irish descent.

They were brought before Chief Justice Sir William Beckett, as was the Italian, Raffaelo Carboni, and the American negro, John Joseph.

The contemporary engraving below shows those brought to trial together in the dock.

and Hayes were next to be acquitted. The Crown law prosecutors advised Hotham that it would be wise to drop further trials, as it was obvious that the jury was intent on freeing each and every man. Hotham replied that if the juries would not do their duty, he could see no reason for failing to do his. But after ten were set free, Hotham gave up. The case was finished.

Although there was a reward of £500 for his arrest, Lalor never stood before a judge; he had been protected by sympathisers, of whom there were many. It was only when an amnesty was granted to all participants in the 'uprising' that he was free to emerge. The diggers had won a great victory over an inept government; they won the

| Timothy Hayes | J. F. Campbell | Raffaello Carboni | Jacob Sorenson | John Manning | John Phelan | Thomas Dignum | John Joseph | James Beattie | William Molloy | Jan Vennick | Michael Touhey | Henry Read |

The Acquittal of all Prisoners
Engraving from *Illustrated Australian
News*, 1887
(PRIVATE COLLECTION)

One of the diggers arrested and charged
with conspiracy and treason after the
battle at Eureka is lifted above the crowd,
following the acquittal of all prisoners.

The juries refused to convict any
of those brought before the courts,
excepting Henry Seekamp, the former
editor of the *Ballarat Times*, who was
charged for inciting the rebellion and
jailed for the crime of sedition.

Lalor was never brought before the
courts. He was taken into hiding where
he remained until after all of his compatriots had been freed.

Both Lalor and Humffray were elected
to the Victorian parliament, where they
continued the push for further reform
of the goldfields administration.

Carboni was appointed to the post of
mining warden, a popular choice among
the diggers.

right to vote in the new legislative assembly, which was formed in
1855; and Peter Lalor won the right to represent them in parliament.

The licence fee was abolished and replaced with a Miner's Right for
an annual fee of £1, and an export levy on gold. This Right gave the
diggers title deed to their claims, allowing them to establish
permanent dwellings, and a permanent sense of community.
Commissioners were replaced with mining wardens, and military
rule was abolished on the goldfields forever.

Hotham lived for only one more year; he died on 31 December
1855. He had been a naval officer of distinction who had inherited an
outmoded system already in decline, and an increasingly vocal community demanding to be free.

*'The stirring of the revolutionary spirit
in Australia, and although the battle was
lost Eureka became a symbol in the
continuing battle for the people's rights'*
– KARL MARX

CHAPTER 12

A LAW UNTO THEMSELVES

Black Trooper's escorting a prisoner, from Ballarat to Melbourne. 1851

COUNTLESS STORIES are recorded in first-hand accounts of the dangers of attack by bushrangers on the roads to and from the diggings.

The simple fact was that 'new chums' fresh from the streets of London, or the green fields of Ireland were walking through the darkened forests, carrying all they owned with them, and it was too great an opportunity for the hundreds of Vandemonians who had come to Victoria. Many an old lag was to make his fortune without ever lifting a shovel.

Severyn Korzelinski, a Polish digger, while on his way to Mt Alexander was accompanied for a short distance through the Black Forest by a rather 'well-dressed man … with pistols and a revolver in his belt'[1]. The bushranger eventually took his leave after he discovered that Korzelinski and his party were Polish. He remarked before he galloped away: 'I wouldn't have wasted so much time on you. It's well known that you Poles never have anything'. This was true, as

Bushranger on His Way Back from the Goldfields
Watercolour by William Strutt
(STATE PARLIAMENTARY LIBRARY COLLECTION, VICTORIA)

This drawing shows a sorry-looking fellow in the charge of three smartly kitted-out Aboriginal troopers.

It was a smart move to train and equip a body of native troops and police. While the diggers resented the appointment of many ex-convicts or ticket-of-leave men to such forces, they did not resent the Aboriginals.

While many a hated felon donned a uniform and relished power to oppress his fellow-countrymen, the Aboriginal troops had no 'cultural' baggage to bring with them to the task, and they were apparently treated with respect.

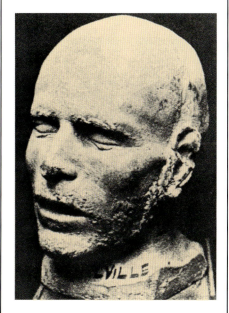

Death mask of George Melville

This cast was taken after the bushranger George Melville was hanged in the Old Melbourne Gaol on 3 October 1853.

Melville was the leader of the gang that robbed the McIvor Escort on 20 July. There are various reports of this daring robbery. Korzelinski records:

> during the battle between the immobilised escort and the bushrangers, six members of the escort and two bushrangers were killed. The bushrangers left the field victorious, with 3,000 ounces of gold. I heard later that an expedition of about fifty settlers and merchants went after the bushrangers, surrounded them and caught them, recovering part of the booty.

The details of the number shot differ with each telling, but one thing is certain: that the bush telegraph carried such news far and wide, and no doubt the daring deeds grew a little each time the story was retold.

most middle Europeans were refugees from their war-ravaged home-lands, bringing little with them to this new country.

Most eyewitness accounts of the diggings refer to bushrangers as one of the greatest worries when travelling. Because of this, few chose to travel alone, often teaming up with a bullock driver or others who knew the route and its dangers.

Bushrangers, escaped convicts or men of low character had been active in the region for many years. In fact, when Captain John Hepburn first passed through the area in 1838 he discovered the remains of a convict who had been buried in the sand where two creeks came together (at what is now the town of Castlemaine). Hepburn recalled later:

> **On the brink of the waterhole at the junction of the creeks known as Barker's and Forest Creeks I buried the skull of a prisoner of the Crown who was murdered by his mates after absconding. It was dug up by the natives twice, and the third time I buried it in the dry deposit in the waterhole.**[2]

Escorts were established to carry the gold from the diggings to the Treasury in Melbourne, yet the government took no responsibility for any loss incurred on the journey. The escorts were heavily armed, but although attacks were frequent most of the gold got through.

It was the lone digger who was easy prey for those with evil intent. Korzelinski remembers seeing ragged skeletons tied to trees on lonely tracks through the forest. Bushrangers would attack lone travellers, taking all they had and leaving the unfortunates to the ants, flies, mosquitoes and other bush creatures. What a miserable end for the unwary or foolish 'new chum', and what a salutary lesson for all those who thought they could go it alone.

On the Ballarat Road, 19 December 1852

Frank McCallum, alias Captain Melville (not to be confused with George Melville) and his companion, William Roberts, held up two diggers, Thomas Wearne and William Madden, on the Ballarat road. Melville relieved them of £33, but gave back £10 as it was close to Christmas and he didn't wish to deprive them of an enjoyable holiday in Geelong. Melville and Roberts made their way on to Geelong, taking what they could from other travellers on the way. They were apprehended on Christmas Eve after they were discovered in a brothel. They had a long list of crimes for which they were wanted, including murder and robberies on the Ovens diggings.

Mc IVOR DIGGINGS, JULY 25. 1853.

On 3 February 1853 Melville was sentenced to 32 years' gaol for his crimes. He was sent to the hulks in Port Phillip Bay, where he was found strangled in his cell in August 1857. Roberts also got 32 years, and was sent to another hulk, the *President*. He was released on a ticket-of-leave on 19 January 1864.

McIvor Escort Robbery, 20 July 1853

The McIvor Escort was held up 14 miles out of Kyneton in central Victoria on its way from the McIvor (Heathcote) diggings. The escort was attacked in broad daylight by a large band of bushrangers, who wounded three troopers accompanying the escort, and killed the driver. They escaped with 2230 ounces of gold.

A reward was posted on Monday, 23 July, offering

£250 for the apprehension and conviction of the parties who robbed the McIvor Branch of the Escort … and a further sum of £250 for the recovery of the stolen property, or a proportional sum, for the recovery of part thereof.

Most of the gang were captured as they were preparing to leave the country. Only £2501 10s. in gold, notes, sovereigns and bankdrafts was recovered, suggesting that most of it had already been taken out

McIvor Diggings, 25 July 1853
(PRIVATE COLLECTION)

This drawing was made only a few days after the attack on the McIvor Escort by a large band of thieves.

They were all eventually captured, and three of the band were hanged before a large crowd in Melbourne. One, George Melville took so long to die that the hangman had to pull down on his legs 'with considerable force before life was extinct'.

– ANDREW SCOTT –
a.k.a. Captain Moonlight

*There may be some confusion in this report by Chandler about the identity of the particular bushranger.

Andrew Scott, alias Captain Moonlite, did range the Victorian goldfields, but it is recorded that he died on the Darlinghurst gallows on 20 January 1880.

Frank McCallum, alias Captain Melville, also made a nuisance of himself around the Victorian diggings, and it is recorded that he strangled himself with a neckerchief in his prison cell in August 1857.

The other Melville, George, robbed the McIvor gold escort, and he did die on the gallows.

It does seem that Chandler has confused the Captains and the Melvilles, and attributed this crime to poor old Andrew Scott.

What is in no doubt is that those on the road were well aware of who was about, who to look out for, and who to avoid.

The niceties of formal introduction may well have been eschewed once the bullets started to fly.

of the colony. Some of those caught committed suicide before being brought to justice; only three of them were tried, convicted, and sent to the gallows.

One of the victims of the hold-up later described his attackers:

you might see them starting on a campaign, on the great roads leading out of Melbourne to the Mines. There are a pair of them, well mounted, and wrapped up in great coats, they have a quiet reserved air, and keep a little aloof from the main line of traffic. They always go armed with loaded revolvers; but these are kept concealed.[3]

The bushrangers (William Atkins, George Wilson and George Melville) were executed before a large crowd on Monday, 3 October 1853. Melville's wife took his body and displayed it, decorated with flowers, in the window of an oyster shop in Bourke Street, Melbourne, where they had been living. This added attraction brought hundreds to the shop out of morbid curiosity. Whether it did much for business is unknown, but after that the bodies of those executed were buried within prison walls.

The threat of such punishment did little to deter the determined bushranger. So many old lags were abroad in the bush, and so many had suffered such indignities from transportation, floggings and deprivations of all kinds, that the long arm of the law and eventual retribution held no fears for them. Such felons were past redemption and often past caring; they had been taught that their own lives held little value, and they cared little for the lives of others.

John Chandler's diaries* record the following encounter with some poor unfortunate travellers who had the misfortune to make the acquaintance of a notorious bushranger:

In the morning we saw some who had been stuck up; they were camped on the road. Captain Moonlight [sic] and the others had taken all their money, revolvers, ammunition, and whatever they wanted, leaving them without money to buy provisions. He stuck up every one along the road, and the troopers seemed to keep well out of his way. It was not far from this place where they robbed the escort a year or two before, and killed some of the troopers. We unloaded and got safe back with our money. I put my money in a leather bag and when we camped, I dug a little hole in the ground and put the bag into it, and then drew my dray wheel on top, keeping some in my pocket so as not to raise suspicion, for if they thought you planted it, they would have shot you in a moment. Moonlight was captured soon after, and he committed suicide in gaol.[4]

Capture of Bushrangers at Night by Gold Police
Watercolour by George Lacy, c. 1852
(REX NAN KIVELL COLLECTION, R4113.
BY PERMISSION, NATIONAL LIBRARY OF AUSTRALIA

What a surprise to be so rudely awoken, even the mongrel straining on his leash did not make enough noise to warn these 'wild boys' of the arrival of the police.

'Mad Dan' Morgan

Morgan kept a butcher's 'shambles' at Barker's Creek, near Castlemaine, where he was often seen in the company of his white bulldog. He was arrested only once in all his long bushranging career, for the robbery of a hawker on the Castlemaine goldfields in 1854.

He was sentenced by Judge Redmond Barry to twelve years' hard labour, the first two to be spent in irons. He always protested his innocence of the crime for which he had been convicted, and on his release on a ticket-of-leave in 1860 he began a long and bloody campaign of revenge against the police and the society that had incarcerated him. He ranged far and wide, and clocked up a huge number of heinous crimes that were attributed to him. He was eventually surrounded by police and killed in a shoot-out at Peechelba Station on the Ovens River on 9 April 1865.

Morgan's body was mutilated: the head was severed at the request of the Coroner, Dr Dobbyn, who wanted it for scientific research; locks of his hair were souvenired; and his facial skin and hair flayed from the flesh for Police Super-intendent Cobham so he could 'peg it out and dry it like a possum skin'; his scrotum was removed for use as a money pouch. The police were disgusted by such ghoulish souvenir hunting.

The public treated Morgan in death as poorly as he had treated those whom he had murdered. He was a curiosity, feared in life, and humiliated in defeat.

'Mad Dan' Morgan photographed at Wangaratta, following his death in a shoot-out with police at Peechelba Station on the Ovens
(COURTESY VICTORIA POLICE PRD)

There were few bushrangers more hated than Morgan. Although he always protested his innocence of the only crime he was ever convicted of, the years spent behind bars left an indelible mark. His fellow-inmates described him as 'an isolated and bitter man', who on his release in 1860 went on a rampage of revenge on the community who had taken away his freedom.

He was shot and killed in 1865.

The gun in his hand, a 50-calibre, five-shot Dane, Adams & Dean (Lon) Dragoon percussion double-action revolver, popular with soldiers on the Crimea, was lent to him by John Kirk, a fellow-digger at Barker's Creek.

As Walter Wilson recalls in the *Records of the Castlemaine Pioneers*:

> **Kirk lent his revolver to Morgan, the bushranger, who never returned it, and it was found in his possession at the time he was shot dead.**[5]

Small copies of this photograph were made by the police at the time and sold to souvenir hunters.

A Butcher's Shambles nr. Adelaide Gully at Forest Creek
Lithograph by S. T. Gill, Macartney & Galbraith, Melbourne, 1852

It is not hard to imagine that the character depicted could well be Morgan with his bulldog by his side.

Walter Wilson recalled:

I knew Morgan well by sight … on Sundays used to visit the Robert Burns Hotel. He had invariably a white bull-dog with him, and it and its master seemed a sulky pair.[6]

Ballarat, 16 October 1854

Four digger mates walked into the Bank of Victoria on Bakery Hill, and, with unloaded pistols, held up the clerk at the counter. They walked out with 350 oz gold and about £14,300.

Henry Garrett, a stonemason from Geelong, and diggers Henry Marriott, Thomas Quinn and John Boulton had planned the robbery the previous day in their tent at the Gravel Pits. The robbery was bold and brazen, and went very smoothly for them; they then divided the money and the gold between them, and went their separate ways. Garrett went south immediately, boarding a ship bound for England; Quinn and Boulton went to Melbourne, where they sold their share of the gold to the London Chartered Bank; Marriott stayed in lodgings in Ballarat.

But before long their daring cheek bought them undone. Quinn and Boulton returned to Ballarat, where Boulton went back to the Bank of Victoria and attempted to draw a draft on London for £1,450. He tried to use some of the money he had stolen, was identified, delayed, and captured. It was one down and three to go, and the police rounded up Marriott and Quinn very soon after. By this time Garrett was 'safe' in England, but the Victorian police traced him there. The story goes that he was bailed up by Detective Henry Webb in the streets of London when Webb used the Australian bush cry of 'coo-ee' (others suggest Webb simply yelled out 'Garrett'); either way, Garrett gave himself away, and was brought back to Australia where he received a ten-year sentence.

When he was released on a ticket-of-leave in 1861, he travelled to the New Zealand goldfields, and was soon up to his old tricks. Garrett was considered by many to be the first New Zealand bushranger.

Black Douglas

One name featured prominently in the records of many a traveller on the roads to and from the diggings, and that name was Black Douglas.

Douglas was a powerfully-built negro who had jumped ship at Port Phillip. He and his bushranging band made their headquarters at Alma, near Maryborough. They were supposed to be working on the diggings, but made their gold by stealing from tents and shops. This was easy work, as tents were left untended during the day and the shops at night. They would create a disturbance in front of a shop late at night and, when the owner came to see what was going on out front, others would slit the rear canvas wall and help themselves.

Owing to a cost-cutting measure and the resultant reduced presence of police on the goldfields, diggers were eventually forced to band together in mutual protection societies, just as their digger brothers had done in California years before. At Alma they took the law into their own hands. One night they surrounded Douglas and his cronies, tied them up, and burnt their tents. Douglas put up a good fight, but was eventually overpowered. He was sent by cart to Maryborough, but several hundred miners, taking no chances, escorted him there.

There are several versions of his demise or disappearance from official records. Korzelinski, who had been on that field, recorded that Douglas was taken from Maryborough to Melbourne, and hanged. Richard Thimbleby, a digger at Diamond Gully near Castlemaine, recalls that Douglas was captured in 1855 at Fryer's Creek, near Castlemaine, where he was taken into the hospital at the Camp (Thimbleby was himself in the hospital with 'brain fever' after sticking his head in a bucket of water to cool down). He writes in his letter to *The Castlemaine Pioneers and Old Residents* in October 1904 that the hospital warder, Isaac George, keen to take a look at the notorious bushranger, had left the door to the small wooden building unlocked, and Black Douglas disappeared.

Johnny Gilbert
(*PRIVATE COLLECTION*)

John 'The Canadian' Gilbert was a dashing young man who knew the Kellys, rode with Gardiner and Ben Hall, and is immortalised as 'Jack Marsden' in Rolf Boldrewood's novel *Robbery Under Arms* (see page 168).

He was killed by police on 13 May 1865, and lies buried on a hillside near Binalong, NSW, in what was once the police paddock.

(*AUTHOR'S PHOTOGRAPH*)

'Bold Ben Hall'
(COURTESY NSW POLICE PDR)

Hall had a cattle farm near Wheoga, a wife and a young son, when he was arrested, at the age of 25, with Frank Gardiner on suspicion of a wagon hold-up near Forbes.

He was held in gaol for a month before the charges were dismissed. When he returned to his farm, he discovered that his wife had run off with a policeman, his house was burnt and his cattle gone.

He took his revenge on the roads around Forbes until he was killed on 6 May 1865. His body was riddled with between 15 and 30 bullet holes.

(ABOVE RIGHT)
Frank 'Darkie' Gardiner
(PRIVATE COLLECTION)

Gardiner rode onto the Kiandra goldfields in 1859 on a stolen horse. There he ran a butcher's shop, selling meat to the hungry diggers. He found it easier to steal his meat than buy it, and was eventually arrested for cattle duffing in January 1861. He stood before the magistrate, was bailed, and absconded from the district in May.

His derring-do, and spectacular robberies gave him the status of folk legend; after many adventures he was eventually imprisoned, pardoned and deported.

His was exiled to China but absconded yet again, and ended up in California, where he apparently settled down and ran a saloon in San Francisco.

Another writing in the same collection of letters from old pioneers recalls 'that notorious robber, Black Douglas' was chained to the logs at Pennyweight Flat alongside sixteen other diggers who had been apprehended for being without a licence. Another claims that Douglas was apprehended following an unsuccessful series of raids on groups of diggers who were taking their gold to Melbourne. The diggers were well prepared for such a raid; they had replied to Douglas's intentions with muskets and pistols. Douglas and his band were taken by troopers the following day while attacking a roadside inn. This report states that Douglas was 'sentenced to 14 years but is impossible to confirm as records of his trial and punishment have long since disappeared'.

Whether hanged or shot, captured or chained to the logs, Douglas seems to have at least captured the imagination and incited the fears of countless travellers on those lonely roads. His name was the name known by all who entered the Black Forest and his demise the stuff of legend.

J. F. Hughes:

on the second day we entered the Black Forest, noted then as the haunt of the celebrated 'Black Douglas'.[7]

William Ottey:

before we started next morning we heard of bushrangers, Black Douglas and his gang were about, and as the majority of us were armed we felt pretty plucky ... I think if anyone had looked black at us we would have done a bit of shooting, but if, on the other hand a revolver had been pointed at us, I have my doubts of the pluck holding out.[8]

Eugowra, near Forbes, New South Wales, 15 June 1862

The Lachlan Escort was held up by Frank Gardiner and his gang near Eugowra, 27 miles from Forbes. When the coach slowed to pass some bullock drays at the edge of the roadway, the gang of eight men, all with blackened faces and wearing red serge shirts, appeared alongside. One of the gang shouted 'Fire', and a volley of shots splintered the walls of the coach. The horses took fright and bolted, capsizing the coach. Three of the police guard were wounded in the brief

exchange of fire, others took to the bush for refuge. The gang escaped with gold boxes containing 2717 oz gold, £3700 in cash, and several mailbags. The haul was worth over £14,000.

Gardiner had some notorious accomplices that day: Johnny Gilbert, Harry Manns, John Bow, Alexander Fordyce, Dan Charters, Johnny O'Meally, Charles Darcy, and the charismatic Ben Hall. The news of the robbery – it was the biggest and boldest holdup in Australia's history – caused a sensation. Gardiner escaped north with Ben Hall's sister-in-law, Katherine, the wife of settler John Brown. They opened a store in Aphis Creek, Queensland where he went straight – for a time. In fact, while he was there he was so well regarded that local diggers left their finds with him for safe-keeping. In March 1864 the police, following a trail left by Katherine, finally tracked him to Aphis Creek. On 17 May 1864 Frank Gardiner was sentenced, at last, in the Central Criminal Court in Sydney to a total of 32 years.

Gardiner served only ten years before the government reviewed the harsh sentences dealt to those at this earlier, tougher period of colonial rule. He was pardoned by Henry Parkes in 1874, but was exiled to China. He sailed as far as Hong Kong, hopped on an

Bailed Up
Oil on canvas by Tom Roberts, 1895
(ART GALLERY OF NEW SOUTH WALES COLLECTION)

This painting was inspired by both a story Roberts had heard when he was painting his famous *Shearing the Rams* at a sheep station near Inverell, NSW, and reports of the Eugowra robbery. Roberts decided to create an imaginary image of an event from the 'wild colonial' days.

Inverell's Cobb & Co. coach driver, 'Silent-Bob Bates', had been held up by the notorious bushranger, Captain Thunderbolt, in the 1860s. His retelling of the story, in his typically laconic style, was the inspiration for the seemingly-relaxed attitude of the bushrangers and the occupants of the coach.

For accuracy, Roberts painted the landscape background on the Eugowra road near where the escort had been attacked.

Portrait of bushrangers:
Michael B(o)urke
Ben Hall
Frank Gardiner
King of the Road – John Gilbert
& John Dunn(e)
Oil on canvas by Patrick Maron, c. 1894

(REX NAN KIVELL COLLECTION, R4408.
BY PERMISSION, NATIONAL LIBRARY OF AUSTRALIA

These likely lads were all at Lambing Flat at the time of the attack on the Chinese camp.

All but one died young – Burke (aged only 17) shot by a gold warden, Hall riddled with bullets, Gilbert gunned down, and Dunn hanged.

Gardiner escaped to California, where it is believed he died of pneumonia in 1904.

The Way Her Majesty's Mails & the Public Protectors Are Served in New South Wales
Hand-coloured lithograph
Paul Jerrard & Son, for Messrs Newbold & Co., London, c. 1860, from *Sketches of Australian Life and Scenery*, after a drawing by S. T. Gill

(REX NAN KIVELL COLLECTION, U2820.
BY PERMISSION, NATIONAL LIBRARY OF AUSTRALIA

American ship, and landed in San Francisco. Ironically, it was in San Francisco that vigilante groups had formed only a few years earlier to rid that town of the 'Sydney Ducks', the notorious groups of 'old lags' from Australia in the rough'n'ready days of that Californian province. But things must have changed. Gardiner, under the assumed name of Frank Smith, set up in business and opened a saloon and restaurant, the Twilight Star, on Kearney Street.

There are several versions of Gardiner's demise: that he was shot in a gambling fight in Colorado, or died from pneumonia in 1904. Gardiner, Gilbert and Hall had all been at Lambing Flat (Young, NSW) in 1861 at the time of the riot when the diggers attempted to drive the Chinese off that goldfield. The Lambing Flat diggings in the heart of the Riverina district of central New South Wales had collected 'not less than five hundred of the most notorious thieves, forgers, foot-pads, gamblers, horse-stealers and escaped convicts'.

It is no surprise that this group of hot-heads, so far away from the reach of the law, was almost uncontrollable when they decided to take action. These notorious scoundrels, Gardiner, Gilbert and Hall, who revelled in their notoriety, were eventually hunted down, one by one, and shot, imprisoned or deported.

Gilbert lies in a lonely grave near Binalong, shot at the age of 25 by police. Hall, aged 28, shot by police, lies in Forbes cemetery. It is believed his last words were 'I am wounded – shoot me dead'.

165

Lynch Law and Larrikins

One of the greatest fears on the Australian goldfields was that the diggers would adopt the American style of summary justice, known as 'lynch law'. The Californian goldfields had been well out of the reach of the law; as a consequence the diggers there took it upon themselves to dispense their own brand of rough justice. Many an unfortunate miscreant was taken and strung up, with few questions asked.

Vigilante groups had formed in the Californian seaports to deal with the criminal element that had washed up on their shores. Prominent among them were scores of old lags from Van Diemen's Land and ex-convicts from Sydney, none of whom had any respect for either life or the law.

At this time California was governed from afar by the politicians of the United States, whereas Australia was under military rule. It must have been a pleasant surprise for 'Australians' to find such a free-wheeling democratic society, but then a shock to discover how swift and decisive was American summary justice when the citizens took control of their own safety.

Just as in California, crime on the Victorian diggings was rife and the police so incompetent that protection committees were formed, and swift justice dealt to those who offended. Murder, robbery, horse stealing, claim jumping, hold-ups, shootings and beatings were common. The prudent diggers stuck close to one another, and kept their powder dry, just in case they were called on to defend themselves.

W. H. Wilson wrote on 26 September 1890:

One Sunday night, while the five of us were lying down in the same tent, we heard footsteps coming towards us, the opening was thrust aside and a man stepped inside with a revolver in his hand and said 'Bail up!' An old soldier was lying near the opening and sang out:– 'He's a bushranger!' and seized the intruder by the legs. This sudden act threw

The First Trial and Execution in San Francisco (California) on the Night of 10th of June at 2 o'clock (1851)
W. C. K. (artist), Justh, Quirot & Co. (lithographer & publisher)
(REX NAN KIVELL COLLECTION, S10127. BY PERMISSION, NATIONAL LIBRARY OF AUSTRALIA)

The caption to this lithograph reads as follows:

John Jenkins, a Sidney [*sic*] man, entered the store of McV on long Wharf in the evening of 10th of June & carried off a safe. After he was captured he was brought to the corner of Sansomie & Bush Sts. where he was tried by a jury of the highest respectability, and condemned to hang.

The execution took place on the Plaza on the same night at 2 o'clock.

Immediately after sentence of death was passed upon him he was asked if he had anything to say, he replied: No, I have nothing to say, only I wish to have a cigar & brandy & water, which was given him.

Diggers of Low Degree
Lithograph by S. T. Gill, H. H. Collins & Co., London, 1853
(REX NAN KIVELL COLLECTION, S170. BY PERMISSION, NATIONAL LIBRARY OF AUSTRALIA)

There were plenty of unsavoury characters on the goldfields. Other diggers were wise to keep their eyes open and their powder dry.

Bourke Street West in the Forenoon
Wood engraving by Frederick Grosse
From *Australian News for Home Readers*,
24 March 1864

The diggings brought all kinds together, and there were plenty of young men, full of vigour, bursting with high spirits and pockets filled with gold, who wanted to do nothing more than to spend both their energy and their money – and most of all to impress anyone who cared to watch their antics.

William Howitt writes rather disparagingly of the goings-on in the streets of Melbourne:

The whole street swarms with diggers and diggeresses. Men in slouching wide-awakes with long untrimmed hair and beards, and like navvies in their costume. Some have horse-whips in their hands, and are looking at the exploits of other diggers on horseback with a knowing air.

Although this engraving does not necessarily depict bushrangers or criminals in action, yet these 'wild colonial boys' care little for the niceties of society or for the arm of the law. This same freewheeling, devil-may-care, larrikin streak has always been part of the Australian character, where every man is equal as long as he has the money to prove it.

the scoundrel, and as he fell his revolver flew out of his hand and on to my stretcher. We secured the fellow with rope, whipped him and kicked him almost to a jelly.[9]

Judge Barry, in sentencing the felon to 15 years, complained of the brutal treatment meted out to the unfortunate miscreant. The old soldier replied that 'the next time he saw a bushranger he would kill him if he could'.

Beatings of this kind were common, yet there is only one instance where an American-style lynching has been recorded. A Vandemonian was captured by diggers after he had killed his partner when they were divvying up their gold. Although he pleaded to be taken to the Commissioner for trial, he never made it. He was taken and strung up to the nearest tree. Over 4000 diggers gave the murdered man a solemn burial, then cut down his killer, threw him in a hole, and covered him with dirt.

It seems that the crime of stealing from a mate was the worst of all possible offences, against the ideals of mateship, dependence and trust, born on the goldfields.

There were many other incidents where diggers nearly met their Maker at the end of a rope:

we wandered about Forest Creek. We had not gone far before a digger with a pistol in his hand shot by us; he was followed by an immense mob, hooting, yelling, and screaming, as only a mob on the diggings can. It was in full pursuit, and we turned aside only in time to prevent ourselves from being knocked down in the confusion.

'Stop him – stop him', was the cry. He was captured, and the cry changed to, 'String him up – string him up – it's useless taking him to the police-office'.

When asked of the mob what the man had done the reply was:

[He] shot a man in a quarrel at a grog-shop.

Portraits of Charles White, author
of *Story of Australian Bushranging*,
c. 1894
Oil on canvas by Patrick William Marony
(REX NAN KIVELL COLLECTION, R4396.
BY PERMISSION, NATIONAL LIBRARY OF AUSTRALIA)

This unusual composite portrait includes
an imaginary portrait of the fictional
character Captain Starlight.

Starlight was one of the characters in
Rolf Boldrewood's classic Australian novel
Robbery Under Arms, and the bushranger
Johnny Gilbert was also immortalised in
this story as the character 'Jack Marsden'.

Boldrewood (T. A. Browne) was
a squatter in the Western District of
Victoria when the Victorian goldrush
began, and like so many others at that
time was fascinated by the social
revolution that followed. He later
became a police magistrate and a goldfields commissioner, but his lack of
mining experience caused some criticism
of his administration.

However, his experience of the
diggings, the criminal classes (Browne
had arrived in Australia, aged five, aboard
his father's ship, which carried a cargo of
convicts), and the bush, served him well
in the creation of this classic tale.

This painting features portraits of:
Charles White
Dr Pechey
Trooper Hipkiss
Matthew Gibney
Frederick Lowry
Tom Clarke
Charles Rutherford
Inspector Stephenson
J. Hawthorne
Martin Cash
Hugh Bracken
Francis Augustus Hare
Ben Hall
Captain Starlight

(OPPOSITE)
Arrival of the Gold Escort in Melbourne
Watercolour by William Strutt
(STATE PARLIAMENTARY LIBRARY COLLECTION, VICTORIA)

Carrying the chests into the Treasury,
Spring Street; from sketch taken from
nature in 1851 [*sic*].

The mob continued to howl for justice:

String him up – string him up – confront him with the body, … at this
moment the firmly secured and well-guarded culprit passed by, to be
confronted by the dead body of his adversary. No sooner did he come
into his presence than the corpse found his feet, 'showed fight', and
roared out, 'Come on', with a most unghostlike vehemence.[10]

It appears that the pistol shot had simply grazed his forehead, and
no serious injury was sustained. The fugitive took advantage of the
lull in the proceedings, and 'declared that the wounded man had been
robbing him'. The tables had now turned, and the 'dead man' took to
his heels and disappeared into the bush.

Although there were many who would have been prepared to shoot
first and ask questions later, a large number of practising lawyers
offered swift recourse to the protection of the law when it was
desired. The legal system in place on the goldfields may have frus-
trated the diggers for most of the time, but it must have also saved
many from an unlawful demise.

– THE ESCORTS –

GOLD was carried from the diggings to the Treasury by way of armed escort.

One of the most remarkable was the escort under the command of the redoubtable South Australian Chief of Police, Alexander Tolmer, who carried over £188,000 worth of gold from the Victorian diggings back to the Adelaide Treasury. Tolmer battled against swamps, floods and bandits as he opened up the overland route.

Much of the gold Tolmer carried was won by South Australian diggers who consigned their nuggets back to the South Australian Treasury, which at the time gave the diggers a higher price for their gold than could be gained in Melbourne.

In fact there was such a severe shortage of sterling left in Adelaide after half of the population had taken off for the diggings, that South Australia was almost bankrupt. The South Australian Government Assay Office began to mint its own coins under the Bullion Act, which they believed allowed them to exercise the Royal Prerogative of Coining if … 'urgent necessity exists'.

The first escort from the diggings was despatched to Adelaide in

– ALEXANDER TOLMER –

November 1851 carrying 94,000 ounces of gold.

In January 1852 the first escort to Melbourne arrived at the Gold Offices in William Street. There was great excitement as three heavily laden drays drew up to discharge their precious cargo. Each dray carried two boxes of gold, each of which had to be carried into the office by six men. After only three months since the declaration of the goldfields at Mt Alexander that week's deposit at the gold office was 105,000 ounces.

The following day almost all of the staff of clerks and draftsmen in Hoddle's Survey Office resigned and set off to try their luck at the diggings.

In July seven drays, 17 foot soldiers and six troopers delivered 83,582 ounces to Melbourne. Between May and December 1852 the South Australian Escort carried 224,220 ounces out of Mount Alexander and a further 363,384 ounces were taken to Melbourne.

The escorts were constantly in danger of attack from bushrangers who lurked along every highway waiting for an unguarded moment.

The McIvor Escort, carrying gold from the diggings east of Bendigo, was robbed of 2230 ounces on 20 July 1853 (see page 158) and on 15 June 1862 the Lachlan Escort was attacked near Eugowra (see page 163). 2717 ounces and £3700 in cash was taken. There are numerous other reports of the escorts coming under attack on the roads, yet the huge amount of gold carried compared with the small amount taken indicates that the escort remained the safest way diggers could get their gold to the Treasury.

arrival of the Gold Escort in Melbourne. conveying the chests into the Treasury. William Street from sketch taken from nature in 1851 by William Strutt

THE CELESTIALS

'Rule Britannia! Britannia rule the waves! No more Chinamen allowed in New South Wales!'

— cry heard across the New South Wales diggings

'No Chinese – Roll Up! Roll Up!'

— cry heard at Lambing Flat, 30 June 1861

O N 2 FEBRUARY 1848 the brig *Eagle* landed the first ship-load of Chinese workers in San Francisco. The Chinese were always ready to supply much-needed labour wherever there was demand. The workers who landed in San Francisco came not to dig for gold but to till other fields.

It was much the same story in Victoria. About 150 Chinese labourers had been working for the squatters around Port Phillip long before the gold rush, but once the discoveries were known it was not long before they too were caught up in the rush to the diggings.

Might Versus Right
Watercolour by S. T. Gill, c. 1854
(*MITCHELL LIBRARY COLLECTION*)

This watercolour depicts the Buckland River Riot, which took place on the Beechworth diggings on 4 July 1857.

A mob of angry diggers attacked the Chinese camp, and drove the Chinese into the river and from the diggings. An unknown number were killed, many injured, and their belongings destroyed.

A similar attack at Lambing Flat on 30 June 1861, near Young in New South Wales, was the genesis of the White Australia Policy, which disallowed migration of any 'coloured' peoples to Australia for over a century.

The Chinese District
Wood engraving

(BENDIGO ART GALLERY COLLECTION)

Governor Hotham had demanded from the Consuls in Chinese ports that an equal number of Chinese women migrate with the men, and proposed an extra tax on 'single' male migrants that would be levied on the shipowners who carried them to Australian ports.

However, there were only two Chinese women in the Colony of New South Wales, and only one is recorded on the Bendigo diggings. The Governor believed that the Chinese indulged in sexual practices of the darkest kind, and was fearful that all-male immigration would corrupt the youth of the colony. He believed that:

the goldfields will be trained in vice and profligacy, and the moral growth of the colony blighted.

Yet the Chinese fascinated the Europeans. They offered a taste of the exotic and the unusual.

In their camps all sorts of recreational services were on offer, from prostitution to the pleasure of the pipe.

From the *Annals of Bendigo*:

Opium smoking seemed to be carried on in almost every shop and dwelling, and, truth to say, there was the smell of opium everywhere and in everything throughout the whole encampment ... Several men were seen overcome by the narcotic, apparently in a deep and quiet sleep.[1]

In both California and Australia the Chinese applied their muscle to the goldfields with as much energy as any other man, and at times with more diligence and a level-headed dedication that was often wanting in the Europeans.

By 1850 tens of thousands of Chinese were in California, yet an official census taken in March 1854 counted only 2000 in Victoria, although in that year thirty-seven shiploads had landed in Australia. In 1855 sixty-one ships disembarked their human cargo. By the end of 1855 Victoria enacted legislation to curb Oriental immigration. The Victorian government imposed a levy of £10 per head on each Chinese arrival, and limited the number to one Chinese per ten tons of shipping.

The *Act to Make Provision for Certain Immigrants*, proclaimed on 24 October 1857, was a purposely created device to halt Chinese immigration. Along with restricted entry into Victoria, the Act also empowered the government to collect a fee of £4 from all Chinese working and living in the colony. This did not stop them from entering Australia in their hundreds; shipowners simply sailed a little further west and landed their cargo in South Australia. By the end of 1857 over 14,000 Chinese had landed at Guichen Bay, near Robe in South Australia, and made their way overland to the diggings. The Act had failed in its intention.

The government sought to put pressure on South Australia and New South Wales to agree to legislation similar to Victoria. South Australia fell into line, but New South Wales left the gates open for cheap 'coolie' labour. The Chinese still poured into Australia, this time through NSW, and by the end of the 1850s their number had grown to almost 40,000. Considering how poorly they were treated by both the government and the Caucasian diggers, it may seem surprising that they continued to come. For them it was not a great colonial adventure, they came as a form of indentured labour, working for labour-supply contractors, paying off their debts against their earnings. This type of contract arrangement was described by Sir Henry Parkes as 'nothing short of slave labour'.

Reports at the time suggested an almost unbroken line of Chinese, carrying their goods slung from bamboo poles across their shoulders, that stretched from South Australia to the central Victorian diggings. One observer recalled: 'They were winding across the plain like a long black mark, and as I passed them every one behind seemed to be yabbering to his mate in a sing-song tone'.

On the early diggings, when gold was plentiful, the Chinese were largely left to themselves. They were industrious, working together in gangs and sharing all they had. They worked the poorer ground left abandoned by the European diggers, who were ever ready to rush away to new finds. The Chinese picked meticulously over these untended claims, often recovering more gold than was ever taken by the previous owner.

It was when the easy gold became scarce that the Chinese began to be openly resented by the Europeans, especially those who tried to return to their abandoned claims, to find them being worked successfully by the 'Celestials'. It was not long before the European diggers sought to reclaim the territory they believed belonged to them.

William Denovan, the diggers' leader at Bendigo, was foremost in showing his discrimination against the Chinese. In July 1854 he had attempted to bring the diggers at Bendigo together *en masse* to drive the Chinese from that field. He had chosen 4 July for the expulsion, but after he was called to a meeting with 'Bendigo Mac', an authoritarian Police Magistrate on the Bendigo diggings, he acted to avoid the planned confrontation, by displaying the following public notice across the diggings:

> Brother Diggers,
> as a FALSE REPORT has appeared in the Columns of the
> Advertiser injurious to my personal liberty, relative to the Chinese
> question, I call upon the Digger throughout Bendigo to refrain from
> taking steps against the Chinese on the 4th of July.
> A MONSTER MEETING,
> – Wm D. C. DENOVAN

It appears that Denovan, although carried away with the power of his own oratory, had been made aware that he had unleashed emotions among the diggers that were less than desirable. The Chinese, fearing an assault, had posted armed sentries around their camps. In Castlemaine they offered rewards for the murder of several of their own headmen who were suspected of collusion with the authorities

John Chinaman
Watercolour by Harold John Graham, c. 1882
(Rex Nan Kivell Collection, R9866/57. By Permission, National Library of Australia)

– THE COOLIE –

The word 'coolie' comes from a merging of two Chinese words: koo meaning 'to rent' and lee meaning 'muscle' – to rent muscles, to work. In Chinese culture the labourer ranks higher than the merchant class but below scholars and farmers. The labourer is respected and free to choose his own employment. The term 'coolie' was applied as a pejorative, meaning 'bonded labourer', which is understandable, as many who came to Australia worked in this manner.

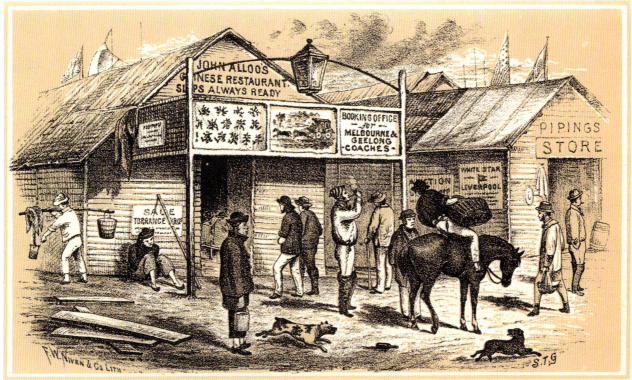

JOHN ALLOO'S CHINESE RESTAURANT, MAIN ROAD, BALLAARAT.1853

John Alloo's Restaurant, Ballarat
Lithograph by F. W. Niven & Co., from
a sketch by S. T. Gill, 1853, from W. B.
Withers, *History of Ballarat*, 1887

The Chinese generally built their camps
well away from the Europeans. They
created small townships of tents and huts,
huddled together with very little space
between them.

Although the Chinese always presented
themselves as clean and tidy, the fronts of
their dwellings always kept with pride, the
alleys that ran between them at the rear
were often filthy and vermin-infested.

This was just another aspect that added
to the resentment of the Chinese by other
diggers, giving yet another reason
to demand that the Chinese be forced
from the diggings.

over the enforcement of the tax. Denovan became concerned for his own safety, and it was up to him to defuse the situation.

The Chinese were resented for the style of their dress, their culinary tastes, their cultural habits, their pigtails, their religious rituals – in fact, the Europeans found them easy to revile for almost any reason at all.

Quang Chew, a prominent Chinese, spoke passionately in defence of his countrymen in an address to the Governor in 1855:

Wherefore have we Chinese, humbly disembarked upon your pleasant shores, given just cause for your anger? … Why should our gardeners, cooks, animal trainers, conjurers etc. etc. see themselves driven away when they could become such useful members of the colony? The whole question is this: Will it be unwise to allow 20,000 Chinese to come to Australia? Will it be necessary to send back whence they came those who arrive from so far and who are all such respectful people?[2]

On 4 July 1857 a group of disgruntled miners decided to rid the Buckland River diggings, near Beechworth in north-eastern Victoria, of the 'Oriental menace'. They attacked the Chinese camp: they swept through the gorge, smashing and burning as they went; they destroyed tents, stores and even a joss house, as they drove the Chinese into the river.

It is not known how many lives were lost in this attack, but several Chinese died of exposure as they were forced to remain in the chilly waters of the Buckland until police arrived from Beechworth.

Chinese Camp, Beechworth
(BURKE MUSEUM BEECHWORTH COLLECTION)

Chinese business establishments line the road on the Beechworth diggings.

The left side of the road, shown here, was known as 'The Canton Camp', the right as 'The Peking Camp'.

These 'hotels' were open to all who had the money to spend within, and were frequented by both European and Chinese alike.

The first flag reads 'Sun Quong Goon Hotel', the second, 'Wye Kee Hotel' and the third, 'Hang On How Hotel'.

The Peking Camp was demolished only five years after this photograph was taken, when the Beechworth Lunatic Asylum consolidated its 'reserve' for agricultural use.

The following description from the *Annals of Bendigo* describes a similar Chinese Camp, 'of over 1000 souls', that stretched along Bridge Street near the Bendigo Creek:

> The village was of an oblong form, through the centre of which ran one main street, consisting of between fifty and sixty buildings ... there were a number of cross and back lanes, all very narrow ... the streets and lanes were kept pretty clean, but in some of the back slums there were disgusting and unwholesome collections of rubbish and filth, and the attempts which had been made at drainage had been very defective so much so that most of the drains had become a highly offensive nuisance.
>
> An inspection of the various dwellings was extremely interesting. There were gambling-houses, joss-houses, eating-houses, and smoking-shops, as well as private habitations. A cook-shop was of considerable size, a novel description of building, being a tent of two stories, and an inspection of the arrangements occupied some time. Cooking operations on an extensive scale were being carried on the ground floor and in the adjoining kitchens. Tables were laid out in the lower story, and the upper one seemed devoted to persons of the bettermost class.

As was the practice in California, Australian diggers also took great delight in parting the Chinaman from his pigtail; it was the ultimate insult and relatively easy to achieve, while having a long-lasting effect on the poor victims. Following the Buckland River riot it was recorded that some diggers even kept pigtails as trophies, and some pigtails were said to have had large bits of skin and skull still attached.

Although the Chinese were resented by most Europeans, the perpetrators were brought to trial. However, only three were convicted of the crime of unlawful assembly, and one of riot. All three served prison terms of nine months only. Such punishment was no deterrent to the active discrimination against the Chinese, which continued right across the diggings.

On 27 July 1857 the diggers at Golden Point near Castlemaine attempted to drive the Chinese from that goldfield. Just as at Buckland, they destroyed the goods belonging to the Chinese, jostling any who resisted. Hundreds rushed to join in, shouting 'Down with the Chinese – expel them from the goldfields'. They were hoping to 'encourage' the Chinese on Golden Point to move out to join other larger Chinese camps at nearby Pennyweight and Moonlight Flats, leaving Golden Point to the Europeans. Although the British government had previously signed a treaty with the Chinese Emperor to protect its citizens abroad, the Australian diggers were in no mind to honour that treaty.

The Europeans sought to impose any legal means to drive the Chinese away. A 'capitation tax' was imposed on them (this was later to become a residence tax), and this impost proved a heavy burden for most of them.

On the Bendigo diggings the first of the Chinese Residents' Licence tickets were issued at the beginning of 1858, but by May only 165 Chinese had paid the fee and held the piece of paper that gave them the right to remain. Several were arrested, but over 1000 Chinese

– William Denovan –

Denovan was a vocal agitator on the Bendigo field. He had expressed his opinions on the miner's licence at every opportunity, as well as his opinion on the 'Chinese question'.

Denovan and another agitator from Ballarat, Henry Holyoake, were on their way to Ballarat to pledge the support of the Bendigo diggers to the cause when the news reached them at Castlemaine that the Eureka stockade had fallen. A meeting was held at Castlemaine, and the Forest Creek diggers moved to continue in their demands for justice. Denovan returned to Bendigo, proudly wearing a red scarf, which had been given to him by an admirer, wound around his neck.

He was greeted with cheers at every turn, although he was closely shadowed all the way back to Bendigo by a trooper who darted behind him from tree to tree.

Denovan also agitated against the Chinese, but when things started to get out of hand in Bendigo he was prompted to defuse the situation.

After Eureka he was prevailed upon by the Chinese leader in Bendigo to carry their petition for equal rights to the Governor. Although at first refusing, he changed his mind. He later became a defender of the rights of the Chinese in much the same way as he had fought for the European digger.

demanded that either the detainees be released or they be arrested also, as they, too, could not afford the newly imposed tax.

Denovan must have had quite a change of heart. He became one the Chinese diggers' biggest supporters in their fight to have the discriminatory 'residency' taxes lifted. He assisted in the presentation of a petition, signed by the Bendigo Chinese, to Sir Henry Barkly. The petition, which, curiously, Denovan first declined to carry to Melbourne on behalf of the Chinese, read:

> That your petitioners are anxious to be placed on the same footing of social liberty as all other alien races living on the goldfields.
>
> That your petitioners, although they strive to be industrious and economical in their habits, find great and daily increasing difficulties to obtain sufficient means whereon to subsist. That their average daily earnings do not exceed half a dwt of gold per man, out of which they are now required to pay over and above their share in export duty on gold the sum of £4 each man per annum, in the shape of special taxes to the revenue, a sum which your petitioners regret to inform your Excellency they are no longer able to pay.
>
> Your petitioners have, therefore, hastened to throw themselves at the feet of your Excellency, and to implore your protection.

The Mount Alexander Mail reported that the Chinese in Castlemaine had been given 24 hours to pay the tax. Only one man paid. Although the gaol was too small to hold them all, over one hundred were arrested and held in the Camp. The same action took place on the Spring Creek diggings near Beechworth.

Denovan wrote to the *Bendigo Advertiser* on 22 May 1859:

> I am as much opposed to extensive immigration of Chinese into this colony as ever I was, but it does not necessarily follow that ... I should be in favour of maltreating those already here ...[3]

Obviously buoyed by this seemingly reconciliatory note, the Chinese asked again, and Denovan finally agreed to take their petition to the Governor.

Behind the resentment lay the prejudice that stems from the difference in culture between the 'Christian' majority of Europeans and the 'pagan' minority of the Chinese. The difference was tolerated until economic factors entered the equation.

Sir Henry Barkly added his opinion of the Oriental diggers:

> The Chinese, because of total dissimilarity of habits and ideas obstructed the miners, whose dislike grew with envy and jealousy; others

condemned the Chinese because they were, like many others, sojourners who contribute little to the permanent settlement or prosperity of the colony; still, others including the Statesman and the Christian, viewed with extreme anxiety these all-male immigrants, pagans in religion, and addicted, as was loudly asserted, to unnatural practices.

Even the peculiarities of the Chinese barbershop attracted interest, and this description from the *Annals of Bendigo* appeared to regard even the most domestic of practices as worthy of critical attention:

> The operation of shaving in one of the numerous Barber shops was an event of much interest. From the peculiarity of the manipulation, and the strangeness of the instruments employed ... the eyebrows and even the eyelashes were trimmed, ... the cheeks, the ears, the throat ... and the operation was twice gone over with different descriptions of razors.[4]

The Protection Ticket enactment of the previous year was superseded by a residence tax of £4 per annum. The government was not so cynical that it could allow a tax to remain with the title of 'Protection Ticket', when it did little to protect the Chinese at all. The residence tax was hard on the poorer Chinese who, like the diggers at Eureka only five years earlier, began to organise resistance to this imposition with the help of professional agitators connected to Chinese secret societies.

Off to the Diggings – Flemington near Melbourne
Watercolour by Samuel Charles Brees, c. 1856

An almost-unbroken line of Chinese diggers pass the Flemington Hotel, heading for the Mt Alexander diggings near Castlemaine. This scene can be contrasted with images of Europeans making the same journey, where it was 'every man for himself'.

The communal enterprise of the Chinese can be seen in this drawing, each man taking his turn, making his progress along with every other person, moving purposefully towards their collective goal. It was this sort of behaviour that separated the Chinese from others, and they were resented for it; as well as for the difference in their eating habits, their religion, their clothing, their bamboo hats, their pigtails, their opium smoking, their hard work, their diligence.

Revival of the Fine Old Australian Sport of Licence-Hunting
Melbourne Punch, 1854
(PRIVATE COLLECTION)

The caption to this contemporary cartoon reads :

> Up here all of us, and especially our jurymen, are looking forward with great pleasure to the prospect of a good Chinese hunting season.
> Under the proposed new laws the sport will gain much extra éclat, by being carried on with official sanction and patronage, and will not as hitherto, merely by sufferance. I send you an anticipatory sketch by a local artist.

The troopers are depicted here up to their old tricks. After Eureka and the disappearance of the licence fee, the sport of digger hunting had also disappeared. Now, with the introduction of the residence tax, the troopers could pick up where they left off.

Boxing Day Procession, 1895, Ford Street, Beechworth
(BURKE MUSEUM, BEECHWORTH COLLECTION)

Although the Chinese were at times treated harshly by the European diggers, they remained very civic minded in all of their dealings on the goldfields.

The thousands of Chinese stuck together, worked together, played together; they banded together for cultural reasons as well as for self-protection.

Many had travelled from the same village in the same province, and remained connected by history, or a family or community bond. Very few travelled with female company, and many Chinese were to marry European wives, staying and making their future in Australia.

On public holidays in both Beechworth and Bendigo the Chinese paraded through the streets of the towns they had adopted, raising money for local charities.

In this case the Chinese of Beechworth raised donations from spectators of their procession, which was in turn donated to the Ovens Hospital and Benevolent Home for the Aged.

Curiously, many of the old diggers who would benefit in turn from the generosity of the Chinese would have been the same diggers who had actively protested against their presence on the goldfields.

Notices were seized that were to communicate the message:

CAUTION. After this no Chinese would allow to take out the Residence Ticket, if they do they will be punished by apprehension to the Sze Yip Club House severely, without pardon.

If a Chinese may be arrested by having no ticket we will with the exertion of our strength help him and find him all the expenses during the time of his being kept in the prison. £200 reward for killing the headman.[5]

It appears that the headman, Ah Coy, had been running protection rackets, deceiving his countrymen with the lie that opium trading was a capital offence, and demanding £1 a week as danger money for engaging in this trade. He seems to have been caught up in the wave of ill feeling that was sweeping through the Chinese camps.

The Chinese, like their European 'brothers', had banded together in protest. The United Confederacy of Chinese was formed to represent the Chinese in the same way that the diggers had rallied under the Southern Cross flag to protest for their rights on the Eureka diggings. The Chinese again sent delegates

嘉和人在

The Lambing Flat Flag

The flag carried on 30 June 1861 at Lambing Flat (Young), NSW, was a tent-fly that had been expertly painted by a digger on the field. The flag bore a white cross on a brilliant blue ground. Five stars were also painted, one in each quarter and one at the centre of the cross, which, although diagonal, was reminiscent of the Southern Cross flag flown at Ballarat only a few years earlier.

Each corner of the elegant design was embellished with golden decoration, and the words 'No Chinese – Roll Up, Roll Up' formed a typographic border around the blue square, and was fringed with gold.

The decorated tent-fly was more in the style of trade banners carried by unionists than that of a true flag. It required two men to support its weight when the miners rallied behind it on the march to the Chinese camp.

(OPPOSITE)

Sun Loong, The Bendigo Chinese Dragon

(PHOTOGRAPHS BY GEOFF HOCKING)

The central Victoria City of Bendigo has two Chinese dragons: one now on permanent display in the Chinese Museum, the other paraded through the streets of Bendigo every Easter Monday, just as the older dragon was for over 100 years.

The second Sun Loong was brought from Hong Kong in 1970 to replace the 'old' Sun Loong, who was beginning to appear a bit frail after a century of service.

The new dragon was given to the city by Mr Allen Guy (a descendant of Chinese who came to Bendigo during the goldrush), with the proviso that it never leave Bendigo, and remain under the protection and control of the city.

Each Easter the Sun Loong is woken in a fiery ceremony, complete with fireworks and exuberant dances by smaller dragons just in time for him to be prepared for the Monday procession.

The dragon is carried by volunteers from the city, including many who are descended from families who were part of the original story of the Chinese in Bendigo.

to Melbourne to request exemption from the residence tax of £4 per head that the government had levied against them. They argued that the tax was only justified to cover the expenses of the protectorate on the goldfields, they certainly felt that they were not getting much protection for the fee that they were charged; but the Chief Minister replied that the intention of the tax was really to put an end to Chinese immigration.

Disputes between the European diggers and the Chinese continued to fuel the rage that burnt across the diggings from Victoria to New South Wales. The governments of both colonies, while appearing to abide by the letter of the law and attempting to keep the peace, seemed eager to provide the kindling for the eventual conflagration.

Among all of the disquiet, discrimination and dissent Chinese continued to land on Australia's shores, yet they were increasingly treated as social pariahs.

It was at Lambing Flat, near Young in New South Wales, that the worst instance of violence against the Chinese took place. The government had stationed soldiers from the 12th Regiment, accompanied by a squad of artillery, on the diggings following continuing attacks against the Chinese since December 1860, when vigilante groups had driven Chinese diggers from the Lambing Flat field. In the months between December and the July of the following year two Chinese had been murdered, and hundreds of others attacked. But the government had taken the view that the situation was under control, and the troops were pulled out on 24 May 1861.

Just one month later, on Sunday, 30 June, the diggers, under the umbrella of the Miners' Protection League, and marching to the strains of a 'military' band, swept into the Chinese camp, carrying a banner bearing the stars of the Southern Cross and the words 'No Chinese – Roll Up, Roll Up', destroying all before them.

This report is from the *Illustrated Sydney News* of 5 August 1861:

meanwhile matters were approaching a crisis: fifers and drummers were obtained, and flags bearing sentiments were hoisted. Fire-arms and other weapons were procured; public-houses and booths were rushed, and plenty of Dutch courage imbibed. All these precautions were

Chinese Man on the Goldfields
Watercolour by Eugène von Guérard,
1854

(DIXSON GALLERIES, STATE LIBRARY OF NEW
SOUTH WALES)

considered necessary by thousands of brave men [?] in order to successfully attack a few hundred defenceless Chinese.

The poor Asiatics made scarcely any resistance. All who could do so secreted their gold, and many of them lost their lives for refusing to tell where it was; others who were not quick enough in getting out of their holes and drives were buried alive in them – just for fun; and such of the tents and goods as were not appropriated by the civilizers were collected in heaps and burned, and thus the work of murder and robbery went bravely on.

Troops were called to Lambing Flat from surrounding districts, and three men were eventually arrested for inciting riot. The diggers demanded that their mates be freed, and attempted to release them from the police lock-up. They fired at the police horses and the police fired back, dropping one digger in his tracks, shot straight through the head. As at Beechworth, the Europeans arrested seemed to escape the full weight of the law – at Lambing Flat only one digger was gaoled.

On 9 December 1873, following a dispute over wages and hours of labour between miners and the proprietors of the Lothair mine at Clunes in central Victoria, it was reported that Chinese labourers were to be brought into Clunes as strike-breakers or 'scabs'. Once the news was abroad, the miners gathered together and determined to 'resist the invasion'. Telegrams sent on 8 December said that the Chinese were aboard five coaches being sent up from Ballarat and from Creswick. Over 1000 miners assembled with their wives and children at the junction of the Ballarat and Clunes roads, about one mile from the town. Fire bells rang the alarm incessantly, and a barricade was erected across the road. The miners waited all night, and it wasn't until about 8 o'clock the following morning that the first coach came into sight. A storm of stones and bricks rained down upon the coaches, and the miners charged, assaulting the Chinese on board. The persistence of the miners and their wives forced the police guard to withdraw, and the coaches turned back to Ballarat.

– CHINESE VS THE LAW –

The Chinese were frequently before the courts, commonly charged with trying to dispose of spurious or adulterated gold or for stealing.

On the Bendigo diggings in February 1857 three Chinese were charged with 'occupying Crown Lands without being licenced to do so'.

Although they were let off with a warning, the magistrate, 'Bendigo Mac', felt that it was about time an example was made of some of the Chinese. Before long another Chinese, the unfortunate Ah King, came before him, charged with stealing four hats from a store in Bendigo; he received a three months' sentence. Another, Ah Yan, was sentenced to six months for the theft of five panama hats. Ah Tong and Ah Chang were both sentenced to one month each for stealing seven pairs of 'trowsers' from Campion's Store in Pall Mall, Bendigo.

Some Chinese even had a go at bushranging, but were not all that successful.

In New South Wales in 1859 a large and stout Chinese bailed up a Mr Ball, from Cathcart, and demanded he hand over his money. Ball took to the assailant with a whip, and chased him away.

Another unlucky fellow who had bailed up several people in the Mudgee district shot the policeman who came to capture him. The policeman survived, and escaped to a nearby farmhouse where he raised the alarm. The 'Oriental bushranger' was eventually captured and hanged.

Chu Ah Luk was one of the few Chinese hanged in Victoria. He had killed his fellow-countryman, Ah Pud, in a store at Campbell's Creek. Poor Ah Pud had simply asked Chu Ah Luk for 10 shillings that he was owed, but when he refused to pay Ah Pud threatened to take his clothes from him. Chu Ah Luk stabbed Ah Pud, and fled. He was later captured in Ballarat, brought back to Castlemaine, and hanged.

Considering the large number of Chinese on the goldfields and the treatment they received at the hands of the Europeans, the incidence of crime was small, and was usually for minor offences, such as stealing chickens or clothing, and mostly for the simple reason that the Chinese were destitute. The *Bendigo Advertiser* reported in 1858 that 'there is in reality more actual distress among the Chinese population than is generally supposed'.

Disturbances at Clunes, Miners Resisting the Introduction of Chinese Labourers
Wood engraving by Samuel Calvert, *The Illustrated Australian News*, Ebenezer and David Syme, 31 December 1873

(La Trobe Picture Collection, State Library of Victoria)

The diggers' hero, Peter Lalor, who had fought so hard for the rights of the miners in 1854, was partially responsible for the troubles at Clunes. As director of the Lothair Mining Company he had refused the miners' demands that they be allowed more than a single day off per week from digging. This refusal sent the workers to strike for fourteen weeks.

His attempt to break the strike by bringing Chinese miners from Ballarat caused the riot.

---

*Sergeant Larner was the leader of the small band of police who had escorted the coaches to the Clunes barricade. In the first barrage of rocks he had been hit on the head, and fell from his horse. With blood streaming from his wound, he leapt on to the barricade and thrust his pistol into the chest of one miner, who did not flinch in defence of his rights.

Once the miners had achieved their aim, they went about their business and the district returned to its 'former quietude'. This was the first time in Australia's history where violence and resistance of the law was the solution to a labour dispute. The general public condemned the action:

> the successful attempt to resist the law, and to prohibit by force of arms the exercise on the part of the employers of their unquestionable right to get labour where they pleased, caused a great shock to the public feeling of the colony, and it was felt that a very objectionable example had been set, and a dangerous precedent established.[6]

The miners and their wives had fought a 'great battle' to save their jobs and livelihoods, they had stood up to the bosses, had stared into the barrels of the troopers' guns, never flinching, not backing away from the fray, and once again the poor Chinese were the victims. What was in essence a working-men's struggle, labour against capital, became another chapter in the ever-expanding chronicle of the Australians' distrust of the Chinese.

The events of 9 December 1873 were celebrated for many years with a victory ballad composed to celebrate the great day where the people of Clunes rose up to defend themselves:

Mother Bailey was in front,
With her apron full of stones,
Determined if she could
To break some of their bones.

The Chows were driven back
All a-quiver and a-quake,
With Larner* and his escort
Following in their wake.

F.MARRYAT DELINEAT

J. BRANDARD LITH

THE BAR OF A GAMBLING SALOON.

While the Chinese were eager to take their place in goldfields society, they never escaped constant harassment. In Tamboroora, near Mudgee in New South Wales, as a lark, a gang of Chinese had been sold the lease to a mining claim that in fact belonged to a group of European diggers. Two of the diggers who actually owned the claim had been in the town for several days on a spree. When they returned to their claim, they found their shafts filled in and a number of Chinese busily engaged in mining where their claim once was. They were shocked to discover that the Chinese had murdered their mates and collapsed the shaft on their bodies. They gathered together a mob of other diggers, and took their revenge – some lark!

In California the Chinese retreated to the towns, using their muscle to win riches in other ways. They established laundries, restaurants, and market gardens, and, although few Chinese women accompanied the men to the goldfields, they were prominent in the importation and supply of prostitutes for the pleasure and entertainment of the European miners. In San Francisco, to 'See the world' meant a trip to Chinatown where a pagan morality was to be enjoyed. Wherever the Chinese went, their habits infuriated the blinkered prejudice of conservative Christian moralists. In Australia the Chinese also retreated into the towns, following much the same pattern as in California.

A Gambling Saloon in Sacramento
Lithograph by Frank Marryat,
from *Mountains and Molehills*
(COURTESY OF THE BANCROFT LIBRARY,
UNIVERSITY OF CALIFORNIA, BERKELEY)

The Chinese took their place in frontier society alongside the Europeans. They worked hard, played at the same games and drank in the same bars, but were readily discriminated against as soon as things got tough for the Europeans.

While the Chinese were prepared to work long, hard and diligently for their gold, the Europeans expected to be able to pick it up easily from the ground, and for there to be a never-ending supply of easy money.

When the gold started to run out, they turned against the Chinese, who always followed them onto the diggings, reworking the old claims the Europeans had discarded, and the Chinese were forced off. When the Chinese looked for employment in the towns, the Europeans tried to force them from there as well.

Yet the Chinese persisted, claiming a lasting place in both Californian and Australian society.

Chinese Miners on Board a Cobb & Co. Coach

(Castlemaine Art Gallery & Historical Museum Collection)

This coach is piled high with both bodies and goods as a large group of miners depart from Ballarat, headed for Castlemaine.

Interestingly, all of the Chinese are wearing European hats, while their bamboo 'coolie' hats are tied securely at the back of the coach. Maybe the wind-draft caused by the speed gained by this six-horse-powered coach would endanger the security of the large circular hats, and the Chinese had exchanged style for safety.

This photograph has also been considered to show the strike-breaking miners on route to Clunes. If so, it would have been a wise move to have hidden the trademark bamboo hats from European gaze.

Chinese Gardener
Watercolour by Harold John Graham, c. 1882

(Rex Nan Kivell Collection, R9866/56. By Permission, National Library of Australia)

Yet there were still new goldfields being opened up, and still plenty of opportunity for those with muscle for hire. The discovery of gold in Queensland led to a mass migration to the north, and the same old problems followed.

A group of diggers on the Queensland goldfields, at the height of Chinese troubles there, became very suspicious of one storekeeper after half of their gold had been stolen:

> A meeting was held and suspicion fell upon a Chinaman who kept a general store … it was arranged that half a dozen of them visit his store the next morning and overhaul it … every cask, sack, box and article of clothing in the place was closely examined … [as nothing] could be found … the Chinaman become more bold, shrugged his shoulders and [even complained] of the treatment he and his goods had been receiving.
>
> Not being able to find the lost gold, the men were determined to have something to take with them … looking around they saw a great many German sausages hanging from the roof … 'Let's have one of these saveloys each, Joey,' said one of the men … 'Half one of these big 'uns is enough for me,' said Joey, and whipping out his knife he divided it in two on the counter. The moment he put his knife through the skin, out poured the gold.[7]

The storekeeper, Ah Silah Joy, ran from the shop, chased by the irate diggers, who quickly apprehended him:

> They dragged him back to a clump of trees near the camp … his pigtail was cut off, and his hands tied behind his back with it. He was made to stand on top of a bucket with his back to a tree. His ears were nailed fast to the tree and the bucket kicked from under his feet.[8]

In Queensland the Chinese were treated just as poorly as they had been on other fields during the 'roaring days'.

Towards the end of 1868, after the European diggers began to fall back upon earlier abandoned diggings around Gympie, the cry of 'Roll Up, Roll Up' was heard again. Just as had been done on earlier diggings in Victoria and New South Wales, the Queensland diggers swept through the camp at Chinaman's Flat in an attempt to drive the Chinese from the field. Although the Chinese were considered by the Gympie Times to be 'orderly and harmless ... and we presume there can be no objection to them', the diggers were looking first for a 'Mongolian' scapegoat on which to vent their anger.

The Chinese continued to arrive on the diggings even after the easy alluvial gold ran out. They were already suffering constant harassment on every goldfield, but the continuous migration caused the angry and resentful European miners to attempt to drive them all from the diggings.

Ah Joy was left hanging in this manner until police arrived the following day.

The swift 'justice' meted out to the Chinese resembles the work of the vigilantes who cleared the San Francisco Bay area of unwanted Australian nuisances.

But the Chinese did not disappear: they remained in the towns, they developed good solid businesses, many married and raised families with the blood of the East and of Ireland flowing through their veins (the Chinese tended to marry young Irish girls, who were keen to leave 'service' and to live free in the young colony). The Chinese left a legacy that has persisted for over a century. They, like the diggers at Eureka, forced change, as they too demanded their rights in the new egalitarian society born of the goldfields.

**Chinese Merchants at Gulgong,
New South Wales, c. 1870**
(Mitchell Library NSW, Holtermann Collection)

After the riot at Lambing Flat, Governor
Cowper placed restrictions on the
Chinese in New South Wales, and some
were even refused miner's licences.

The resourceful Chinese soon found
other means of survival. As merchants
they were usually successful, some
became restaurateurs, some market
gardeners, some herbalists.

Many married, raising Chinese-Irish
Australians.

– NED KELLY –

*In 1870, the first foray by the
young 14-year-old Ned Kelly into
the business of bushranging was
to bail up a Chinese and steal
10 shillings from him.
It was reported that, upon
striking the man with a stick,
he informed him that he was
going to be a bushranger.*

*When first it was I landed here, folks rushed to Bendigo,
And went and pitched in Eaglehawk, where lots were made,
    you know.
Where lots were made, you know, but those days are now
    gone by;
Those days are now gone by, my boys; getting rich is all my eye.
Getting rich is all my eye, my boys; the Chinese swarm around,
The Chinese swarm around my boys, puddling every bit of
ground. And nuggets are not found, my boys,
    like when I landed here.
And nuggets are not found, my boys, like when I landed here.*

THE END OF THE ROARING DAYS

S THE ALLUVIAL GOLD RAN OUT across the goldfields and the creeks no longer flowed with nuggets, companies were formed as investors rushed to finance the shift to deep-lead mining. The wild days of the gold rushes gradually disappeared. The Australian traditions of independence and mateship forged on the diggings entered a new era, with miners organising to protect themselves once again from exploitation, not from the government but from the 'bosses', the investors and speculators whose decisions made in smoke-filled, mahogany-lined gentlemen's clubs far from the Antipodes ensured the viability or the extinction of the diggers' livelihood.

The 'red republicanism' so feared by Earl Grey metamorphosed into collectivism as mining unions became established. The workers did not forget the hard lesson of Eureka when they had joined together to fight under the Southern Cross flag.

In Victoria the settlements of Bendigo, Ballarat, Creswick, Clunes and Maldon flourished, and the landscape became dotted with towering poppet-heads as miners dug deep into the earth in search of the quartz reefs and gravel beds far beneath the surface.

Thousands of once-free diggers became employees. Their lives, once spent in the sun with the creeks swirling at their knees, were now confined in dark and airless shafts as they blasted and drilled away at the gold-bearing quartz. Ironically, many diggers who had fought so hard for the right to be free from autocratic overlords were now chained to the mine owners and the promise of a weekly pay packet.

The incessant thump and hammer of the massive quartz-crushing plants thundered day and night from Castlemaine to Kalgoorlie, stopping only on Sunday. When the mines ceased at midnight on Saturday an eerie quiet fell across the field; many were unable to sleep in the deathly silence, and were relieved when the roar took up again at midnight on Sunday to mark the beginning of the new working week.

The rush to the diggings in 1851 had been a great colonial adventure, but as the alluvial gold had all but played out by the end of the 1850s, and great centres such as Ballarat, Bendigo and Bathurst settled into domesticity, the later rushes to the north and to the west became a different type of adventure.

Sandhurst from Camp Hill, 1886 Oil on canvas by James Edwin Meadows

(COLLECTION – BENDIGO ART GALLERY)

VICTORIA
Across the Great Divide

BALLAARAT

Ballaarat from the Black Hill, 1868
Wood engraving by Robert Bruce, *Illustrated Australian News*, July 1868
(REX NAN KIVELL COLLECTION, S2399. BY PERMISSION, NATIONAL LIBRARY OF AUSTRALIA)

Ballarat

At first, inexperienced European diggers rushed from place to place seeking the easy gold, the gold that lay in the creeks, or glistened in the gravel beds. A rush would lose its appeal as quickly as it had begun: when another rush was on, diggers simply abandoned the claims they had in favour of any new patch of ground where others professed to have found the latest rich source of gold.

The troubles at Ballarat had largely stemmed from the lack of alluvial gold after the first rush had passed. When Cornishmen arrived in their hundreds in 1852 to find the diggings all but deserted, they put their experience in the Cornish tin-mines to work, and tunnelled deep into the earth.

The truth was that the real wealth at Ballarat lay deep beneath the surface in the ancient gravelled streams that were long buried. The newly arrived professional miners saw those who remained were still getting gold as they dug deeper and deeper into the clay, following the creek-bed lines.

– BALLAARAT –

Common usage has shortened the official spelling of Ballaarat to Ballarat. The name is from the Aboriginal word meaning a grassy, well-shaded spot on the bank of the creek – 'a resting place'.

How inappropriate this meaning became after the influx of diggers in 1852. What had been described before the rush as one of the prettiest spots imaginable soon resembled the site of a great battle, with craters and holes littering the landscape.

NOTABLE NUGGETS

– THE CANADIAN –
1319 oz
Canadian Gully, Ballarat
31 January 1853
D. & J. Evans, J. Lees, W. Poulter
& W. F. Green

•

– LADY HOTHAM –
1177 oz
Dalton's Flat, Ballarat
8 September 1854
McDonald, Irwin, Cock,
Radcliffe, McPhillamy, Day,
Lyons & Bryant

•

1011 oz
Canadian Lead, Ballarat
2 January 1853
Gough, Sulley & Bristow

•

– KOHINOOR –
834 oz
Ballarat
August 1860
Kohinoor G. M. Co.

•

– LADY DON –
606 oz
Ballarat
12 November 1866
Lady Don Co.

Shafts over 100 feet deep were dug through the waterlogged ground until bedrock was struck. Some of the shafts were so rich they soon became known as 'jewellers' shops', and the second rush to Ballarat began. The three main leads at Ballarat – the Eureka, Gravel Pits and the Canadian – were described by W. B. Withers as 'the Golden Trinity that made Ballarat famous throughout the civilised world'.

When English novelist Anthony Trollope visited Ballarat in 1872 he wrote:

> It struck me with more surprise than any other city in Australia. It is not only its youth … but that a town so well built, so well ordered, endowed with present advantages so great … and the like should have sprung up so quickly with no internal advantages of its own other than gold.[1]

J. C. Patterson also described the Ballarat township only a decade after the first discovery, praising the community that had grown with enterprise into respectability:

> the money that in other mining districts took the form of unbottomed shafts and unfinished drives – of machinery built to be thrown down again, and mines only now being brought to paying point – built long lines of handsome streets, erected foundries, flour mills, and breweries and brought into cultivation such large tracts of territory that while Ballarat claims to excel Bendigo as a gold-fields, the country around it aspires to be regarded as the leading agricultural district of the colony.
>
> It has supplied itself with the machinery for its own mines; it produces the implements with which its own fields are tilled; it grinds its own corn, and brews its own beer … the result of all this is well-directed energy, and the local circulation of the stores of gold obtained from the deep gutters, has been a sound and healthy trade in Ballarat itself.[2]

Patterson's 'well-directed energy' may have been a reminder to the contemporary reader that Ballarat had not always directed its energies where good and loyal citizens should, that there was a stain on the character of the town that hardwork, enterprise and patriotic loyalty would eventually erase. Patterson continued:

> there is an abundance of employment at fair wages, for all who are willing to labour, and the still unexhausted alluvial in the shallow gullies affords a living to the weak and unskilled, and to the swarms of Chinese to whom Ballarat East is being rapidly abandoned.[3]

The company mine, its managers and shareholders, may have held the key to the future, yet, in Ballarat, the 'Eureka' spirit lived on.

Arrival of the Geelong Mail, Main Road, Ballarat May 2nd 1855
Watercolour by S. T. Gill, 1880
(CITY OF BALLARAT FINE ART GALLERY COLLECTION)

Quartz Crushing Battery, Black Hill, Ballarat
Lithograph by F. W. Niven from a sketch by S. T. Gill, 1854, from W. B. Withers, *History of Ballarat*, 1887
(CITY OF BALLARAT FINE ART GALLERY COLLECTION)

The first quartz crushing battery was set up at the base of Black Hill in 1855. Mining activities stripped the hilsides of trees, leaving them almost bare.

Those gents in Melbourne
    do this grand, and pooh!
    pooh! Ballarat;
But we ought to make them
    understand we don't believe
    in that.
And when Sir Henry Barkley
    first to visit did deign,
He found the township beat
    Sandhurst and the flat
    slew'd Castlemaine.
We astonished his nerves,
    deny it who can,
And sent him to town
    a Ballarat man.

'The Bendigo digger,
    try as hard as he can,
No use at deep sinking with
    a Ballarat man'.

— ROBERT THATCHER

Concert Room, Charlie Napier Hotel, Ballarat, June, '55.
Thatcher's Popular Songs. Watercolour by S. T. Gill, 1855
(REX NAN KIVELL COLLECTION, R8789. BY PERMISSION, NATIONAL LIBRARY OF AUSTRALIA)

190

Deep Sinking, Ballaarat
Lithograph by S. T. Gill, James J. Blundell & Co., Melbourne, 1855

– The Artist of the Goldfields, Samuel Thomas Gill –

S. T. Gill is the most recognised of all the artists who recorded life on the diggings.

He was born at Perriton, in Devonshire in 1819 the son of a Baptist minister and schoolmaster. His early training with W. J. Hubard's Profile Gallery taught him skills of drawing and observation that became the hallmark of his works on the goldfields.

Gill and his family migrated to South Australia in 1839. It was in Adelaide that Gill began to seek commissions for his portraits and he was commissioned to record the homes of the squatters and the streets of early Adelaide.

He soon joined the rush to the diggings, where he captured the very tenor of all life there – the fights, the troopers, licensing tents, diggers on a spree, digger's weddings, destitute and disap-

Samuel Thomas Gill, 1919~1880

pointed diggers, from Forest Creek to Bendigo, Ballarat and Eaglehawk.

Gill's drawings are the most human and often the most humorous of all images made at the time. Yet his life was filled with pathos. Like his image of the 'unlucky digger', Gill took to the bottle and fell on hard times. On 27 October 1880 while alone, destitute and drunk, 61-year-old Gill collapsed and died on the steps of the General Post Office in Melbourne. Described as 'an habitual drunkard' he died from a rupture of the aorta.

The *Herald* reported the sad and lonely death of Samuel Thomas Gill:

who once occupied an opulent position … has of late been in reduced circumstances.

The Argus described him as 'one of the notables of the land of gold'.

Mining Operations at the Black Hill,
Ballarat
Engraving by Robert Bruce, Ebenezer and
David Syme, from *Illustrated Australian
News, 18 July 1868*
(La Trobe Picture Collection,
State Library of Victoria)

– WELCOME NUGGET –

The Welcome Nugget was found at
Bakery Hill, Ballarat, on 15 June 1858
by Richard Jeffrey, working with a
company called the Red Hill Gold
Mining Co., formed by 22 Cornish
miners.

At the time of its discovery the
Welcome Nugget was the largest piece
of solid virgin gold to be found
anywhere in the world. It was measured at 20 inches long, 12 inches wide
and 8 inches thick, and weighed 2195
oz.

The morning after its discovery, the
miners carted the Welcome Nugget
through the streets of Ballarat, in a
wheelbarrow, to the Treasury (where
the Art Gallery now stands). The lucky
diggers were followed by a large crowd
amazed at the sheer scale of the horse-
head-shaped golden lump resting in the
barrow.

It was put on display, and visitors
paid a shilling to see it before the
Ballarat gold-buying firm, Wittowski
Bros, bought it for £10,500. It was
taken to England, where it was again
put on display in the Crystal Palace.

In November 1859 it was purchased
by the Royal Mint, and melted down
for sovereigns.

Speculators on 'The Corner'
at Ballarat
Engraving from *Picturesque Atlas of
Australasia*, Sydney and Melbourne, 1888
(Private Collection)

'The Corner' was an open-air stock
market, at the time equal to the New York
Stock Exchange. More stock was traded
here in the 1860s than anywhere else in
Australia.

– O'Farrell from Ballarat, the Failed Assassin –

HENRY JAMES O'FARRELL was another of the sons of Erin who wrote their name into the history of Ballarat. O'Farrell was a hay and grain merchant who came to Ballarat in the 1850s.

A red-faced and excitable Dubliner, he spent his afternoons at 'The Corner'. He was a shrewd investor, buying cheap and selling dear. But eventually he saw the value of his stock holdings in Ballarat mines collapse.

However, he continued to buy and sell, and then to drink, mostly to drink, as he soon spent most of those afternoons at the bar of Royal Craig's Hotel. He eventually left Ballarat. In Sydney on 12 March 1868 O'Farrell made his mark in history. Prince Alfred, second son of Queen Victoria, the Duke of Edinburgh, had just enjoyed a picnic at the Sailors' Home at Clontarf, and was about to watch a corroboree when O'Farrell stepped from the admiring crowd and shot him in the back.

The prince fell to his knees crying, 'Good God, I'm shot. My back is broken.'

As Mr Vial, a Sydney coachbuilder, grabbed O'Farrell from behind in an attempt to take the gun from him, another shot was fired, striking bystander George Thorne. The crowd turned in search of the assailant, and attacked Vial, whom they thought was the would-be assassin. They soon discovered their mistake, and the mob moved against O'Farrell, beating him, while yelling 'Hang him, lynch him.' He was almost torn apart. A sailor found some rope, threw it over a tree and called for O'Farrell to be hanged on the spot. The police managed to rescue him from the angry mob; his clothes were ripped to shreds, and he was carried, bruised, bleeding and unconscious, to the steamer *Paterson* anchored nearby.

The prince survived. He was carried to his tent where doctors from HMS *Challenger* and the *Galatea* treated him immediately – the bullet had struck his indiarubber braces, which deflected it past his spine and into his abdomen, missing all vital organs.

O'Farrell was tried for the attempted assassination of the young prince, convicted, and executed at Darlinghurst gaol five weeks later.

O'Farrell was one more of the defiant Irishmen who seemed to forgive the English for nothing, and like so many before, and after, was prepared to die in yet another attempt to right the wrongs done to the Irish nation.

O'Farrel [sic] *in Darlinghurst*
Pencil drawing attributed to Viscount Francis Charles Needham Newry, c. 1868
(*R6193. NATIONAL LIBRARY OF AUSTRALIA COLLECTION*)

Attempted Assassination of H.R.H. the Duke of Edinburgh at Clontarf, N.S.W.
Wood engraving by Samuel Calvert, 1868
(*NATIONAL LIBRARY OF AUSTRALIA COLLECTION, S4491*)

The Prince was shot in the back as he attended a picnic in Sydney.

His assailant was the disaffected, failed goldmining investor from Dublin, Henry James O'Farrell (above), late of Ballarat.

(PHOTOGRAPHS BY GEOFF HOCKING,
REPRODUCED BY PERMISSION
OF SOVEREIGN HILL)

Both of the great Victorian mining centres of Ballarat and Bendigo continue to celebrate the richness of their goldfields heritage.

Sovereign Hill, at Ballarat *(above and right)*, is a faithful recreation of a typical mining town. It features a nugget-salted running creek, a canvas-and-calico diggers' camp, and a bustling township that hugs the gravel roadway leading to the minehead towering over the entire 'field'.

The Central Deborah Gold Mine, Bendigo *(below)*, on the Deborah reef, is an original deep-lead mine. Visitors can ride in one of the cages, to explore the shafts that cut across once-rich quartz reefs, in this working mine far below the city of Bendigo.

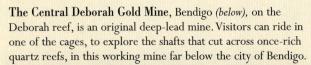

(PHOTOGRAPHS COURTESY OF CENTRAL DEBORAH GOLD MINE)

*Jackson's Store & Gold Office
at View Point, Bendigo*
(BENDIGO REGIONAL LIBRARY COLLECTION)

A photographer's cart rests opposite
Jackson's corner, the scene of so much
protest in 1853. The name on the cart
is Batchelder; the same name appears
on the photographer's saloon on the
California goldfields shown on p. 32.

'Bold Bendigo' Thompson
(COURTESY, FRANK CUSACK BENDIGO)

Bendigo was named after ex-sailor, cum
bullock-driver, James Mouat, who was
known around the district to be handy
with his fists, so was nicknamed,
'Bendigo', after the British prize-fighting
champion, William Thompson.

Thompson was one of triplets born
to a Nottingham lacemaker in 1811. The
triplets were, in fun, nicknamed Meshach,
Shadrach and Abednego. Little William's
nickname was then corrupted to Bendigo.
At the height of his fame, he only ever
lost one fight; he was known as 'Bold
Bendigo'.

James Mouat's portrait can be seen
among 'The Pioneer Gold Discoverers
of Bendigo' on page 198.

The Bendigo Creek (Sandhurst)

When William Tulloch visited the Bendigo diggings he described the
more established encampment:

> In fact, Bendigo is a large city, where a population of 40,000 lives in tents
> and huts instead of houses. Almost every tent has its large fire place and
> chimney, constructed of logs, at one end of it … It is curious to see the
> various rude constructions of these
> huts and chimneys. Some huts are
> built of solid trunks of trees, laid
> horizontally – in fact, the log-huts of
> America reconstructed here … you
> may generally distinguish the abodes
> of the native of Ireland, by their pic-
> turesque resemblance to the cabins
> of the Green Isle, being more
> remarkable for their defiance of sym-
> metry than any others. They seem to
> be tossed up rather than built, and
> are sure to have sundry black poles
> sticking out of the top, and bits of old
> sacking or old breeches hung up
> before them, here and there, to keep
> the wind from driving all the smoke
> down into the interior.

Gold Diggers Using a Puddling Machine at Bendigo
Wood engraving by Walter Mason, J. R. Clarke, Sydney, 1857
(REX NAN KIVELL COLLECTION, U822.
BY PERMISSION, NATIONAL LIBRARY OF AUSTRALIA)

GOLD DIGGERS USING A ' PUDDLING MACHINE" AT BENDIGO.

'Bendigo Mac'
From the *Annals of Bendigo*
Lachlan McLachlan, Police Magistrate of the Bendigo district from 1853 ('Bendigo Mac'), was a stern disciplinarian whose credo seems to have been taken from the saying 'desperate evils require desperate remedies'. He was censured often for the rigour, severity and clear discrimination with which he administered the law of the day.

Once an officer with the Van Diemen's Land police force, he had considerable knowledge of the criminal classes, and knew the history of many of the old lags who came before him in his Bendigo court.

McLachlan would accuse a prisoner brought before him with:

'I know you, you scoundrel, your name's so-and-so; you were at Norfolk Island in such a year;' ... of course the prisoner would be at quite a loss to account for the police magistrate's knowledge of his past career.

If the charge was trivial, 'Mac' would turn to his favourite henchman ... 'Sergeant Richards, see that this ruffian leaves the district within 24 hours; if not bring him here again'.[4]

At one time it was possible to scoop up pannikins of gold from the Bendigo Creek, and gold was even found trampled into the mud at the little stockyard. But it was after this alluvial gold had all but petered out that Bendigo really came into its own. Mining companies were established to raise the funds to dig deep into the earth. Great wealth was returned to investors, as tons of gold lay well below the surface. Based on this wealth, the town grew — line after line of giant steel poppet-legs were strung out across the landscape as Bendigo, 'Bold Bendigo', living up to its namesake, tried never to lose the fight for gold.

Eaglehawk and the North

In 1856 a storeman found himself stranded about 60 miles north of Bendigo in the granite country around Mt Hope. Fearing that his goods would spoil and he would lose his investment, he started the rumour that he had found gold there. When the news of this bogus find reached Bendigo another rush started. It was in the height of summer, and this hoax cost the lives of fourteen diggers, who perished in their haste to be the first to stake out a claim on Mt Hope.

In Eaglehawk, as for most other rushes, the surface gold soon ran out. The town survived when, in 1855, rich quartz reefs were located as the miners began to dig deep beneath the gullies. The Eaglehawk mines continued to work, their batteries filling the valleys around with mountains of grey sand, until the last, the South Virginia, closed in 1950.

– THE QUARTZ KING –
George Lansell 1824–1906

George and Edith Lansell at home
(COURTESY Q. C. BINKS COLLECTION)

GEORGE LANSELL arrived in the Bendigo district from Echunga, in South Australia, in 1853. He was a candlemaker by trade, who, with his brother, established a butchery, store and soap factory at Bendigo's View Point.

After the first alluvial rushes had begun to fade and companies established to finance deep mining, it was Lansell's unfailing faith in the value of these deep Sandhurst reefs that eventually made him the richest man in Bendigo. His investment in, and often sole ownership of, a large number of mines returned him rich rewards. At one stage it is recorded that he was making £1000 per day from his investments.

With the proceeds of his favourite, the 'Big 180' *(right)*, which at one time was the deepest mine in Victoria, bottoming out at just over one kilometre, he built the mansion 'Fortuna' in Chum Street, Golden Square.

Fortuna was a three-storeyed Italianate mansion, built on the site of Ballerstedts' home, which Lansell had bought from the successful German miners. It was one of the most extravagant homes in the colony, and set among one of the most appropriately named districts on the goldfields.

In 1879 Lansell left Bendigo and travelled to England. He may have been escaping from an unhappy first marriage to a chronic and, at times, abusive alcoholic, Bedelia Mulganney. George left her in their St Kilda Road mansion, where she died on 20 September 1880, aged 38. He established himself in the Grand Hotel, Charing Cross, London, in company with his housekeeper, Edith Basford, a young widow from a respectable Bendigo family.

Edith became the second Mrs Lansell, he was 57, she 27, on 12 August 1882, and their first son, George Victor, was born two months later.

In leaving Bendigo Lansell may also have been escaping the wrath of the Bendigo mining community who, although he had led the movement to reduce miners' wages, were incensed that he had let his mines on the New Chum Reef flood, creating a domino effect, closing other mines and throwing hundreds out of work.

The fortunes of Bendigo went into a decline, and the civic leaders of Bendigo prepared a beautifully illuminated petition containing 2,628 signatures, which was sent to London requesting his return.

Many believed that he had some mystical power over the Bendigo mines, and were delighted that, on his triumphal return to his 'kingdom', Bendigo once again began to flourish.

After he died in 1906, all his employees received a parcel of shares in his mines, and trust funds were established to support widows and orphaned children of Bendigo miners. In death, as in life, George Lansell was the benefactor of those who had helped make his great fortune.

(BENDIGO REGIONAL LIBRARY COLLECTION)

Sandhurst in 1862 Oil on canvas by Thomas Wright, 1862 *(COLLECTION – BENDIGO ART GALLERY)*

(1st row, from left) Edward Pepprell, Walter Sandbach, Patrick P. Farrell, James Mouat, William C. Coleman,
Abraham Motherwell, John Paton, William Stewart, Joshua Norris, George M. Newman, William Sandbach,
(2nd row) Frederick Fenton, Henry Frencham, Margaret Kennedy, William M. Johnson.

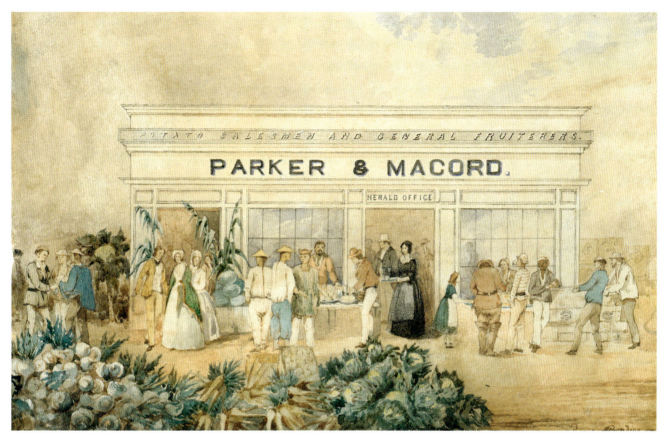

Parker and Macord, Potato Salesmen and General Fruiterers, Bendigo
Watercolour by George Rowe, c. 1857
(REX NAN KIVELL COLLECTION, R11529. BY PERMISSION, NATIONAL LIBRARY OF AUSTRALIA)
This observant watercolour by Rowe shows that a number of women had settled on the diggings in the early years. As usual the Chinese are in evidence – a few likely lads lounge about outside the shop.

Eagle Hawk Gully, Bendigo   Watercolour by S. T. Gill, c. 1852
(COLLECTION – BENDIGO ART GALLERY)

(OPPOSITE)

The Pioneer Gold Discoverers of Bendigo, Early Days
From the *Annals of Bendigo*

Bendigo was justly proud of its achievements. It had grown into a bustling city that had won over 450 tons of gold, making it the quartz-mining capital of the world.

Those who had been lucky, or provident, or both, also felt justly proud of what they had become. Many ordinary working-class men and women had the wealth to live like lords. In the substantial buildings they left, they showed they were intent on making sure that their names were recorded for posterity.

This illustration shows aspects of digging life, a reminder of the pioneering days: *(clockwise, from top)* Off to Bendigo, Issuing Licences, A Whim, The First Shaft at Bendigo, The Gold Escort, Hut and Store at the Mines, Washing Off, Deep Sinking, Puddling; *(centre)* Horse Puddling Machine, and Digger Hunting 'Joe Joe'.

Spring Creek Goldfield, Beechworth, c. 1861

(BURKE MUSEUM BEECHWORTH COLLECTION)

Miners are seen building a water race along the severely-degraded gully just to the west of the township. Sluice mining had stripped the sides of the gully and tons of soil were washed into the old creek-bed.

Beechworth

William Craig witnessed the legendary ride into Beechworth of the parliamentary candidate, the diggers' friend and local storekeeper, Dan Cameron:

> The stream of population … was moving in the direction of the Ovens, where it was reported that gold was being unearthed in large quantities. An interesting feature of this rush was the intense excitement that ensued upon the rumour that gold was so abundant that even the miners' horses were shod with it![5]

Although Craig claims that the horse was borrowed from a travelling circus at the Ovens at the time, and that the shoes were merely gilded iron, and the 'horse trained to lie on its back in the circus ring and flourish his heels in the air', the audience believed that those shoes were gold.

Cameron hired the horse from Brown, the circus owner, who 'saw a chance of making an honest penny out of the Cameron election', and Dan's election committee took great pains to publicise, far and wide, his exuberant ride to the polling booth 'on a horse [shod] with golden shoes'. Thousands poured onto the streets to witness the event.

> 'Shoes of gold at the Ovens!' announced the newspapers in large letters. 'Shoes of gold!' echoed business men in Melbourne as they hurriedly despatched large consignments of goods to meet the requirements of the new rush. 'Gold-shod horses!' murmured crowds … along the high road … exclaimed thousands of people in far-off lands.[6]

Craig suggested that it was the worldwide reporting of Cameron's folly that caused thousands to leave their homes and rush to these diggings – only to be disappointed. He claims that it was a 'store keeper's and shanty keeper's rush', and that there were more profitable diggings elsewhere.

Miners' celebration on the Beechworth Diggings, c. 1857

(BURKE MUSEUM BEECHWORTH COLLECTION)

Miners celebrate their luck in finding a rich strike out on the Nine-Mile, just out of Beechworth.

Beer by the bucket and quart-pot are the order of the day for this relaxed and joyous occasion.

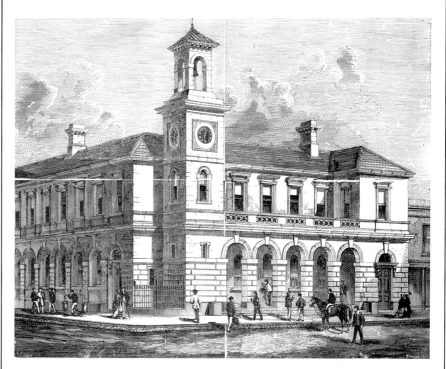

The Beechworth Post Office, 1867
(BURKE MUSEUM BEECHWORTH COLLECTION)

The handsome clock on this impressive post office tower has chimed the hour, without fail, since its construction in 1859.

When the town received its mains water supply in 1874, local dignitary, Frederick Brown, propelled a jet of water clear over the post office, much to the delight of all the local residents who turned out for the occasion.

Miner at Cock's El Dorado Mining Claim, 1897

(BURKE MUSEUM BEECHWORTH COLLECTION)

Bourke Street. The Start for Beechworth
From *News Letter of Australasia*, 'A narrative to send to friends', No. 59, July 1867

(LA TROBE PICTURE COLLECTION,
STATE LIBRARY OF VICTORIA)

The Cobb & Co. Coach is shown leaving from outside the Coaching Office and the Albion Hotel on the journey to the diggings at Beechworth.

BOURKE STREET. THE START FOR BEECHWORTH.

Post Office, Beechworth
**Hand-coloured lithograph by A. J. Stopps,
from a daguerrotype by Acley & Rochletz
James J. Blundell & Co., Melbourne, c.1856**
(REX NAN KIVELL COLLECTION, U2303.
BY PERMISSION, NATIONAL LIBRARY OF AUSTRALIA)

Chinese Burning Towers, Beechworth
(PHOTOGRAPH BY GEOFF HOCKING)

These towers are typical of those built in almost every cemetery across the goldfields where Chinese gathered. After the attack on the Buckland River, the Chinese fell back into Beechworth, and set up a large community there.

The burning towers were built in 1883 in the cemetery that holds the remains of 2000 Chinese who never returned to their homeland.

Contrary to popularly-held opinion, cremations were not held in the burning towers. Paper tokens were burnt, gifts of food and wine were placed within, the purpose being to sustain the departing spirit on its journey to Heaven, carried on the smoke of the paper prayers. Firecrackers were exploded to frighten any devils away.

Many a young larrikin had a good feed of pork, washed down with rice wine, after the funeral party had long departed.

(LEFT & ABOVE LEFT)
**Spring Creek Goldfields Beechworth,
c. 1857**
(BURKE MUSEUM BEECHWORTH COLLECTION)

(OPPOSITE)
Robert O'Hara Burke
Oil by William Strutt, 1862
(PRIVATE COLLECTION)

The Buckland River diggings were set among the foothills
of the Victorian Alps. Here diggers rioted against the Chinese,
driving them into the freezing river in July 1857.
(LA TROBE PICTURE COLLECTION, STATE LIBRARY OF VICTORIA)

– Our First Victorian Hero! Robert O'Hara Burke –

IRISH-BORN ROBERT O'HARA BURKE had served in the Hungarian Hussars and with the Irish Constabulary before joining the Victoria Police in April 1853.

He was stationed on the Beechworth diggings between 1854 and 1858 where, as Senior Inspector of Police, he was instrumental in bringing order to the Buckland River diggings after the attack on the Chinese in July 1857.

Burke was transferred to the Police Camp at Castlemaine in November 1858.

He was an impressive man, described as

a gentleman in the prime of life ... tall, well-made, with dark brown hair; his broad chest was decorated with a magnificent beard ... fine intelligent eyes, and a splendidly formed head.[7]

He sported a sabre cut, gained in the Austrian Army, which made him most attractive to the ladies, who seem enchanted by this bold adventurer.

Burke was 'born to lead' and enjoyed the admiration and loyalty of those who served beneath him, and of those he served.

Although he was almost incapable of maintaining any sort of normal order in his own affairs, had little knowledge of navigation, no experience at exploration, no bushcraft skills worth mentioning, it was his attractive and eccentric personality, and his Anglo-Irish pedigree, that ensured his name was put forward to lead an exploration to the Gulf of Carpentaria that left Melbourne on 20 August 1860.

Burke had used the interior of his house at Beechworth as his journal, writing notes to himself in English, French and German, scrawling bits of letters, memoranda, and poetry along the walls. He asserted: 'I cannot keep any record in a systematic manner, so I jot things down like this.' Just the man to lead the ill-fated exploring party across the desert in 1860.

Clunes and Creswick

Creswick was to become the scene of pioneering workplace reform in the mines, yet it was also the scene of the worst mining disaster on the goldfields when water burst through the face of the south-west drive of No. 2 shaft in the New Australasian Mine, on Tuesday, 12 December 1882.

The deep mines sought ancient river beds far below the surface, and the miners had been shovelling out the loose gravel sandwiched between layers of basalt and shale when the tunnel burst. Thousands of litres of water poured over the two men who were at work at the face, they ran and warned the plateman, who, showing great courage, ran a further 500 metres back down another drive to warn his cobbers. A further twenty-nine men struggled through the rapidly rising waters, but only two of these managed to swim to safety in the total darkness, guided by ventilation pipes.

The others climbed to the highest point in the tunnel, but as the air slowly ran out they collapsed and fell unconscious into the water. It took all the pumps on the surface two days to lower the level sufficiently for rescuers to enter the dark and watery tomb; twenty-two of the twenty-seven left below ground were found dead.

Fifteen thousand attended the funerals the following day, and a relief fund was established that raised £75 per family for the seventeen widows, and the seventy-five children left fatherless.

A board of inquiry agreed that inaccurate surveys had led the mine manager to mistakenly allow tunnelling too close to older, water-

The Port Phillip Gold Mining Company's Claim and the Town of Clunes
Wood engraving by Samuel Calvert, Ebenezer and David Syme, from *The Australian Illustrated News*, 19 June 1869

There was limited alluvial gold on the Clunes diggings, and it was not until 1856, when the English company, Port Phillip & Colonial, began to follow the quartz reefs, that any real wealth was taken from Clunes.

By the end of the century the gold had all but played out, and the town, which had once been the fifth largest in Victoria, saw investments disappear, along with much of its population.

NOTABLE NUGGETS
– LADY LOCH –
617 oz
Sulky Gully, Creswick
23 August 1887
Midas Gold Mining Co.

– CRESWICK GOLD –
The combined output of the major mines at Creswick was
1,697,500 oz gold.

Union leader, W. G. Spence

(From 'Early Creswick' by John A. Graham, 1942)

Spence was brought up on the diggings at Jackass Flat, near Creswick. Although he had little education he was an inquiring and hard-working lad. He loved to read, with a fondness for history, philosophy and politics. He was particularly influenced by the utilitarian ideas espoused by John Stuart Mill.

In 1874 Spence was actively involved with the trade union movement helping to create the Creswick Miner's Union. His union activities took him far and wide. He became in turn General Secretary of the Amalgamated Miners Association and the President of the Amalgamated Shearers Union of Australasia. A member of the Australian Labor Party, Spence was elected to the first Federal Parliament in 1901.

Captain John Hepburn

(La Trobe Picture Collection, State Library of Victoria)

filled workings. Following the Disaster Inquiry it was recommended that all mines were required to have better mine signalling and escape routes.

Union leader W. G. Spence made Creswick the cradle of the trade union movement in Australia. Just as the miners at Clunes had banded together in December 1873, and defended their jobs against the Chinese, the miners at Creswick fought the bosses for their fair day's pay. In the 1880s miners worked an eight-hour shift for 4s 6d. An extra shilling, a hardship allowance, was paid to the men who worked at the mine face; these 'face men' often worked all day lying in the wet mud, shovelling gravel over their heads to their mates behind. They rarely lived beyond the age of 40. When mine owners sought to employ contractors on 4 shillings per foot, rather than on an hourly rate, the miners once again joined in mass protest.

The spirit that led to the wearing of the red ribbon at Bendigo and Ballarat was reborn in protest at the avaricious mine-owners and their shareholders. The combination of water rising in the mines and continued organised labour resistance resulted in the eventual demise of the big mines.

Jim Crow
Daylesford, Blackwood and the Central Highlands

Some diggings took their names for obvious reasons: the name of the discoverer of the rush or the squatter's run, or simply from the topography or some remarkable feature of the landscape. Others, like the Jim Crow diggings, were a little more cryptic in the origin of their name.

The district, first opened in 1838 by seaman-turned-squatter, Captain John Hepburn, was often difficult to negotiate. The hills and gullies were abrupt, then deep, twisting and turning, and falling away again into creeks rushing with the mineral-rich waters that were later to bring a different kind of prosperity to the region. Some said that the diggers had to adopt a kind of crow-like hopping gait to navigate the hillsides, and this name stuck; other reports were that it was named after the chief of the natives nearby, but who or what gave him this uncharacteristic name?

Hepburn had celebrated the discovery of the excellent natural spring water, but the discovery of gold overshadowed the benefits of the springs for a further thirty years. A small bath-house was

Simmons Reef, Mount Blackwood,
57 miles from Melbourne, Victoria
Oil on board by Elizabeth Shepherd, 1858
(REX NAN KIVELL COLLECTION, T320.
BY PERMISSION, NATIONAL LIBRARY OF AUSTRALIA)

An inscription on the back of this painting states that Shepherd was on the goldfields between September 1855 and February 1884.

As the field had only opened in February 1855 and was not at its peak until September when it saw an influx of 15,000 diggers, Shepherd must have been among this rush.

constructed at 'Hepburn Springs'; it became fashionable for travellers from Melbourne to take the railway to the European-styled mineral baths set in the middle of the Australian bush.

The rushing waters fed by these springs were often far beneath the old creek-beds that were the source of wealth on other fields, and the diggers here often tunnelled straight into the hillsides following these beds, rather than driving shafts from above.

John Chandler, a carrier by trade, had been offered a good price to get a load up to Daylesford, but

> When we got to the ranges, we had some very bad hills to go up and down, and one siding. We had the greatest difficulty to keep from cap-sizing. We got safe in with our loads and came back another way. We stopped at a spring for dinner. The water bubbled up like a fountain. It made the tea so strong we could hardly drink it. This is now the famous Daylesford mineral waters. We did not think much of it. At the foot of Mount Franklin we passed a tribe of natives. There was a lot of lubras and piccaninnies. We generally found it best to give them a wide berth, for they are such bold beggars that they will clean you out of all your tobacco, rum, tea, sugar, etc., and if you are alone and any way timid of them, then look out for yourself.[8]

William Howitt also writes of the Aboriginals encountered on his journeys through this region:

> we were surprised to see a number of natives haunting about [a] grog-shop in European costume; but learnt that they were from the aborig-ines station ahead of us, called Parker's Station, from the Protector. The place in which they were found did not argue much for their progress in civilisation ...[9]

and, with disgust, the digger lounging at the same tent:

The Protector, Edward Stone Parker
(LA TROBE PICTURE COLLECTION,
STATE LIBRARY OF VICTORIA)

Parker was Government Protector of Aborigines, and established his station in the Mt Franklin region.

Parker Street in Castlemaine is named after him.

The Great Eastern Tunnel
Jim Crow diggings, c. 1858
Photograph by Richard Daintree

(LA TROBE PICTURE COLLECTION, STATE LIBRARY OF VICTORIA)

The tunnel cut into the hillside on the Jim Crow diggings was 1500 feet long. A long flume and waterwheel are shown in this photograph.

Richard Daintree was one of the many contemporary photographers whose work covered almost all of the Australian diggings, from Victoria to Queensland.

A Puddler in the Bush

(PHOTOGRAPH BY MARY THOMPSON, CASTLEMAINE)

The ruins of a puddler in bushland near Castlemaine.

A puddler was a circular trough cut into the ground, in which a horse tramped around and around, crushing, stone and dirt into a watery slurry from which gold was extracted.

NOTABLE NUGGETS
– JOHN BULL –

The John Bull nugget was found in White Horse Gully on the Jim Crow diggings, between Castlemaine and Daylesford, by three poor sailors. The lucky fellow who actually discovered the John Bull, only inches below the surface, had only been on the diggings for a fortnight. The nugget weighed 45 lbs, and was eventually sold by the sailors for £5,000 and taken to London, where it was put on public exhibition.

•

600 oz
Yandoit ~ February 1860
A German and 2 Poles

•

600 oz
Yandoit ~ April 1860
4 Irishmen

a tall, dirty, unshaven, gallows-looking fellow who appeared at the door with a basin of broth, or liquid of the sort ... and answered our inquiries in the same favourite style of surliness.[10]

Howitt passed Hepburn's homestead, which he described as one of the largest he had ever seen, and mused on the good fortune that this master of a merchant-vessel had encountered when he traded 'ploughing the seas [for] grazing the Crown lands of Victoria'. He wondered when a digger would ever find a nugget so large that he, too, would be able to buy large tracts of land for 1 shilling an acre.

The area saw a great influx of southern Europeans; Italians established themselves in factories and farms; middle-European Jews came in their hundreds, drawn by the similarity of the 'mountain' region to that left far behind. The hardy little Cornishmen, whose expertise in deep underground mining was never equalled, followed the introduction of deep quartz mining.

What a mixture these diggings became! All the world was there – sober, hard-working Protestants working side by side with exuberant Italian Catholics, careful Jews and solid Presbyterians, the Tipperary mob, larrikins and ladies; all hopped about these diggings with a 'Jimcra' gait.

Mt Alexander (Castlemaine)

Mt Alexander was at the heart of Dr Barker's Ravenswood Run, a vast sheep-grazing station, typical of the holdings taken up by scores of squatters following the opening of the district by Major Mitchell's expedition of 1836.

The alluvial diggings in the shadow of the mount lasted for several years, but after new rushes opened up to the north and north-west, and the larger centres developed deep-lead mines, the district now known as Castlemaine settled into a new era of prosperity.

The first regional railway steamed through the valley in 1861 bringing commerce and enterprise of a different kind to the goldfields, as Castlemaine developed its expertise in engineering and metal founding that had been learnt on the diggings.

Robert O'Hara Burke was transferred to Castlemaine in 1858. It was the local foundry-owner J. V. A. Bruce who was instrumental in ensuring Burke's selection as leader of the disastrous expedition to the north in 1860. It was the honour of the citizens of Castlemaine to lead the funeral procession* through the streets of Melbourne on 21 January 1863, when Burke's bones were finally laid to rest back in Victoria.

View of the Castlemaine Diggings
From an original watercolour drawing by George Rowe, 1857
(PRIVATE COLLECTION)

This engraving shows miners working in the old watercourse of Forest Creek.

The creek was eventually moved away from the growing township (at the right of this drawing) as Castlemaine went to an inordinate amount of trouble to realign its landscape.

Hills were cut down, gullies filled, and street levels cut away as the townsfolk sought to impose an ordered town-grid over the undulating terrain.

*The funeral procession was led by Castlemaine Councillor F. Gingell, the advance guard of the Castlemaine Dragoons, 40 men led by Captain Anderson, the Castlemaine Volunteer Band, and then came the 50-strong Castlemaine Rifle Corps.

If Burke had survived he would have been Commander of the Dragoons.

Forest Creek   Watercolour by S. T. Gill, 1852
(La Trobe Picture Collection, State Library of Victoria)

On the left are the office of the *Argus* newspaper and Bryce Ross's Agency Office on the
Red Hill at Chewton, Forest Creek diggings. The trooper is following the track heading
towards the Camp, nestled between the hills, at Castlemaine in the distance.

Mt Alexander Gold Diggings from Adelaide Hill   Watercolour by G. T. Angas 1852
(Rex Nan Kivell Collection, U76. By Permission, National Library of Australia)

Store at Chewton, c. 1860
(Chewton Historical Museum Collection)

Chewton grew up on the site of the first Forest Creek diggings. It was also the site of the first Commissioners' Camp on Adelaide Hill.

The Camp moved into Castlemaine in October 1851, but Chewton remained an important junction as the diggings fanned out in all directions from this point: to Golden Point, Fryer's Creek, Forest Creek, Moonlight and Pennyweight Flats.

Bryce Ross established his 'Newspaper' office in Chewton.

Fryer's Creek, Near Castlemaine
After a sketch by S. T. Gill, 1852
(Private Collection)

NOTABLE NUGGETS
– HERON –
1008 oz
Fryers Creek, ~ 29/3/1855
Davis and Harriss

•

648 oz
Taradale, ~ 27/5/1856
**J. Williams, Geo. Stapleton
and Jno. Matthews**

•

600 oz
Fryers Creek, ~ 1854
Finder Unknown

The Garfield Wheel, c. 1898
*(Castlemaine Art Gallery
& Historical Museum Collection)*

The waterwheel that drove the crushing mill at Quartz Hill near Chewton was the largest in the Southern Hemisphere: diameter, 72 feet; one revolution every 45 to 50 seconds.

– Antoine Fauchery –

Photographer Antoine Fauchery travelled to the diggings from his native France in 1853.

Unlike many photographers who restricted themselves to portraits of eminent figures or *carte-de-visites*, Fauchery created tableaus of diggers working the creeks, groups of natives, and panoramic views of the townships and ravaged diggings that were often interpretative creations rather than simply captured observations.

He pioneered the use of a lens, designed in Vienna, which gave sharp focus to the background making the subjects in the foreground appear almost in relief. His views of the towns and of the diggings are sharp all over. He called his prints taken in this way 'Stereomonoscopes'.

Eugène von Guérard, who was travelling with a large group of French artists and intellectuals, recorded that 'Fougery' was in Ballarat in 1853 after coming to Australia from California with his wife. Neither so-called 'facts' were true: they had not been in California, and his travelling companion was not actually his wife at the time.

Like so many other diggers, Fauchery had success and failure, and after going broke he used his few remaining pounds to set up a restaurant in Melbourne, catering for the large number of French diggers passing through. His takings from this helped fund his return to Paris, where he and his companion were finally married. They returned to Australia in 1857.

Antoine Fauchery

(LA TROBE PICTURE COLLECTION, STATE LIBRARY OF VICTORIA)

Chewton Diggings
Photograph by Antoine Fauchery, 1858

(LA TROBE PICTURE COLLECTION, STATE LIBRARY OF VICTORIA)

Tarrangower (Maldon)

Once the easy pickings ran out Maldon did not go into decline. There were incredibly rich veins running just below the surface, and mining companies were soon formed to tunnel into the earth.

The Nuggetty Reef, north of Mt Tarrangower, was discovered by young Alexander Pettit in November 1855. He and a couple of his mates quietly worked the reef until their secret got out in January 1856. Over the next five years £1,000,000 worth of gold was taken from these rich, yet mostly shallow, reefs. Little gold was found beyond 250 feet, making sustained deep mining quite a challenge.

In Maldon they worked around the clock, the sound of crushing batteries constantly pounded the air, and three times a day the streets were filled with hot and thirsty miners as they were hauled to the surface at the end of their shifts.

The town has remained virtually unchanged since the roaring days and it was honoured by the National Trust of Australia in 1966, when it earned the title of Australia's First Notable Town.

The Kangaroo Hotel, Maldon

The Kangaroo at Maldon still stands today. Surprisingly, it is the only hotel so-named in Australia.

Most hoteliers seemed more intent on honouring their past than embracing their future, with pubs named – The Shamrock, Brian Boru, Old England, The Royal and Caledonian; there is even a Pig & Whistle in Central Victoria.

(*All Photographs, Courtesy of Maldon Historical Museum*)

Beer label, Maldon Brewery

Several breweries were established in Maldon at the foot of Mt Tarrangower, where springs provided pure water, perfect for a good brew.

Carman's Tunnel

Between November 1882 and December 1884 the impressively named Great International Quartz Mining Company (No Liability) drove a 570-metre tunnel into the south-western side of Mt Tarrangower.

The miners expected to cut across reefs that ran within the mountain, but for all their hard work chasing drives, opening crosscuts, galleries, following quartz veins, digging shafts, cutting, timbering and laying tracks – they found nothing. Just as well they had added 'No Liability'!

A quartz crown was found on top of the mountain, but yielded only 2 oz per ton. It was declared 'not proving payable', and abandoned.

The long, dry tunnel, 2.5 km from Maldon, later restored, is accessible to the public.

Miners on the Nuggetty Reef

A group of Maldon miners pose along the rail-track of their small single-wheeled mine-head on the Nuggetty Reef.

– THE WELSH SWAGMAN –

Joseph Jenkins (1818–98) was born in Cardiganshire, West Wales. His family had been farmers and men of letters, numbering some recognised Welsh poets among them.

He farmed at home until he married, when he moved to farm at Trecefel, Tregaron. The Jenkins had nine children, a prosperous farm, and Joseph held a position of respect in the community.

He held strong views on farming methods, favouring crop rotation, harrowing rather than deep ploughing, and was an advocate of the powerful properties of manure. He even badgered machinery makers for a combined dung-cart and distributor some sixty years before they were to become generally available.

At 51 years of age Jenkins packed his swag and set out for Australia, leaving his wife and seven surviving children behind.

He arrived in Port Phillip in March 1869 and had travelled up to the Mt Alexander goldfields by the end of April.

After trying his hand at digging, he eventually settled in a hut in the bush near Lewis Road at Muckleford. He worked for many years around the district, helping farmers, clearing roads, digging the Maldon drains, and cutting great heaps of firewood.

All this time he recorded his adventures in his diaries. These records, which include many of his poems and songs, form the basis of the book *Diary of a Welsh Swagman,* in which he also extols the virtue of manure, unable to comprehend why the colonial farmer, complaining of the poor quality of the Australian soils, ignored the beneficial produce of their beasts.

He returned to Wales, aged 76, to spend the next and last four years of his life surrounded by his grandchildren.

The Maldon Market Place   Watercolour by David Drape, c. 1855

Warnock Bros., Beehive Stores, Main Street, Maldon, c. 1900

The Maldon Mines   Watercolour by David Drape, c. 1855

Thomson & Comry's Stores, Tarnagulla, c. 1865

Poster calling Diggers to a Meeting at Dunolly

FELLOW-DIGGERS!

A MONSTER
MEETING
Will be held TO-MORROW,
SATURDAY,
AT ELEVEN O'CLOCK, IN THE GOVERNMENT ROAD,

To take into consideration the Government Orders respecting this Road.   All who have Claims are specially ordered to attend.

R. L. GARDNER, Chairman.   J. GORDON, Secretary.

PRINTED AT THE "ADVERTISER OFFICE." NEAR THE CRITERION HOTEL, GOVERNMENT ROAD, DUNOLLY.

The Golden Triangle

The district known as the Golden Triangle takes in the extraordinarily rich alluvial fields of Dunolly, Tarnagulla, Moliagul, Wedderburn, Rheola, Inglewood and Kingower. The number of significant nuggets taken from this region leaves all other goldfields well behind.

The Welcome Stranger nugget, the largest ever found in the world, was unearthed by John Deason and Richard Oates in 1869, at Moliagul, a small farming community in the heart of this coarse-gravelled, black-treed, harsh, dry country. All around this area great nuggets were discovered from the early days of the goldrush right up into the first decade of the twentieth century – the area justly earned its title as the 'Golden Triangle'.

NOTABLE NUGGETS

– WELCOME STRANGER –
2284 oz
Moliagul, ~ 5 February 1869
John Deason & Richard Oates

– BLANCHE BARKLY –
1743 oz
Kingower, ~ 27 August 1857
R. & J. Ambrose, S. & C. Napier

– NOT NAMED –
– 1363 oz –
Old Lead, Dunolly, ~ October 1857

– VISCOUNT CANTERBURY –
1114 oz
Berlin-Rheola, ~ 31 May 1853
S. Schlossman & J. Davis

– MARYBOROUGH –
1034 oz
Blackman's Lead, ~ 22 January 1853
J. Dinon & Jas. Edinton

– POSEIDON –
953 oz
Tarnagulla, ~ 18 December 1906
Woodall, Condron, Brookes & Eva

–VISCOUNTESS CANTERBURY –
912 oz
Berlin-Rheola, ~ 3 October 1870
Felstead & Party

– 893 oz –
Berlin Rush, ~12 March 1869
Pat & Jas. Hoare

– KUM TOW –
795 oz
Berlin Rush, ~ 17 April 1871
Loo Ching & Pty.

– 782 oz –
Evans Gully, Kingower, ~ February 1861

– LEILA –
675 oz
Poseidon, ~ 3 January 1907
C. Smith, J. Rodgers & G. Stephenson

(Top)
Martin's Timber Yard, Dunolly, c. 1865

(Centre)
Main Street, Inglewood

(Courtesy, Allan M. Nixon)

Although some substantial buildings grace the streetscape, others are still roofed with canvas. In the centre a large gum-tree is posted with notices: *'The Diggers' Intelligencer'* was a common feature across the diggings.

(Bottom)
Linger & Die Diggings, Tarnagulla, 1896

(Photographs Courtesy Central Goldfields Shire, Historical Museums Collections)

Lucky diggers at their windlass, Tarnagulla, 1902

Diggers, Lockett and Scholes, pose at the head of their shaft after finding a 27 ounce nugget.

– THE PRECIOUS NUGGET –
c. 1864
From *Cassell's Picturesque Atlas of Australasia*, 1889
(Private Collection)

The Precious Nugget was discovered on 5 January 1871 on the Berlin-Rheola diggings by Ah Chang & Co. The nugget, weighing 1717 oz, was the fourth-largest found on the Victorian goldfields. Its value at the time was £6,868.

Walhalla and Wood's Point

Wood's Point, Mines on Morning Star Hill, c. 1864

William Gooley claimed to have been the discoverer of the Upper Goulburn goldfield in May 1861. However, at the same time there were countless numbers of diggers prospecting the icy streams of the Victorian Alps, as one by one the diggings opened up – Wood's Point, Gaffney's Creek, Jamieson, Matlock, Stringer's Creek and Walhalla.

In 1862 two experienced bushmen led a party of prospectors following the Goulburn River to its source, high in the Victorian ranges. At a fork in the river, one, a German named Dittmer Brehrens, took the left branch, and his companion, Corry, took the right. After considerable struggle, fighting his way through almost impenetrable scrub, Corry gave up. He cut across the mountain hoping to meet up with Brehrens. As he slipped down the other side he dropped into a secluded gully where he discovered the ground strewn with quartz, which showed a 'plentiful supply of gold'. He immediately staked out a claim and set to work.

His companion soon caught up with him, and it was not before long when others joined in the rush to what must have been the most difficult of all the goldfields to access.

At times bushmen and diggers would attempt to open a way through the dense bush by burning a path before them with a fire-brand. When Duncan and Colin McDougall, who had been among Brehrens and Corry's exploring party, attempted to bring in machinery for quartz-crushing, the carriers they had engaged refused to

(OPPOSITE)

Waterwheel in the Walhalla Valley
From *Cassell's Picturesque Atlas of Australasia*, 1889
(PRIVATE COLLECTION)

Mine workings snake through the valley, making every inch of level ground pay.

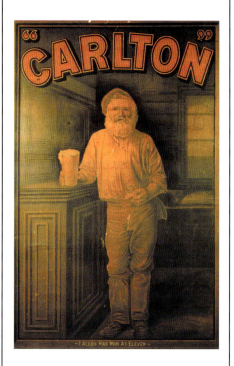

'I allus has wan at eleven'
(COURTESY CARLTON & UNITED BREWERIES)

This famous poster for Carlton Beer was based on a photograph taken around the turn of the century by Melbourne-based photographer, G. M Sinclair.

Sinclair had gone into a bush pub at Walsh's Creek, an old gold diggings in the Upper Yarra/Warburton region, north-east of Melbourne, where he observed this old fossicker, Sam Griffin, approach the bar and raise a glass of beer to his lips with what appeared to be almost spiritual dedication.

When he had drained his glass he let out a long sigh of deep satisfaction. Sinclair commented, 'You seem to be enjoying your beer, my friend?' Sam replied, 'I do indeed sir, I allus has wan at eleven'. A photograph was taken, and later adapted by a commercial artist to the now-famous poster for Carlton.

There is an amusing rejoinder to Sam's reply. He may have said that 'He allus had wan at eleven', but the original advertisement continued, 'It's something wot's gotta be done, cos if I don't have wan at eleven I allus has eleven at wan!'

WALHALLA GOLD MINE.

The mountainous terrain of the upper Goulburn diggings was so difficult to access that packhorses were at first the only way to carry in supplies.

The English novelist, Anthony Trollope, toured these goldfields on horseback, and found the track into Walhalla so steep that at times he could hardly remain in the saddle. Imagine his surprise when he discovered a piano and billiard table in the hotel on arrival.

An enterprising carrier, Louie the Frenchman, carried dancehall girl, Kitty Cane, up the hillside into Walhalla for 9d a pound, which wasn't such a bad deal for him, as Kitty weighed 22 stone!

The crushing machinery designed for McDougall & Company's Morning Star Mine was made to measure. No single piece of the eight-head stamping battery could weigh over 200 lbs, as each had to be carried on horseback, and had to be assembled on site.

Although the entire crusher weighed less than 3 tons, it took them over three months to carry it up to Wood's Point, and almost a year to bring the entire project to completion.

Advertisements from the *Walhalla Chronicle*, 1897

push their horses any further. The McDougalls had to do it themselves. They named their mine 'The Morning Star', and although they were only able to cart in a 'clumsy little machine, with wooden shanks to the old-fashioned water-engine, [it] turned out more gold than the large-stream driven batteries of Ballarat and Sandhurst'.[11] By the end of 1866 the claim had paid out over £164,000.

The mines in the often snow-covered mountain gullies of eastern Victoria were exceedingly rich; the Long Tunnel Mine, at Walhalla, at the time of its closure in 1913 was the single largest producer of gold in Victoria, yielding 13.5 tons of gold between 1865 and 1911. The shaft of the Long Tunnel was 1100 yards deep, and the tunnel extended over 5 miles underground.

The gullies were so steep on this goldfield that little flat ground was available for building. The settlement at Walhalla followed the meandering watercourse, winding in and out of the valley, some buildings even straddling the creek.

When the miners wanted a place for recreation they simply removed the top of a hill, truncating it to provide a level playing field. The Walhalla Cricket Ground is still today only reached by a climb of over 600 feet. It was on this field in 1907 that Warwick Armstrong, captain of the Australian cricket team, bet that he could hit a six by landing it on the roof of the Star Hotel. (He didn't quite manage it, and was caught out on the boundary for 12.)

In the cemetery some of the diggers are buried in graves cut vertically into the hillsides, so valuable was horizontal space.

Where once stood proud forests, barren hillsides remained. The Long Tunnel itself fired eight steam boilers, 24 hours a day. Where lack of water was the bane of some goldfields, at Walhalla there was often too much, with miners forced to work all day in mud and slush, miles underground.

The Balaclava Syndicate, 1932

(Courtesy Q. C. Binks Collection)

A group of investors, their friends and families pose on the hillside at the re-opening of the Balaclava Mine in 1932.

There were not many mines still working on the Victorian goldfields when this photograph was taken, yet there were plenty who still believed in the diggings.

At various times attempts were made to reopen the pits, speculation on the possibilities of reworking the old shafts was always defeated by the element that had caused so many to close – water.

Towards the end of the twentieth century mining took on a new form, when huge drives were opened miles away from the reefs to be worked, and trucks and excavators driven straight in, to eventually reach the working face far underground.

No more winding cables or poppet heads, no more clattering cages or sound of the steam whistle or ringing of bells – all were replaced by the growl of the diesel engine.

Waranga, Whroo & the Balaclava Mine

The Waranga diggings had been troublesome around the time of the 'Red-ribbon' rebellion in Bendigo; diggers on this scrubby, dusty, goldfield cared little for the requirements of the troopers.

To the east of the McIvor diggings, on the undulating plains near the Goulburn River, there was once a bustling township that was home to over 20,000 diggers and their families. Today nothing is left of Whroo but a huge hole in the ground and an abandoned cemetery, whose metal and wooden headstones bear testament to the hardships endured on these rough-and-ready diggings.

There were rich alluvial fields around Rushworth, but it is the story of the Whroo diggings that is the most intriguing.

The discovery of the Balaclava Reef just a few miles out of Rushworth saw mining methods that were most unusual. Shafts were cut down into the hillside following the rich veins of gold-bearing quartz. The miners removed entire veins leaving open fissures in the rock that were propped apart with timbers, leaving the hillside like a giant honeycomb.

An attempt was made to blast the hill apart with an enormous charge of explosive, but this was not successful. All that was left was a hill too dangerous for further shaft mining. A gaping hole, blasted into the side of the hill, allowed the miners to cut away material in what was to become one huge open-cut mine. The earth to be crushed was taken away by tramway through a tunnel cut through 100 yards of solid rock.

The gold won from the Balaclava mine at Whroo financed the building of the majestic Menzies Hotel in Victorian Melbourne.

NEW SOUTH WALES
Beyond the Blue Mountains

Bathurst

Bathurst is Australia's oldest inland settlement, first settled after Governor Macquarie travelled to the 'newly discovered country' in 1815. Although the land was ripe for agricultural development, such development in the region was unusually slow, as several years of successive droughts and economic depression deterred squatters from expanding into a region so remote from the coastal ports.

Just as explorer Thomas Livingston Mitchell was to wax lyrical about the 'great south countrie' he had crossed on his expedition from Sydney into Victoria in 1836, when he titled the central region 'Australia Felix', Assistant Surveyor-General G.W. Evans had also described the rich plains of central New South Wales — as 'the handsomest country I ever saw'.

Ophir at the Junction, June 1851
Lithograph by J. Hogarth, London, 1851, from a drawing by G. F. Angas

(REX NAN KIVELL COLLECTION, S9070.
BY PERMISSION, NATIONAL LIBRARY OF AUSTRALIA)

This almost arcadian scene belies the reality of the rush to these parts. This lithograph was first published in June 1851, just one month after Hargraves had made his discovery, and obviously before the creek had been churned to mud by the thousands of diggers who crowded onto these green banks.

– OPHIR –

Hargraves named the diggings where he found the first gold at Summer Hill Creek, 35 km from Bathurst, Ophir, after the biblical 'city of gold' (as was Ophir County in California).

The Sort to Catch Gardiner –
The Right Man on the Right Horse at the Right Place

No matter where the venturer dared to roam, the possibility of encountering one of the 'Kings of the Road' was real. Although police were stationed all across the colonies, they were not considered too much of a threat to the bushrangers.

Just as Evans had been the first to lay foot on the Bathurst plains and herald the influx of Scottish squatters and sheep-herders, so too did Mitchell herald the migration of the Sydney Scots to take up large squatting runs right across the best tracts of land in Victoria.

The discovery of gold at Ophir, only 35 km from Bathurst, brought thousands onto the squatters' runs in 1851, as did the discovery of gold in the central Victorian highlands see the end of the squatters' reign on those rich plains. The story repeated itself on almost every goldfield: shepherds walked away from their flocks; shopkeepers put up their shutters, packed their wares and headed for the diggings, where their next store was a simple plank set across two boxes and roofed in canvas. Sailors abandoned their ships, police resigned, gaolers threw in their keys, parsons, priests, prosecutors and prostitutes all headed for the diggings where each expected their fortune was to be made.

The diggings around Bathurst, at Young, Forbes, Mudgee, West Wyalong, Parkes and Eugowra are also names that feature prominently in the tales of derring-do on the diggings – a disproportionate number of notorious characters ended up on these NSW goldfields.

'Darkie' Gardiner, Ben Hall, Johnnie Gilbert and John Bow were some of the more famous of the 'currency lads' who roamed these diggings. They were known to be at Lambing Flat at the time of the riots there. The Clarke Brothers (Thomas and John) and their extended family terrorised the area around Yass and Goulburn until they were captured at Jindera in April 1867. 'Mad Dan' Morgan, who started his career in Castlemaine and finished it on the Ovens near Beechworth, instilled fear into the hearts of the honest settlers around Wagga Wagga and Tumbarumba for many years.

The apparent isolation of these diggings drew the misfits, the outcasts, the errant ticket-of-leave men, the bold lads who defied the law and demanded that they too had a right to pursue their destiny as free men. Unfortunately these bushrangers saw the easy way out: if digging was hard, sitting astride a stolen horse and pushing a pistol under the nose of a coach-driver were easy, and there was always gold a-plenty ready for the taking. The law, however, did prevail – and there are numerous lonely graves dotted through the bush.

The rush to the alluvial goldfields of Victoria saw a decline in the population on the Bathurst diggings for a while, but the deeper mining brought great rewards to miners right across the region for many years. Just as in Victoria the towns grew into domesticity, miners became farmers, merchants, manufacturers and traders. The Riverina economy, once based on agriculture, but interrupted by mining, saw the fields shimmer once again with golden grain, and bales of fleece were once again carted to the railheads and to the ports.

Kiandra, the Cold Field

High in the snow-covered mountains of New South Wales gold was discovered in the Eucumbene River in January 1860. The alluvial diggings were all but finished in Victoria and around Bathurst, and the diggers rushed to stand once again in freezing creek-beds, searching for a bit of colour.

By the middle of the year most of the miners were unable to work because of the heavy snow. George Preshaw, who, in 1855, had entered service with the Castlemaine branch of the Bank of New South Wales, was transferred to the Kiandra agency at the beginning of the rush. He was shocked to find the conditions in his new bank (a tent) on arrival:

On entering I saw a young man behind the counter ... he was perched on a piece of bark which rested on two logs, a stream of water running

Bathurst
Lithograph, Woolcott & Clarke, Sydney, 1851, from a drawing by G. F. Angas, 1851
(REX NAN KIVELL COLLECTION, S9064. BY PERMISSION, NATIONAL LIBRARY OF AUSTRALIA)

Bathurst had been settled for almost half a century before gold was discovered.

Unlike the Victorian goldfields there was a well-established township already standing when the diggers passed through on their way to the diggings.

Although a road had been built across the Blue Mountains in 1815, following the tracks of the explorers Blaxland, Wentworth and Lawson two years earlier, the trek to the golden plains west of the Blue Mountains was never an easy one.

The town was officially gazetted in 1833, but development was slow. After the discovery of gold the entire region boomed as, typically, thousands of diggers flocked in search of riches.

The coaching company, Cobb & Co., relocated its headquarters to Bathurst in 1862. The entry into town of its 103 horses, eighty in harness, pulling ten red-painted coaches and two feed wagons was described as being like 'the triumphant entry of a first-class equestrian troupe'. By 1870 the company was running 30,000 horses across the eastern states, all centred on Bathurst.

The General Store, Kiandra, c. 1900

£2,000,000 worth of gold was eventually gouged out of the snow-covered Kiandra hillsides.

– George Preshaw –

George Ogilvy Preshaw had grown up on the Castlemaine diggings, where his father had a doctor's surgery at Campbell's Creek.

He was posted to Kiandra in 1860, and when the gold played out by the middle of 1861 he was transferred to Lambing Flat – the next great rush.

The roads of the Riverina were the favourite haunts of the most notorious of New South Wales bushrangers, and as he crossed the country to take up his new posting at Lambing Flat Preshaw had to be careful to avoid being asked to 'Bail up' on the lonely roads.

On the way a young man on horseback had informed him that:

> Lambing Flat was deserted; that there had been a great 'roll-up'; the bankers had fled for Yass with their treasure; the military had been telegraphed for … the courthouse had been burned down … and the town was in a complete state of uproar.[12]

Preshaw dismissed this news, but on arrival he found it all to be true. He had arrived at Lambing Flat in the middle of the riots against the Chinese.

He telegraphed Sydney for instructions, and was ordered to proceed to Yass where, with all of the other bankers, he waited until peace had been restored.

under him … I was puzzled to account for this, but on examination found it was caused by the snow, which was a foot or two deep at the back of the tent, thawing. The floor was one mass of puddle.[13]

By June the miners devised a scheme to engage all the Chinese in the region to bring up much-needed supplies, as it was impossible for pack-horses to get through.

A great feature of Kiandra was Kidd's Hotel, and its restaurant provided hot meals for the diggers:

> Gold Commissioners, bankers, squatters, swells, come to see the rush, burly diggers just as they had left their work, shanty-keepers, bullies, loafers, and niggers, all pierced with cold and impelled by hunger …[14]

crowded into the single room in which two narrow tables ran the entire length of the building. The nearby Carmichael's Empire Hotel opened a dance-room on 18 September 1860; however, there were only three dance-girls. Diggers who missed out on a female partner had to take a 'hairy-faced gentleman or not dance at all'. The floor was thick with mud, and Preshaw recorded:

> It struck me as a queer sight to see hairy-faced men in pea jackets, and long boots, with pipes in their mouths, dancing together.[15]

The winter had been so harsh that only the hardiest remained. Alongside dancing, drinking and brawling (which they did just to keep warm) the Kiandra diggers were the first in Australia to go skiing, swooshing down the slopes with palings strapped to their feet.

The Kiandra rush only lasted until after an extremely cold spell in the middle of 1861, when the rush to the warmer climes of Lambing Flat enticed the diggers down off the mountain.

The Tambaroora Field

The story of Bernard Otto Holtermann, posed proudly with 'his' famous nugget in his renowned photograph, is an interesting tale of opportunism at its best.

Holtermann migrated to Australia from Germany in 1858. After spending some years at various positions in Sydney and at times abroad, Holtermann eventually joined a fellow-countryman, Louis Beyers, at Hill End, just out of Bathurst.

Hill End and the nearby goldfields community of Gulgong were developing into a rich, deep-lead mining district, and Holtermann and Beyers established the Star of Hope mine there.

At one stage Holtermann was short of funds, and sold his share in the mine to another digger at Hill End, a ticket-of-leave man known as 'Northumberland Jimmie'. He hurriedly bought back his share after Beyers showed him the floor of the mine littered with small nuggets following a successful blast. Jimmie was less than pleased when he discovered the reason for Holtermann's undue haste.

Holtermann appointed himself as mine manager after the Star was floated, and a company was formed on 17 April 1872. Seven months later they unearthed the largest specimen of reef gold ever discovered. Holtermann demanded that the mass should be removed from the underground shaft in one piece. Of course, this was a difficult operation for the miners as the heavy lump had to be dug away from all sides, but Holtermann had a great plan for this piece of gold.

The famous photographic portrait of Holtermann standing next to 'his' nugget was never actually taken. The image that he was to use over and over again for the rest of his days was a montage created by the A&A Co. photographic assistant, Charles Bayliss, from a shot of the nugget taken on the day and a shot of Holtermann leaning against a studio prop. The two negatives were brought together years later, well after the nugget had been to the crusher.

Both Holtermann and Beyers became very wealthy men. Holtermann set about doing good works, became involved in public affairs, constructed buildings and churches, and built a large turreted mansion in Sydney, where he even had a stained-glass window created of this image.

German-born prospector, Bernard Otto Holterman poses with the nugget that made him famous
Photograph by Charles Bayliss

(HOLTERMANN COLLECTION, MITCHELL LIBRARY, STATE LIBRARY OF NEW SOUTH WALES)

The mass of gold and quartz weighing 630 lbs, and valued at £12,000, was unearthed by miners working for Holtermann and his partner, Louis Beyers, in the Star of Hope mine in 1872.

Holtermann used this gold-encrusted quartz monolith as a symbol for the rest of his life.

(OPPOSITE)
Whim and Shaft Houses, Hawkin's Hill

(HOLTERMANN COLLECTION, MITCHELL LIBRARY, STATE LIBRARY OF NEW SOUTH WALES)

The harshness of the weather high up on the central New South Wales plateaus made for some ingenious bush architecture.

On observing these examples of bush carpentry one correspondent wrote:

the horse which works the whim is in every case sheltered from snow and rain by a very picturesque octagon building roofed to a point in bark ... the make of these whims displays no mean proficiency in bush carpentry and the liberality with which they are supported by struts and braces is marvellous.[16]

A&A Photographic Studio in
Tambaroora Street, Hill End, in 1872
(HOLTERMANN COLLECTION, MITCHELL LIBRARY,
STATE LIBRARY OF NEW SOUTH WALES)

Holtermann owned the land that the
studio occupied, and he had an interest
in the company, and in the *Hill End
Observer* that occupied the building
next door.

Photographer Charles Bayliss, who
took over after the death of Henry
Merlin, in 1876, stands in the doorway,
with the studio and darkroom assistant
just behind. Their caravan driver stands
to the left of the doorway, and the young
boy in white is thought to be the driver's
son, as he is often seen in photographs
taken by A&A.

Henry Beaufoy Merlin, 1872
Merlin was the photographer who
established his American & Australian
Photographic Company's Studios at Hill
End.

All of the photographs on pages 224-9
were taken by the company in the early
1870s.

Holtermann invested in all sorts of schemes, one of the most curious being the creation of Holtermann's Life-preserving Drops, which
claimed to cure 'asthma, bronchitis, colds, diarrhoea, dysentery,
fevers, head-aches – cures sore throats, diphtheria, whooping cough,
incipient consumption, sprains, bruises and gout'.

Needless to say, the advertising for the drops featured Holtermann
and 'his' nugget, set among typographic filigree extolling the virtues
of its contents.

Northumberland Jimmie eventually struck it rich in the mine he
worked at Hawkins Hill with Black Nat, an escaped American negro
slave. Nat had travelled to Australia on the same boat as Hargraves
and the brother of James Marshall, who had found the first gold at
Sutter's Mill in California. Jimmie rode into the history books one
day when he shod his pony with golden shoes and trotted through the
streets of Hill End. This act, however remarkable it may have seemed
to the diggers at Hill End, was repeated on several other diggings,
such was the exuberant extravagance of the fortunate digger, no
matter where Lady Luck had found him.

> **– KERR'S HUNDREDWEIGHT –**
> *This nugget was unearthed close
> to Hargraves's claim in July 1851.
> Kerr's Hundredweight weighed
> 75 lbs and contained 700 oz of gold.
> It was broken into three pieces
> for ease of removal.*

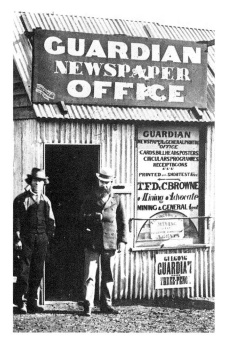

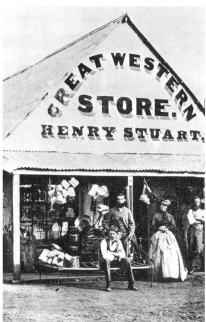

The editor of the Gulgong *Guardian*, T. F. De Courcy Browne, with his runner, Henry Beal, outside the Gulgong office

Browne was a fierce advocate for miners' rights, and suffered many writs for libel in the course of his public duty.

Henry Stuart's Great Western Store

This building on Tambaroora Street, Hill End, still stands today. Stuart sold a huge range of goods from these substantial wide-fronted premises, from griddles to beds, pots to paintbrushes.

Smith's Cheap Jack Tobacco & Fancy Goods Warehouse (Wholesale & Retail)

This, the smallest shop on Clarke Street, Hill End, probably has the most impressive title. All of that in a building that measured only 8 feet across.

(ALL PHOTOGRAPHS HOLTERMANN COLLECTION, MITCHELL LIBRARY, STATE LIBRARY OF NEW SOUTH WALES)

Henry Hilton's Golden Age Hotel

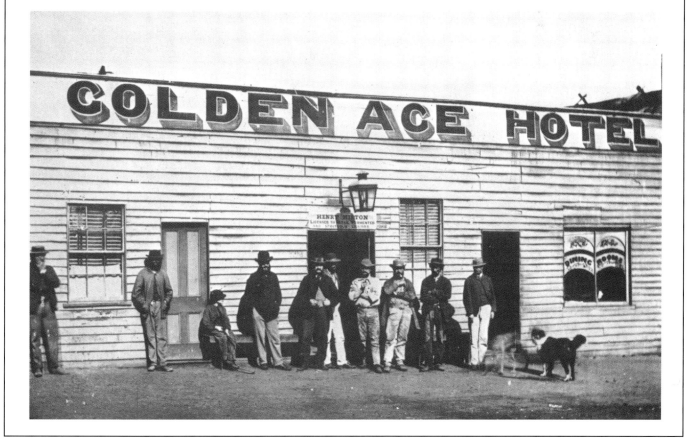

– HENRY LAWSON & GULGONG GOLD –

HENRY LAWSON, 'the bard of the bush', was born in a tent at Grenfell, on the New South Wales goldfields, in 1867.

After his parents split up when he was only fourteen years of age, Lawson moved down to Sydney, where he took jobs working in factories by day, attending school at night, hoping in vain to gain entry to university.

He eventually abandoned this goal, and began to submit his poems to the *Bulletin* magazine. By the time he was twenty, he was a regular contributor to the *Bulletin*.

Lawson's poems and short stories were based on the hardship and privations that he had experienced as a lad growing up on his parents dirt-poor farm on the goldfields. His collected work, *While the Billy Boils,* is full of the wry humour and rough mateship that typifies the Australian bush.

By the time he married at the age of 28, Lawson was already a compulsive drinker. His love of the bottle destroyed his marriage, and was eventually to destroy him.

Lawson was the workers' mate, often embittered by his alcoholism and envious of the growing reputation and apparent financial success of his lifelong 'nemesis', the lawyer-son of a country grazier, 'Banjo' Paterson. His writings express a left-wing egalitarianism that sought to revere the working poor, while debunking the affectations of the 'nobs'.

He was found dead in a rented cottage on 2 September 1922. This son of a Norwegian migrant, who was born poor and died destitute, had so enriched the nation that he was honoured with a state funeral.

Holtermann, Beyers and mates with gold-bearing reef taken from their **Star of Hope Mine at Hill End**
(*HOLTERMANN COLLECTION, MITCHELL LIBRARY, STATE LIBRARY OF NEW SOUTH WALES*)

(*OPPOSITE, CLOCKWISE FROM TOP LEFT*)
Timbered house at Gulgong
Barber T. B. Scurrah, leans against the doorpost of his Shampooing and Hairdressing Saloon in Gulgong. Apparently Scurrah was a man of many talents. Apart from his tonsorial skills, he was also known to belt out a good song, 'Does Yer Want to Buy a Dorg' and 'My Farder Kept a Brewery' being among his particular favourites.

The four men shown here standing in front of the **American Tobacco Warehouse & Fancy Goods Emporium** appear on the first Australian $10 note.

Miners at Gulgong
This group of diggers posing atop their shaft and at the windlass obviously could not afford the luxury of a whip horse, which would have cost them about £50. Here everything is winched up and down by hand. Although this was the norm on the shallow alluvial fields, the deep shafts at Gulgong would have made this a back-breaking and laborious exercise.

Times Bakery, Gulgong
Proprietors Thompson and McGregor pose in the Herbert Street doorway.

Dr Charles Zimmler's Dispensary
Mr White, who had been the manager of Barnes's Mudgee Drug Store, poses for the camera in his doorway opening onto Queen Street, Gulgong.

(*CENTRE*)
Donald's Circulating Library

(*LEFT*)
Granny's Visitor was the title given to this photograph when the negative was first printed.

The old lady (dressed in contrast to the stylish younger one to her right) was the inspiration for Lawson's classic poem 'Black Bonnet'.

(*FAR LEFT*)
Portrait of Henry Lawson, 1867-1941
Oil on canvas by Sir John Longstaff, c. 1900

(*R11550. BY PERMISSION, NATIONAL LIBRARY OF AUSTRALIA*)

(*ALL PHOTOGRAPHS HOLTERMANN COLLECTION, MITCHELL LIBRARY, STATE LIBRARY OF NEW SOUTH WALES*)

Oh, who would paint a goldfield,
    and limn the picture right,
As we have often seen it
    In early mornings light.

The yellow mounds of mullock
    With spots of red and white,
The scattered quartz that glistened
    Like diamonds in light.

The azure lines of ridges.
    The bush of darkest green,
The little homes of calico,
    That dotted all the scene.

Oh, they were lion-hearted
    Who gave our country birth!
Oh, they were of the stoutest sons
    From all the lands on earth!

– HENRY LAWSON

All of the photographs shown here were used by Australian designer Gordon Andrews as part of a collage of images behind the portrait of writer Henry Lawson on the first Australian $10 note.

Lawson grew up on these goldfields, and his stories often reflect the hardship and the pioneering spirit he observed as a boy.

William Henry Corkhill
(TT83)

The photographs reproduced here are from the collection of William Henry Corkhill, whose family had long been acquainted with the Bate family in England (see caption opposite).

Corkhill, who was born in Cumberland, came to Australia with his family in 1854. He visited the Bates at Tilba in 1882, and stayed. He took a position as cheese-maker at Henry Bate's farm, and in 1883 married his daughter, Frances.

Bate had began to construct shops and dwellings for lease near his homestead, and these buildings ranged across the hillside that formed the town of Tilba Tilba. The buildings remained in the Bate family until the first buildings were sold in the early 1970s.

Corkhill also developed a passion for photography, and for the next twenty years he recorded almost every aspect of the district he had grown to love. Corkhill died in 1936, but his photographic record shows a community that changed little in his lifetime, the town owned for so long by the one family remained almost intact into the present age.

Tilba Tilba & Mt Dromedary

In 1877 the Cowdroy brothers found the reef they had all been searching for, about 500 yards from the summit of the granite mountain, at the foot of the last steep rise.

Although the terrain was almost impossible to work, there was a small mining boom that worked the mountain reefs until 1906. The Mount Dromedary Proprietary Gold Mining Co. Ltd pegged its first claim in 1878, and the lease situated close to Cowdroy's yielded 42,522 grains of gold by the end of the nineteenth century.

The Cole family pose under the verandah of their neat little slab-and-shingle hut.

The men worked in the Mt Dromedary mine, which by 1899 employed around fifty people.

(TT186)

Central Tilba, c. 1897

Numerous settlers had had an interest in the region around the Wallago Lake on the New South Wales Coast, 185 miles south of Sydney, since the first Europeans explored the area in the early years of the nineteenth century.

The Curlewis Brothers, who farmed at Ballalaba, staked a claim near Cobargo in 1833, and Dr Thomas Braidwood Wilson sent a party from Braidwood to establish his claim in the same region. In 1839, when Crown Land Commissioner Lambie was on one of his periodic inspections to the region from his base at Cooma, he found the station called 'Tolbedilbo', which consisted of one slab hut, 2 acres of wheat, 301 cattle, and 2 horses, spread over 8 square miles.

The first resident to settle in Tilba Tilba was Henry Jefferson Bate, who arrived in 1869, setting up his farm on a block he called 'Mountain View', near the site of the present settlement of Tilba.

(TT835)

(RIGHT)

Striking miners picnic at Half Way Rock on Mt Dromedary Road, 1898.

SOUTH AUSTRALIA
The Last Rush West

B Y THE END of the nineteenth century the world had become a harder place. Wars across Europe, in America, the Boer War and the Crimea were followed by years of economic depression that created a generation desperate to create its own future.

The romance of the diggings was replaced by the excitement of the stock exchange. Hordes of hardheaded investors jostled each other, frantic to buy into almost any mining venture. There were still great fortunes to be made from deep within the earth, and just as many to be lost. Towards the end of the nineteenth century the great Queensland mines opened, and the Golden Mile of Western Australia also drew thousands more, unable to resist the lure of gold, across the blistering desert sands.

The mining camps of the north and the west became the latest frontier towns, they welcomed a new breed of desperate men, the gamblers, boozers and shady characters, accompanied by scores of freshly painted ladies from Europe and the Orient, ready and willing to keep them company – and to share their wages.

The age of the bushranger may have been long gone, but the spirit of the 'wild colonial boy' was still evident on the hot and dusty diggings far from the eastern ports.

Teetulpa and Brady's Gully

If it was the similarity between the landscape around Bathurst and the hills of Sacramento that encouraged Edward Hargraves to prospect at Summerhill Creek in 1851, it is hard to imagine why Thomas Brady was scratching around in the shale on the desert sands near Waukaringa, in north-eastern South Australia, in 1886.

The landscape there must be one of the most uninviting of all the Australian goldfields. Where Assistant Surveyor-General Evans had extolled the beauty of the Turon, and Major Mitchell championed the 'great south countrie', what poet ever sang of the charms of the Teetulpa field?

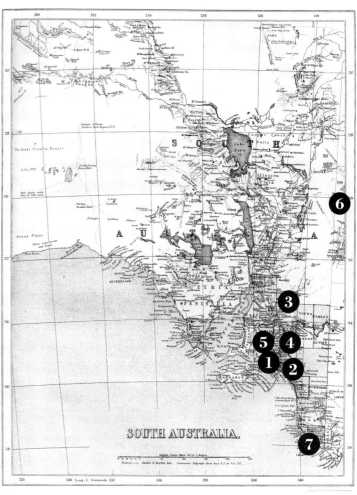

Map of South Australia
From *The History of Australia* by David Blair, McGready, Thompson and Niven, Glasgow, Melbourne & Dunedin, 1878 Lithograph by W. & A. K. Johnston, Edinburgh

(LA TROBE UNIVERSITY, BENDIGO, COLLECTION)

KEY:
1. Adelaide
2. Onkaparinga
3. Barossa
4. Mt Pleasant
5. Gawler
6. Teetulpa (Waukaringa)
7. Robe

The Diggings in the Barossa, c. 1885

(PHOTOGRAPH COURTESY OF THE
STATE LIBRARY OF SOUTH AUSTRALIA)

Gold was first discovered in the Barossa
in October 1868. Some of the claims
there were very rich, yielding at times
as much as £1000 per man.

To gain such a reward required
a lot of hard digging, but by this time
the pressure of the licence fee no longer
applied.

There were, however, few diggers who
could be bothered with such sustained
digging to depths of over 20 feet through
the hard conglomerate and sandstone of
these diggings.

The lure of gold did persist, and
in 1886 there was another great rush.
This time the polite society of Adelaide
stayed at home while the Teetulpa diggings
in the inhospitable desert country, closer
to the New South Wales border, drew
thousands, once again, to scratch about
in the dust seeking their fortune.

The coach journey was slow and wearisome, owing to rough roads and
fagged horses. At sundown, on rising to the crest of a low hill, the passengers beheld at their feet Brady's Gully, then in its infancy. There was
nothing attractive in the view. Few goldfields, perhaps, have been so
devoid of picturesque features as that of Teetulpa … hardly any trees
were to be seen, and no water ever ran in the watercourse, except during
heavy rain. In all directions could be seen reefs of white quartz standing
out in clear relief amid the prevailing colours of blue and salt-bush.[17]

Just to the north lay a great sandy plain, the only vegetation some
acacias that stood where water sometimes flowed after heavy rain.
The rush began in one such watercourse. The upper soil had been
washed away in a strong flood, exposing the auriferous gravel and
loose sand. Brady took shelter in that gully in a rare downpour and,
after the rain had cleared, a shaft of sunlight lit up a piece of gold
exposed by the rain.

The rush that followed saw 5000 diggers make the hot and dusty
journey from Adelaide (200 miles to the south), and pitch their tents
under the blazing desert sun.

Lack of water was the bane of this goldfield, the closest being at
Tonkin's Well about 2 miles from the diggings, and all the wash-dirt
was carried to the well for washing. Eventually water was pumped up
to holding tanks at the southern end of Brady's Gully.

Provisions were also scarce. However, one enterprising butcher
drove a small mob of 60 sheep to the diggings each day, and a baker's
cart carried 400 loaves a day 16 miles to the hungry diggers. All were
sold within minutes of their arrival. The baker could get as much as
2 shillings for each 2 lb loaf, and the fresh loaves were almost 'worth

their weight in gold' to the baker, who didn't even have to lift a shovel to make his fortune.

There were some fortunes to made on this field. One hot day a digger was lying stretched out on his claim in the creek-bed scraping at the gravel with his butcher's knife. Sweeping aside the gravel, he uncovered 'The Joker', a nugget the size and shape of a man's hand; it weighed 30 oz and was worth £120.

Afraid that others would see what he had found, and swarm across his patch, he sat bolt upright and placed his hand over the nugget. Another digger, working in the claim next to him, looked up, 'Found anything?' he asked.

'No! Seen the colour, that's all', he replied. He asked the digger to throw him his coat, which was lying close to the next claim. He said he wanted to have a smoke.

'Here you are, mate. But what's the matter? You look pale. Don't you feel right?' enquired the digger as he handed him his jacket.

'I'm all right; only the sun is a bit hot', he replied. Unable to contain himself any longer, he placed his coat over the nugget, laughing uncontrollably, until he became almost hysterical. Those around him thought he had a touch of the sun, and when he had calmed down he picked up his coat — and nugget — and went to his tent.

It was another ten days before the news of the discovery of 'The Joker' was broadcast, but few knew where his claim was to be found. A few days later nuggets were also found at Goslin's, an abandoned 'duffer' of a claim, where in one day a lucky digger unable to find a spot at Brady's scratched £100 worth from a nest of nuggets found in a hole in the rock.

The spirit of the first rushes in the eastern colonies was rekindled at Teetulpa. This goldfield was not dominated by managers and share-holders watching their investments grow from the comfort of a gentlemen's club in the city, this was a goldfield of muscle and men, of sweat and toil, of dirt and dust — and more dust — and mateship.

The diggings once again offered the spirit of adventure that men could not get standing behind a shop-counter in the city, or chasing behind some fat squatter's sheep. No matter how hard the work was, the pioneering life provided adventure for the lucky, and disappointing memories for those who failed.

Baker's Cart Arrives at the Diggings
From *Cassell's Picturesque Australasia*, 1889
(LA TROBE UNIVERSITY, BENDIGO, LIBRARY COLLECTION)

There was little enough water but no fuel sufficient for the diggers to make even their own damper on the Teetulpa goldfield.

As on most of the later diggings in the desert or the outback, the simple necessities of life proved to be the most difficult to obtain, expensive for some, and most profitable for others.

Aerated Water Factory on the Diggings
(PHOTOGRAPH COURTESY OF THE STATE LIBRARY OF SOUTH AUSTRALIA)

Teetulpa City

(PHOTOGRAPH COURTESY OF THE
STATE LIBRARY OF SOUTH AUSTRALIA)

The desert country offered almost
nothing for the comfort of the diggers.
All provisions had to be carted in, all
food, grog, goods and gear carried across
the desert to the tent city.

Diggers Crowd the Water Course at Tonkin's Well, 1886

(PHOTOGRAPH COURTESY OF THE
STATE LIBRARY OF SOUTH AUSTRALIA)

The diggers had to carry the dirt from
their claims on Brady's Gully to wash at
Tonkin's Well, 2 miles from Teetulpa.

Gold Diggers Camp, c. 1895

(PHOTOGRAPH COURTESY OF THE
STATE LIBRARY OF SOUTH AUSTRALIA)

A digger and his wife pose proudly
beside their makeshift canvas home
on the goldfields.

   Although these diggings were some
of the roughest, hottest and driest, there
was no need for a woman to stay away
from all the excitement.

WESTERN AUSTRALIA
The Goldfields of the Desert

G old had been found in the Kimberley area in the mid-1880s, and rich deposits had been discovered beneath the shifting sands of Southern Cross (Coolgardie) in 1892, but it was not until an Irishman, Patrick ('Paddy') Hannan, found the first small nuggets at Kalgoorlie on 14 June 1893 that the great rush to the western goldfields began.

At that time Australia was in the grip of economic depression, banks were failing in the east, the boom that had followed the first gold rush forty years earlier had burst. Where once labour had been impossible to find, there were now masses of unemployed and disappointed diggers desperate for work.

The great mines of Bendigo and Ballarat were closing down, one by one, the investors eventually defeated by water flooding into the deep underground tunnels. When the miners joined together to demand a fair day's pay for a hard day's work, and to demand to work only eight hours a day, deep mining became a precarious investment. The free-wheeling great colonial adventure had soured.

The finds in the west caused a rebirth of the digger spirit, as thousands of eager diggers once again rushed to the fields. They came overland by bicycle, by dray, on horseback, wagon and camel caravan.

The diggings on the western edge of the great Nullarbor Plain were not all like the verdant granite hills in the east, but beneath the desert sands lay the 'richest square mile on earth'. In time, over £100,000,000 worth of gold was won from these dusty fields.

The Golden Mile

A story typical of the hardships and the excitement encountered by miners on the Golden Mile is that of one miner's trip from the Bendigo goldfield to the West, recalled in the following excerpts from the diary kept by William Hocking (the author's paternal grandfather). The Hockings had migrated to Australia from Penzance in Cornwall, with William aged one, and he had grown up steeped in mining culture and the fellowship of the tight Protestant mining community that worked the Bendigo shafts.

In 1902 William Hocking set out to make his pile in the west:

Bendigo, 29 January 1902 - Having made up my mind that God willing I would go and try my luck in the West like a lot more I left working at the Great Southern Bendigo on January 29.[18]

After a train journey to Melbourne, William boarded a steamship bound for Fremantle, with one stop at Adelaide on the way. He was

Discoveries in Western Australia

1885 – The Kimberley
Mr E. T. Hardmann, W.A. Government Geologist found gold in the Kimberley district

1888 – The Pilbara
17 September 1892 – Coolgardie
Arthur Bayley & William Ford

14 June 1893 – Kalgoorlie
Patrick 'Paddy' Hannan

Bendigo miner, William Hocking, kept a diary of his journey to the west and his time on the East Murchison goldfields.

Excerpts from his diary, which were entered between January 1902 and August 1903, are reproduced in this chapter.

(HOCKING FAMILY COLLECTION)

Map of Western Australia, 1878
From *The History of Australia* by David
Blair, McGready, Thompson and Niven,
Glasgow, Melbourne & Dunedin, 1878
Lithograph by W. & A. K. Johnston,
Edinburgh

(*La Trobe University, Bendigo, Library Collection*)

KEY:

1. Southern Cross
2. Coolgardie
3. Kalgoorlie
4. Leinster
5. Lawlers (East Murchison goldfields)
6. The Kimberley

The diggings of the west were far
away from any established townships
when first discovered. Southern Cross
(as Kalgoorlie was then known), was
a dry, dusty settlement in the middle
of nowhere, and with almost nothing
to recommend it to anyone. Of course,
the lure of gold changed everything.

It was still miles from anywhere
until the railway came to Kalgoorlie
and Coolgardie in 1896, and remained
dry and dusty until a 560-km long
pipeline brought water to the desert
towns in 1902–3.

The scarcity of water had made sanitation difficult, and the 'colonial disease'
of typhoid took over 1000 lives between
1894 and 1899.

Bendigo miner, William Hocking,
recorded in his diary his observations
of the long, slow train trip in 1902 from
Perth:

Thursday 13th – saw a thing done that
I have read about – Train stopped –
Guard got off with mail Bag & walked
over to a Public House – stoped [*sic*]
a bit came out & off we went again –
very slow travelling; this new line just
opened but not yet taken over by the
Raily Dept. slow travelling here – some
of the line not ballasted – bit bumpy –
saw several camels from the train feeding
at Kookynie – saw large number of Camels
also Afgans [*sic*], Blackfellows – arrived
Malcolm 11-30.[19]

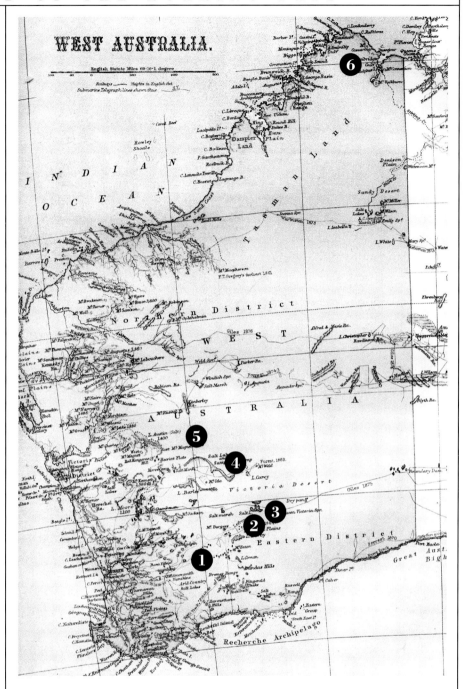

surprised to meet quite a large contingent of other miners from
Bendigo on board, and, although he was too seasick to join them in
the second saloon for Sunday service, he recorded in his diary that 'I
was up on deck and heard it all, felt it done me good, the singing was
nice'.[20]

A large number of the Bendigo deep-lead miners were Cornish
Methodists, whose life revolved around work, church and family; and
for the Methodists, singing ability was of utmost importance. William
takes particular note to record in his diary the varying ability of the
different congregations he joined up with on his journey to the west.

Miners from all over Australia were making their way west, but not
all were of the same persuasion, which seemed at times to shock

young William. After arriving in Fremantle, and a few days 'knocking about' in Perth he took an overnight train for Kalgoorlie:

> travelling all night. Grand country to travel through up till the time I could see ... at east Northam 2 chaps got in, one I used to work with back Little 180 Bendigo – Paddy Sullivan and his brother – all went well until we got to Southern Cross and there 6 navvies got in with their swags – off the Pipe track going to Coolgardie – the language they were using being terrible and the beer flowing freely. Got out and changed carriage at Boorabbin – found it more pleasant than such disgusting company ... one told me that I would not be on the fields long before I drank also, Lord forbid that such be the case.
>
> Got on coach at 1-25 pm arrived Leonora 3 pm ... left again 4-25 pm full load on, on the way to first stopping place saw Geo. Roberts who used to drive Lansell's Big Battery Engine about 2 miles out – reached Diorite King 8-30 pm.[21]

The train journey continued for several days, stopping at Doyle's Well and Poison Creek, and then on to Lawler, where he

> had to stop at a Hotel – no other places in these parts and was put in Bar parlour – did not smell too sweet – had three Austrians for companions and hear the Billiard Balls and the drink going on till about 12 o'clock.[22]

He spent some time on the goldfields before he was able to find employment, but eventually was taken on to work the nightshift at the Leinster Mine about 20 miles from Lawler:

> of all the mines I worked in the Leinster is the worst – Hot as fire and everything so slushy and greasy – have to keep washing your hands and tools. Put in timber. Drinking water and the heat turned me up but put the shift, cannot help drink in here. How the mine is so Hot and only 160 feet deep surprises me ... all hands go up to surface for crib when they fire. Have to leave it for 1/2 an hour or more for the smoke to clear and when you go down the smoke is very thick.[23]

Miner's Camp, West Australian diggings, c. 1902

(*HOCKING FAMILY COLLECTION*)

A group of Cornish miners from Bendigo pose outside their scrub and canvas camp on the East Murchison goldfields; William Hocking is on the right.

The difficulties faced in the construction of this shanty and other forms of abode are recorded in his diary:

> I went out into the bush for a stroll looking for poles for a tent but never found any long enough ... after breakfast went out looking for poles – went 2 or 3 miles got 5 after a terrible amount of trouble and left 3 behind thinking to go back for them – near got bushed this mulga scrub being very difficult to distinguish it

and after a terrible thunderstorm at 4 o'clock one afternoon

> the rain simply pours. My bed and blankets, boots and my portmanteau got all wet, over your boot tops in the tents – had to dig a drain all round to let water away – a typical West Australian experience ... the tent being new let the water through.[24]

Paddy Hannan Statue, Kalgoorlie
Photograph by Aaron Bunch, 1995

(*REX NAN KIVELL COLLECTION,
BY PERMISSION, NATIONAL LIBRARY OF AUSTRALIA*)

Bayley Street, Coolgardie, 1894
Photograph by Roy Millar

(Roy Millar, Kalgoorlie, W.A., Album 283, Rex Nan Kivell Collection, NK10699, By Permission, National Library of Australia)

When Arthur Bayley and William Ford made their first discovery they found 6 lbs gold in the first three hours of digging.

By the time they rode into the little settlement of Southern Cross on 17 September 1892, Bayley was carrying more than 30 lbs of the precious metal in his saddlebags.

Within six months 1000 men had rushed to peg their claims in the desert sands. By the end of 1893 Coolgardie was declared a town, and the first two-storeyed building was under construction.

Coolgardie grew rapidly, like so many other gold towns, but it was a hard place to live for the almost-entirely male population.

Its isolation from the main coastal settlements and the absence of women led to the usual alcoholism and aggressive criminal behaviour that also typified the earlier eastern goldfields.

He goes on to wonder why he left the grand old mines of Bendigo for the West, and complains of the incessant nuisance of the little black flies that robbed him of his daytime sleep, and the poor quality of the drinking water that constantly turned his stomach:

there is a sly-grog shop here and some of the men get hold of this poison which quickly upsets them … a little excitement – Coach arrival from Lake Way with Gold Escort. Mounted Constable riding behind Rifle and Revolver foot Constable on Coach with Rifle also. This goes through every four to five weeks. Went down and seen it off – Leinster gold went with it. Two nice ingots about 900 oz – Blacks around Lawlers very poor specimens – Mixing with Australians has not done them any good. Women smoke as well as men – terrible cadgers – the disease among them is very bad – The Leinster is a great place [for] stacks of flies, ants, insects get in amongst the bread, weevils in the flour – Menzies, Boulder or Coolgardie far before this place – would never bring a woman here, not a fit place but the Lord's way is not ours – What a grand lesson to learn like the Apostle Paul 'In whatsoever state to be content (but it's a hard one)

March 28 – They have put poppet legs up at the claim – up about a week or more (Iron) looks more like a mine now and they are skidding the shaft and going to put cage on as soon as it is ready …

June 14 – Man committed suicide cut his throat – drink again.

June 23 – Heard 2 men suffocated at Mt Sir Samuel (dynamite fumes) were working in a winze firing out, one went down away a good while so his mate went down and he never came up so a third man went down after them – but by this time there were a few men there who got him up but he was pretty bad.[25]

William moved up to the mines at Moyans after underground workers were put off at Leinster, and for a number of weeks continued to present himself at the mines several times a day until he was lucky enough to be picked to start on the night-shift:

Nov 9th – Went to Church Sunday evening, good congregation. Very fair singing.

Nov 10th – up twice to the mine looking for work at 8-half past, no show – over 30 there at night concert in aid of Wesley Church we stood outside and heard it all. Some of the singing was fearful.

Nov 11th – up again twice no chance.

Nov 12th – up again twice no show. Bob Matthews got a start night-shift on machine.

Nov 13th – up again twice no show – really thought we would have been on – its disheartening. There's such a crowd there every time over 20 men every day for the week …

Nov 16th – to my great surprise was told to come on Sunday night night-shift on the machines … got on allright up a rise at the 500 foot level …[26]

In the early months of 1903 the diaries show that shifts were becoming irregular, one day short here, a half day lost there until the heat, dust and flies drove William to hop aboard the train for Perth on Easter Monday, 13 April 1903:

May 6th – [came up] by the Express and arrived at Golden Square [Bendigo] a little after 8pm after 15 months absence none the worse for my trip. Thankful to God for all his mercy toward me in sparing me to get back home amongst all my loved ones again.[27]

– LASSETER'S REEF –

In 1897 an Afghan camel-driver found the exhausted body of Harold Bell Lasseter sprawled in the dust near the central Western Australian border.

Recovering in a surveyor's camp, Lasseter claimed that he had discovered a glittering gold-bearing reef almost 6 miles long near the border in the Petermann Ranges. Although the rock samples that Lasseter had in his pockets when he was found proved to be encouraging to the surveyor, when questioned on the precise whereabouts of his reef Lasseter himself proved to be somewhat taciturn.

For the next thirty years he kept the location of the reef to himself, until in 1930 he was able to raise the funds and mount an expedition, with himself as guide, back to his mythical reef.

Before long, however, there was dissension within the expedition party, and Lasseter struck out on his own, taking a few camels with him. As he departed he cried out, 'If I don't find the reef, I'm never coming back'.

His departing remark proved prophetic: he was never seen alive again. Bob Buck, an experienced bushman, led a search party and claimed to have discovered Lasseter's body in a cave at Winter's Glen. Buck returned with Lasseter's papers, which like those other ill-fated adventurers half a century earlier, Burke & Wills, had been buried beneath a tree marked 'DIG'.

Further expeditions have been mounted over the years, but none have ever found the glittering reef that drew Lasseter to his lonely death.

Coolgardie, Bayley Street, Northside, 1894

Outside Hannan's Warden's Court, Kalgoorlie, 1895
Photograph by Roy Millar

At the beginning of the rush most buildings were crude shacks created from scrub or whatever materials were at hand.

Later, corrugated iron was the easiest building material to carry across the desert plains. By and by the hessian-covered shacks and iron buildings were replaced with timber, brick and stone, the towns losing their frontier appearance and taking on the respectable look of a prosperous mining town.

These fine looking iron premises were in the main street of Coolgardie; camels brought supplies to the goldfields from as far away as South Australia.

Harold Bell Lasseter and Family

The final note written by Lasseter to his wife suggests the hopelessness that can surround those seduced by the dream of gold:

> I am paying the penalty with my life, may this be a lesson to others ... Good Bye Rene darling wife mine and don't grieve ... but it does seem cruel to die alone out here – my last prayer is 'God be merciful to me as a sinner and be good to those I leave behind' ...
> xxx Harry x

The next entry in his diary records:

Arrived Rufton New Zealand on Monday night Aug 10th 1903, stopped at Railway Hotel two nights ... started work Tuesday, afternoon 18th August ... [28]

William married Emily Jane Nankervis, and they honeymooned on the New Zealand diggings. He worked at the Otago mines for several years before they returned to Bendigo with the first three of their seven children.

William's story is typical of the thousands of young men who had little more to trade than their muscle, what seemed like an almost spiritual need for hard work, a strong dose of the Protestant work ethic and a burning desire to prove themselves fit and worthy of their hire. He died of miners' phthisis (a common lung complaint caused by inhalation of dust and grit) in 1922.

William and Emily Hocking, in the snow, outside their miner's cottage in Otago, N.Z.

QUEENSLAND & THE TERRITORY
Tropical Fever

Mt Morgan to the Palmer River (Cooktown)

Although there were some rushes to Queensland in the 1850s it was not until the alluvial gold in the southern colonies had played out and companies were searching for new deposits that the Queensland mines came into being. Men with experience on other fields were seeking for opportunities to apply that knowledge and to make their mark in Australia's goldfields' history.

Some of the early rushes to Queensland were disastrous. The worst came early in 1858 when some gold was found at Canoona, on the Fitzroy River (north of where Rockhampton now stands). There was some speculation that this rush was completely fabricated to inject an instant population into the newly separated colony of Queensland.

Over 15,000 diggers came from the south, but, when the rush proved to be a shicer (no good), they were left stranded over 1000 miles from Sydney. There were no provisions, no stores, and very little gold for trading, even if there had been any supplies. The diggers were eventually brought out of the isolated diggings by sea in a rescue operation financed by the Victorian government and through public subscription. Victoria felt an obligation to the large number of diggers from that colony who had been seduced by the promise of riches in Queensland; they also felt some responsibility for the deeds

Mount Morgan Gold Mine, near Rockhampton, Queensland
Watercolour by Ethel M. Turner, c. 1890
(REX NAN KIVELL COLLECTION, T2255. BY PERMISSION, NATIONAL LIBRARY OF AUSTRALIA)

The old Ironstone Mountain behind the two largest chimney stacks has completely disappeared; it is now a huge hole in the ground.

(OPPOSITE)
Portrait of Walter Hall 1913
Frederick McCubbin, 1855-1917, Australia
Oil on canvas, 90.2 x 151.8 cm
Presented by the Walter and Eliza Hall Trust, 1913
(NATIONAL GALLERY OF VICTORIA, MELBOURNE)

Map of Queensland
From *Picturesque Atlas of Australasia*, 1889
(PRIVATE COLLECTION)

KEY:
1. Palmer River Diggings
2. Croydon
3. Charters Towers
4. Ravenswood
5. Mt Morgan
6. Gympie

– Walter Russell Hall –

One of Australia's greatest philanthropists, Walter Russell Hall, made his fortune on the Queensland goldfields.

Walter Hall, born in Herefordshire, England, in 1831, had sailed for Sydney in 1852 with very little sterling in his pockets. He worked for retailer David Jones for a while before he headed south to the Ballarat diggings. He was there at the time of the Eureka rebellion, but was not within the stockade, as was his brother Thomas. He moved on to Bendigo and the Ovens, but with little success. Hall began a carrying agency between Ballarat and Melbourne before he became the agent for Cobb & Co. at Wood's Point.

In 1861 he joined with James Rutherford and others to take over the successful coaching firm from its original owners. Hall eventually became Cobb's Sydney agent.

When his brother Thomas, who by this time was the manager of the Rockhampton branch of the Queensland National Bank, suggested they join with a syndicate to invest in the Mt Morgan mine, Walter took the opportunity that would make them all very wealthy. The Mount Morgan Gold Mining Co. Ltd was registered in Queensland in 1886.

Hall had donated £5000 to help send the Australian contingent to the Boer War; he offered £10,000 to the Dreadnought Fund, which helped establish the Dreadnought Farm and Sydney Naval College.

When he died in 1913, his estate was valued for probate at £2,915,513; the main beneficiary was his wife, Eliza, whom he had married in 1874. When she died, their endowment to the nation lived on in the Walter & Eliza Hall Institute established in Melbourne.

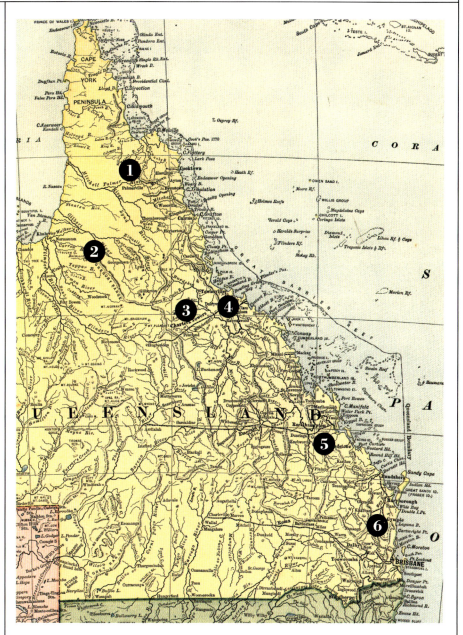

of unscrupulous shipowners and agents who had largely concocted glowing reports of the Fitzroy River goldfield with the express purpose of bringing hearty, working men into the new Colony of Queensland.

The Queensland Aboriginals were hostile to both Europeans and Chinese alike. At the time there many rumours of cannibals eating Chinese killed in the Palmer River area, near Cooktown. The remoteness of the tropical region, and the almost total lack of facilities and difficulties in obtaining supplies, left many diggers stranded, starving, and sorry they had ever stepped aboard a ship bound for the tropics.

Thorvald Weitemeyer was a digger from Denmark who recorded in his diaries his experience of these goldfields:

> When I landed there [Cooktown] looked wild enough. There were some
> thousands of people camped out in tents … all the loafers, pickpockets
> and card-sharpers seemed to have trooped up from Brisbane, Sydney

RAVENSWOOD—CHARTERS TOWERS GOLDFIELD, QUEENSLAND.

and Melbourne ... and the robbing of tents was an everyday occurrence ... although it had been known far and wide that any one who wanted to go to the Palmer must either starve or carry six months rations with him, still many destitute and good-for-nothing people could be seen wherever one looked. Men would walk about among the tents and ... beg. There was a great deal of sickness ... it was a common sight to see men lying helpless, writhing with pain on the ground, some of them bellowing out for pity or mercy ... men would pass such a poor object with the greatest apathy.[29]

The colony was prone to torrential rain, and rivers would flood almost without warning, leaving diggers cut off once again from supplies. One such flood on the Normanby River left a large group of miners stranded on one side of the raging river, while those on the other side had rations to spare: 'There we were, looking across at one another – they shaking their gold-purses at us, and we showing them the flour-bags'.[30]

Two men attempted to cross, and were swept away and drowned. No further attempts were made. Weitemeyer tells of a shipmate of his who had become separated from his main camp by rising waters, and was not found until after the wet season had passed:

His dead body was found in his tent ... he had died of hunger, yet under his head was a bag with eighteen pounds' weight of gold in it ...

The country around is very poorly off for game; besides they had no powder, and so they had been eating their horses, their dogs, and at last their boots! It is a fact that they used to boil their blucher boots for twenty-four hours and eat them with weeds! It takes something to make a Queensland miner lie down and die ...[31]

*I done a lot of prospectin' in Victoria
and New South Wales.
I was one o' the first on New Ballarat,
or Indigo, Chiltern as it is now.
From there I went to the Snowy River,
an' then I took a notion an' went off to
the Port Curtis Rush, an' that's how I
first came to Queensland.*

*I found a good gully or two at Gympie.
After that I travelled over to Western
Creek, and done a bit of prospectin'
all the way.
I was at Gilberton for a bit,
and then at the Cape River.*

*I was at all them little diggins 'round
Rockhampton, and now here I am at
the Palmer.*

*I reckon I've done wanderin'.
I've a goodish bit of gold,
an' I'm not so young as I used to be.
I reckon I'll settle down soon an' get a
good reef as'll keep me comfortable till
I kicks the bucket an' passes in me
checks.*

– ALEXANDER BOYD

Miners pose outside their crude hut
on the Queensland diggings
Photograph by Richard Daintree
(STOCK PHOTOS, MELBOURNE)

Although the great centres of Charters
Towers, Gympie and Mt Morgan returned
huge rewards for the owners, they still
relied on men such as these to cut the ore
from the earth.

Townships grew beside the mines,
stretching out across the valleys.
By 1889 the population of Mt Morgan
had grown to 10,000. While the town
had begun to erect substantial brick and
timber buildings, the itinerant nature of
the diggers meant that many still lived
in bark and canvas huts.

Charters Towers to Croydon

Jupiter Mosman, a young Aboriginal stockman out looking for a stray pack-horse, first found some nuggets on the Burdekin River flats on Christmas Day 1871. Prospectors Hugh Mosman (Jupiter's boss), George Clarke and James Fraser rushed back to Ravenswood to lodge a claim reward.

The district was named after the mining warden of Ravenswood, William Eurbank Melbourne Charters, who first registered the claim. Reminiscent of the hilly outcrops in England known as tors, the area was duly named Charters Tors; it was not long before the name suffered from Australianisation, and was thereafter known as Charters Towers.

Another stockman found the first gold at Mt Morgan, but told no one of his find, and made no claim. About 1880 William McKinley made a find on Ironstone Mountain (as Mt Morgan was then known), but, because he had been swindled out of a claim before, he decided to prospect over the whole mountain until he found the best claim of all. However, when Fred Morgan, the owner of the Criterion Hotel in Rockhampton, got an inkling of McKinley's activities, he himself pegged out a claim. He soon found some good stuff, formed a partnership with his brothers, Ned and Tom, and three other mates

Gold digger's sale, Queensland,
c. 1864–70
Photograph by Richard Daintree
(Rex Nan Kivell Collection, T3218.
By Permission, National Library of Australia)

Most diggers came to the goldfields for only a short time, to get rich quick and return home, set up for life. Most joined into working parties, pooled their resources, and kitted themselves out for the journey.

When they had tired of the adventure, fallen on hard times, or won a prize in this glittering lottery, they sold all their goods before quitting the goldfields – and there were always eager new chums ready to purchase the scarce goods and equipment on offer at a digger's auction. Although premium prices were often paid, it certainly beat lugging the kit for miles through the bush or paying a bullocky for the privilege.

(Thomas Hall, William Pattison and Knox D'Arcy), and they began to mine the mountain.

After four years the Morgan brothers sold out to Hall, Pattison and D'Arcy, who were then joined by Walter Hall; and the Mount Morgan Gold Mining Co. Ltd was formed. It was floated on the stock exchange in 1886, and soon became the talk of the colonies, as at the time only eight men held one million £1 shares each, which in any one's language was a phenomenal amount of money.

Within the first few years the company grew twenty-fold, and over 80 tons of gold taken from old Ironstone Mountain, gold that was described as the purest ever poured in Queensland. Ironstone is no more, so much dirt was cut away that a huge crater lies where once a mountain loomed, and the area is now known as the 'big hole'.

The east-coast ports of Rockhampton, Cairns and Cooktown and Normanton on the Gulf of Carpentaria to the west were established to provide communication and supplies in and out of the goldfields as the population of the separated Colony of Queensland (1859) grew from 30,000 to 100,000 in the first seven years of the gold rush. Normanton became a busy port for a few years after gold was discovered in 1885 at Croydon, 150 miles inland. At the height of this rush 7000 diggers were camped on this scrubby, white-ant-ridden, waterless plain. There were 36 hotels in Croydon during the rush, but today almost nothing remains. Over 21 tons of gold were taken from this goldfield by the end of the century.

Gympie

A field had also opened at Gympie in September 1867, following the discovery there by a wandering prospector, James Nash. Nash had dumped his swag on the banks of the Mary River, lit his fire, got his

---

– GYMPIE –
Approximately 113 tons of gold were taken from the Gympie mines, until the last closed in 1920.

– MT MORGAN –
The Mount Morgan Gold & Copper Mines had produced over £19,000,000 worth of metal, and paid £8,079,166 in dividends, by 1903.

Mullock heaps surround the shafts on the early Gympie field, c. 1868
Photograph by Richard Daintree
(JOHN OXLEY COLLECTION, STATE LIBRARY OF QUEENSLAND)

billy going, and panned a while as he waited for it to boil. He struck it lucky. The *Maryborough Chronicle* described the find as a 'reef loaded with gold like plums in a Christmas pudding'. Within days nearby Maryborough became a virtual ghost town. Gympie grew just like every other gold town – like topsy. Tents were thrown up all over the place; shanty stores, butcher's shambles and rough-and-tumble pubs lined the crooked streets, filled with brawling, drunken diggers who caroused and chased the 'ladies' from dusk until dawn.

There was an influx of over 600 Chinese into Nashville (as Gympie was known at the time). It was their custom to take up claims abandoned by European diggers. The *Maryborough Chronicle* reported on 16 May 1868:

> The Mongolians have lately been arriving in gangs. Their favourite place seems to be the flat at the end of Nash's Gully. They are orderly and harmless and we presume there can be no objection to them.

It was not long though, before the European diggers protested over the success the Chinese had from the abandoned field. The Chinese took thousands of pounds worth of gold from the field, leaving only rubble to welcome the diggers as they fell back on Nashville after the other rushes proved unsuccessful.

By mid-1868 a 'roll-up' was called, and, just as their fellow-countrymen had suffered before them in California, on the Buckland River and at Lambing Flat, the 'Celestials were [sent] flying helter-skelter, taking flying leaps over claims, sometimes into them, when they would be dragged out by their pigtails and cuffed on again'.[32]

The Chinese were driven from these diggings, but came back in greater numbers when the next wet season forced most Europeans out of their old, damp holes.

A great flood rushed through Gympie in 1893 when the Mary River rose to 90 feet above its normal level. All the mines were flooded, and over 120 houses were seen floating downstream. The floods were largely the result of clearing the forests for timbers, and the runoff was incredible. The last of the mines, the North Phoenix, closed in 1925.

James Nash, who found the first gold that started the Gympie goldfields

(JOHN OXLEY COLLECTION, STATE LIBRARY OF QUEENSLAND)

By the time that James Nash was wandering around in the hills of Queensland there had been many attempts to discover a viable goldfield in that new colony.

Wherever men roamed, whether squatter, settler, shepherd or itinerant wanderer, they all cast an eye over the terrain hoping to recognise a gold-bearing landscape.

Every now and then one would be rewarded with a lucky find – and then a rush would start. In the early days few were sustainable, but the rush that followed Nash lasted for almost half a century.

Departure of the Steamship Gothenburg from Adelaide for Port Darwin
Wood engraving from *Illustrated Australian News*, 17 June 1873
(LA TROBE PICTURE COLLECTION, STATE LIBRARY OF VICTORIA)

Northern Territory – The Darwin rush

Gold had been discovered in the Northern Territory as early as 1865, when some 'specs' were taken back to South Australia by a failed government exploration party that had been attempting to establish a settlement at Escape Cliffs. In 1869 the survey party that marked the site of Darwin found gold in the Blackmore and Charlotte Rivers, and some at Tumbling Waters. The discovery that started the rush to Palmerston (as Darwin was then known) came later in 1871, when the construction gangs that were building the overland telegraph found gold at Pine Creek.

Diggers from all over Australia rushed to the north: once again shiploads of diggers sailed from Port Phillip, from Sydney Harbour and Adelaide eager to get at this, the latest rush. No matter how remote the goldfield, an almost insatiable appetite for gold lured the diggers onward. Many also travelled overland, following the newly-built telegraph line into Darwin.

Thousands of Chinese workers, who had been brought into the territory from Singapore as cheap labour, also rushed to the diggings. By 1896 most of the mines were controlled by English companies. Syndicates had been formed at the start of the rush as investors bought up the diggings, using information that was passed down the wire. Most of these were worthless, and most failed.

Port Darwin Rush – The SS Omeo Leaving the Sandridge Railway Pier
Wood engraving from *Illustrated Australian News*, 10 October 1872
(LA TROBE PICTURE COLLECTION, STATE LIBRARY OF VICTORIA)

NOTES

Chapter 1 – Gold! Gold! Gold!

1   From *Hutchings California Magazine*, November 1857.

2   ibid.

3   Secretary of State Earl Grey to Governor La Trobe, 12 January 1852.

4   From the diaries of William Swain; recalled in J. S. Holliday, *The World Rushed In*, Simon & Schuster, USA,1983, pp. 312–29.

5   ibid.

6   From the memoir of Eugene Ring. A New Yorker, Ring began his adventures in California in 1848, after a long illness. He travelled across the Panama isthmus and up the coast to San Francisco, returning to New York in 1851.

7–8 ibid.

9   Swain, op. cit.

10 JoAnn Levy, *They Saw the Elephant: Women in the California Gold Rush*, University of Oklahoma Press, 1992.

11–14 ibid.

15 The Burlingame Treaty was signed between the United States and China, which regulated commerce and immigration. The treaty allowed for a free flow of immigration and travel between the two nations. The treaty was named after Anson Burlingame, a former American ambassador to China who was largely responsible for the negotiations.

Chapter 2 – First Gold in Australia?

1   George Sutherland, *Tales of the Goldfields*, George Robertson, Melbourne, 1880, p. 14.

2   James Flett, *The History of Gold Discovery in Victoria,* Hawthorn Press, Melbourne, 1970, p. 421.

3   ibid, p. 419.

4   John A. Graham, *Early Creswick: The First Century* (Facsimile Edition), Creswick Historical Museum, 1987, Creswick, Vic., pp. 174–5.

5   Flett, op. cit., p. 350.

6   William B. Withers, *The History of Ballarat* (Facsimile Edition), Queensberry Hill Press, Carlton, Vic., 1980, p. 9.

7   C.W. Langtree, Secretary of Mines (1888), in Flett, op.cit., p. 351.

8   William Howitt, *Land, Labour & Gold*, Lowden, Kilmore, Vic., 1972, Letter X, 25 December 1852, p. 93.

9   Antoine Fauchery, *Letters From a Miner in Australia*, Georgian House, Melbourne, Vic.,1965, p. 51.

10 Flett, op. cit., p. 61.

11 ibid., p. 62.

12 From *Cassell's Picturesque Australasia*, first published 1889 (Facsimile Edition), Child & Henry, Fine Arts Press, Gordon, NSW, 1978, p. 790.

13 ibid.

14 Clacy, Mrs Charles. *A Lady's Visit to The Gold Diggings of Australia in 1852–55*, Lansdowne Press, Melb., Vic., 1963, p.124.

15 ibid.

16 ibid., p. 125.

Chapter 3 – The World Turned Topsy-Turvy

1   John Dunmore Lang, *The Australian Emigrant's Manual or, A Guide to the Gold Colonies of New South Wales and Port Phillip*, Partridge & Oakley, London, 1852. p. xvi.

2   John Capper, *Phillip's Emigrant's Guide to Australia,* 1852, p. 18.

3   Lang, op.cit

4   Lang, op. cit., p. 5.

5   ibid., p. 3.

6   Capper, op. cit., p. 21.

7   Quoted in Serle, p. 68, from the diary of W. Rayment. Geoffrey Serle, *The Golden Age*, Melbourne University Press, Carlton, Vic.,1963.

Chapter 4 – The Last of England

1   Henry Kingsley, *My Adventures on the Australian Goldfields*, ch. 1.

2   J. B. Barnes, quoted in Serle, op. cit., p. 49.

3   Kingsley, op. cit.

4   Dante Gabriel Rossetti, *A Victorian Romantic,* London, 1849, p. 114.

5   Advertisement, Truro, Cornwall, England, 19 August 1839.

6   Clacy, op. cit., p. 136.

7   Severyn Korzelinski, *Memoirs of Gold-Digging in Australia*, first published in Cracow, 1858, trs. Robe, University of Queensland Press, St Lucia, Qld, 1979, p. 132. Korzelinski was in Australia between the years 1852 and 1856, and the diaries recalling his adventures on the Victorian goldfields were published in his native Poland following his return home.

8   ibid., p. 135.

9   Howitt, op. cit., Letter X, 25 December 1852, p. 94.

10 ibid., pp. 94–5.

11 ibid., Letter III, 29 September 1852, p. 22.

12–13 ibid.

14 Clacy, op. cit., p. 63.

15 ibid., p. 102.

16 Howitt, op.cit., p. 94.

17 ibid.

Chapter 5 – The Road to the Diggings

1   Thomas Arnot diaries, 7 August 1852, MS 8464, Australian Manuscripts Collection, State Library of Victoria.

2   Howitt, op. cit., Letter XV, 29 March 1853, p. 145.

3   Clacy, op.cit.

4   From Donald Friend, *Hillendiana*, Ure Smith, Sydney, 1956. Friend was a noted Australian artist who rented a cottage in Hill End for many years. He travelled there at various times with fellow-artists Russell Drysdale and Brett Whiteley, whose earlier works celebrated the torn landscapes of this historic goldmining region.

5   Rev. D. Mckenzie, *The Gold Digger, a Visit to the Gold Fields of Australia in Feb. 1852, with Information for Intending Emigrants*. London, 1852.

6   *Records of the Castlemaine Pioneers*, Rigby, Melbourne, 1972, James Robertson, 31 March 1882, p. 47.

Chapter 6 – Under Southern Skies

1   Frank McKillop, *Early Castlemaine,* New Chum Press, Castlemaine, Vic., 1999, Essay 28, p. 81.

2   ibid., Essay 6, p. 25.

3   Howitt, op. cit., Letter XVII, 28 May 1853, p. 171.

4   ibid., p. 175.

5   John Chandler, *Forty Years in the Wilderness*, Loch Haven Books, Main Ridge, Vic., 1990, p. 67. John Chandler came to Australia from England at the age of 11. When gold was discovered, he and his father joined the rush and had some success. He operated as a carter of goods to and from the diggings, and it was this trade that brought him the most success.

6   ibid., p. 83.

7   James Bonwick, *Notes of a Gold Digger and Gold Diggers Guide,* E. Conebee, Melbourne, 1855.

8   Fauchery, op. cit., p. 40.

9   Marjorie Tipping, *An Artist on the Goldfields: The Diary of Eugène von Guérard*, Melbourne University Press, Carlton, Vic., 1992, p. 61.

10 Clacy, op. cit., p. 57.

11 ibid., p. 102.

Chapter 7 – A Glittering Lottery

1   John Sherer, *The Gold Finder in Australia*, Penguin, Ringwood, Vic., 1973, p. 183.

2   ibid.

3   David Tulloch, *Five Views of the Gold Fields of Mount Alexander and Ballarat, in the Colony of Victoria*, Thomas Ham, Melbourne, Vic., 1852.

4   Fauchery, op. cit., pp. 76–7.

5–7 ibid.

8   Sutherland, op. cit., p. 84.

9   John Arthur Phillips, *Gold-mining and Assaying: A Scientific Guide for Emigrants,* John J. Griffin & Co., London, 1852, pp. 38–40.

Chapter 8 – No Place For a Lady

1 Capper, op. cit., p. 172.
2 Clacy, op. cit., p. 137.
3 Capper, op. cit., p. 172.
4 ibid.
5 ibid., p. 173.
6 Clacy, op. cit., pp. 62–3.
7 ibid., pp. 55–6.
8 ibid.
9 Chandler, op. cit., p. 123.
10 ibid., p. 124.
11 William Kelly, *Life in Victoria: or Victoria in 1853 and Victoria in 1858,* Chapman & Hall, London, 1860, pp. 132–135
12 Sherer, op. cit., p. 196.
13 Capper, op. cit., p. 49.
14 Clacy, op. cit., p. 137.
15 ibid., p. 136.
16 Charles Gronn, *Gold! Gold! A Dane on the Diggings,* (ed. Cara McDougall), Hill of Content, Melbourne, 1981, pp. 80–2.
17 *Mount Alexander Mail*, 11 December 1854
18 *Mount Alexander Mail*, 11 December 1854.
19 Gronn, op. cit., p. 91.
20–22 *Mt Alexander Mail*, 11 December 1854
23 Lord Robert Cecil, *Gold Field's Diary, 1852,* Melbourne University Press, Melbourne, Vic., 1935, p. 15.
24 William Craig, *My Adventures on the Australian Goldfields*, Cassell & Co. Ltd, London, 1853, pp. 222–3.
25 ibid.
26 ibid., p. 224.
27 ibid., p. 225.
28 ibid., p. 229.

Chapter 9 – 'Show Us Yer Licence'

1 Howitt, op. cit., Letter XXII, 15 August 1853, p. 216.
2 ibid., Letter XIV, 1 March 1853, p. 131.
3 Chandler, op. cit., p. 50.
4 Edwin Canton Booth, *Australia in the 1870s,* Virtue, London, 1873–76, p. 24.
5 Howitt, op. cit., p. 219

Chapter 10 – The 'Red-ribbon' Rebellion

1 Earl Grey, Secretary of State, 12 January 1852.
2 William Howitt, op. cit., Letter XIV, 1 March 1853, p. 135.
3 David Tulloch, op. cit.
4 Howitt, op. cit., Letter II, 28 September 1852, p. 11.
5 Howitt, op. cit., Letter XXII, p. 224.
6 The Bendigo Petition, State Library of Victoria.
7 Howitt, loc. cit., p. 225.
8 ibid.
9 ibid., Letter XXIII, 27 September 1853, p. 229.
10 ibid.
11 Quoted in *ANZ Gazette*, 17 December 1853.
12 *Records of the Castlemaine Pioneers*, p. 58.

Chapter 11 – The Battle at Ballarat

1 G.W. Rusden, *History of Australia,* 3 vols, Chapman & Hall, London, 1883, p. 680.
2 Raffaello Carboni, *The Eureka Stockade.* Melbourne University Press, Carlton, Vic., 1963; first published 1855.
3 *Argus*, 10 April 1855.
4 Carboni, op. cit., p. 99.
5 From Hotham's despatch to Sir George Grey, Secretary of State, 20 December 1854, quoted in Serle, op. cit., p. 173.

Chapter 12 – A Law Unto Themselves

1 Korzelinski, op. cit., p. 36.
2 Captain John Hepburn, *Letters from Victorian Pioneers*, 10 August 1853,

Public Library, Museums and National Gallery of Victoria, Government Printer, Melbourne, p. 55.
3 Recorded in *Chronicle of Australia,* ed. John Ross, Penguin, Ringwood, Vic., 1993, p. 291.
4 Chandler, op. cit., p. 102.
5 *Records of the Castlemaine Pioneers,* Walter Wilson (essay), 24 September 1886, p. 97.
6 ibid.
7 ibid., J. F. Hughes (essay), 30 September 1887, p. 2.
8 ibid., William Ottey (essay), 25 March 1887, pp. 56–7.
9 ibid., W. H. Wilson (essay), 26 September 1890, p. 157.
10 Clacy, op. cit., p. 97.

Chapter 13 – The Celestials

1 G. Mackay, *Annals of Bendigo 1851–1867,* Mackay & Co., Bendigo, Vic., 1867, p. 61.
2 Fauchery, op. cit, pp. 102–3. Quong-Chew was a fifth cousin of the Mandarin Ta-Quang-Tsung-Loo, who also owned several gardens near Macao. His social standing, combined with his eloquence, entitled him to assume the role of spokesman for the Chinese community.
3 Denovan, in a letter to the *Bendigo Advertiser*, 22 May 1859.
4 Mackay, op. cit., p. 61.
5 Quoted in David Horsfall, *March to Big Gold Mountain*, Red Rooster Press, Vic., 1985, p. 143.
6 *Australasian Sketcher,* 27 December 1873, p. 167.
7 Arthur C. Bicknell, *Travel and Adventure in Northern Queensland*, 1895. Bicknell was an English writer who was in Queensland at the height of the Chinese troubles.
8 ibid.
9 Charles Robert Thatcher, 'When I First Landed Here'

Chapter 14 – The End of the Roaring Days

1 Anthony Trollope, *Australia and New Zealand*, Geo. Robertson, Melbourne, 1873, p. 268.
2 J. C. Patterson, *The Goldfields of Victoria*, 1862., quoted in A. W. Strange, *Ballarat: A Brief History*, Lowden, Kilmore, Vic., 1971, p. 24.
3 ibid.
4 Mackay, op. cit., p. 15.
5 Craig, op. cit., p.195.
6 ibid., p.196.
7 Quoted in Tim Bonyhady, *Burke &Wills: From Melbourne to Myth,* David Ell Press, Balmain, NSW, 1991, p. 40.
8 Chandler, op. cit., p. 111.
9 Howitt, op. cit., Letter XXXVI, 16 May 1854, p. 374.
10 ibid.
11 George Sutherland, op. cit., pp. 73–9.
12 George Preshaw, *Banking Under Difficulties: or Life on the Goldfields of Victoria, New South Wales and New Zealand.* Edwards Dunlop & Co., Melbourne, 1888, p. 56.
13 ibid.
14 ibid. p. 57.
15 ibid. p. 67.
16 Quoted in Keast Burke, *Gold & Silver: Photographs of Australian Goldfields from the Holtermann Collection*, Penguin Books, Ringwood, Vic, 1973, p. 254.
17 *Cassell's Picturesque Australasian*, op. cit., p. 721.
18 From the diary of William Hocking, 1902.
19–28 ibid.
29 Thorvald Weitemeyer, *Missing Friends and Adventures in Northern Queensland,* T. Fisher Unwin, London, 1892; quoted from *Gympie Gold*, Angus and Robertson, Sydney, NSW., 1973.
30–1 ibid.
32 E. B. Kennedy, quoted from *Gympie Gold*, op. cit., p. 107.

BIBLIOGRAPHY

ANDERSON, Hugh (ed.). *Charles Thatcher's The Gold-Diggers' Songbook.* Red Rooster Press, Ascot Vale, Vic., 1980.

BATE, Weston. *Victorian Gold Rushes.* McPhee Gribble/Penguin, Ringwood, Vic., 1988.

BLACKMAN, Grant & LARKIN, John. *Maldon: Australia's First Notable Town.* Hodder & Stoughton, Melbourne, 1978.

BONYHADY, Tim. *Burke &Wills: From Melbourne to Myth.* David Ell Press Pty Ltd, Balmain, NSW, 1991.

BOOTH, Edwin Canton. *Australia in the 1870s.* Virtue & Co., London, 1873–76.

BOWMAN, John S. *The American West Year By Year.* Crescent Books, New York, 1995.

BRIDE, Thomas Francis. *Letters from Victorian Pioneers.* Published for the Trustees of the Public Library, Public Library, Museums and National Gallery of Victoria, Melbourne, 1898.

BURKE, Keast. *Gold & Silver: Photographs of Australian Goldfields from the Holtermann Collection.* Penguin, Ringwood, Vic., 1973.

CARBONI, Raffaello. *The Eureka Stockade.* Melbourne University Press, Carlton, Vic., 1963; first published 1855.

CECIL, Lord Robert. *Gold Field's Diary, 1852.* Melbourne University Press, Carlton, Vic., 1935.

CHANDLER, John. *Forty Years in the Wilderness,* ed. Michael Cannon. Loch Haven Books, 1990; first published by the author, 1893.

Chronicle of Australia, ed. John Ross. Penguin, Ringwood, Vic., 1993.

CLACY, Mrs Charles. *A Lady's Visit to the Gold Diggings of Australia in 1852–55: Written on the spot by Mrs. Charles Clacy.* Lansdowne Press, Melbourne, 1963; first published 1853.

CRAIG, William. *My Adventures on the Australian Goldfields.* Cassell & Co., London, 1853.

Crux Australis (Journal of the Flag Society of Australia), vol. 12/4, no. 52, 1999.

CURREY, C. H. *The Irish at Eureka.* Angus & Robertson, Sydney, 1954.

CUSACK, Frank. *Bendigo: A History.* Heinemann, Melbourne, 1973.

DUYKER, Edward (ed.). *A Woman on the Goldfields: Recollections of Emily Skinner 1854–1878.* Melbourne University Press, Carlton, Vic., 1995.

EVANS, William (ed.). *Diary of a Welsh Swagman, 1869–1894.* Sun Books, Melbourne, 1975.

Family History and Genealogical Record of Thomas Hiscock, Pioneer and Discoverer of Gold in Victoria, 1849. Hiscock & Sons Pty Ltd, Standard Office, Benalla, Vic., 1936.

FAUCHERY, Antoine. *Letters from a Miner in Australia.* Georgian House, Melbourne, 1965; first published in French 1857.

FLETT, James. *The History of Gold Discovery in Victoria.* Hawthorn Press, Melbourne, 1970.

FRIEND, Donald. *Hillendiana.* Ure Smith, Sydney, 1956.

GIBNEY, H. J. & HOYER, N.C. *Taken at Tilba: Photographs from the William Henry Corkhill Tilba Tilba Collection.* National Library of Australia, Canberra, 1983.

GOLDING, D. J. (ed.). *The Emigrant's Guide to Australia in the Eighteen Fifties.* Hawthorn Press, Melbourne, 1973, first published 1853.

GOODMAN, David. *Gold Seeking: Victoria and California in the 1850s.* Allen & Unwin, St Leonards, NSW, 1994.

HAIGH, Christopher (ed.). *The Cambridge Historical Encyclopedia of Great Britain and Ireland.* Cambridge University Press, New York, 1985.

HOCKING, Geoff. *Castlemaine: From Camp to City.* Five Mile Press, Melbourne, 1994.

HOLLIDAY, J. S. *The World Rushed In: The California Gold Rush Experience.* Simon & Schuster, New York, 1983.

HORSFALL, David. *March to Big Gold Mountain.* Red Rooster Press, Ascot Vale, Vic., 1985.

HOWITT, William. *Land, Labour & Gold, or Two Years in Victoria with Visits to Sydney and Van Diemen's Land.* Lowden, Kilmore, Vic., 1972; first published 1855.

KAPLAN, Fred. *Dickens: A Biography.* Hodder & Stoughton, London, 1998.

KELLY, William. *Life in Victoria: or Victoria in 1853 and Victoria in 1858,* Chapman & Hall, London, 1860,

KERR, Colin and Margaret. *The Gold Seekers.* Rigby, Australia, 1975.

KORZELINSKI, Severyn. *Memoirs of Gold-digging in Australia,* trs by Stanley Robe. University of Queensland Press, St Lucia, Qld, 1979; first published Cracow, 1858.

LANG, John Dunmore. *The Australian Emigrant's Manual, or A Guide to the Gold Colonies of New South Wales and Port Phillip.* Partridge & Oakey, London, 1852.

LERK, James A. *Bendigo's Mining History 1851–1954.* Bendigo Trust, Bendigo, Vic., 1991.

LEVY, JoAnn, *They Saw the Elephant: Women in the California Gold Rush.* Archon, Hamden, Ct, 1990

McDOUGALL, Cora (ed.). *Gold! Gold! Diary of Claus Gronn: A Dane on the Diggings.* Hill of Content, Melbourne, 1981.

MACFARLANE, Ian. *Eureka: From the Official Records.* Public Record Office of Victoria, Melbourne, 1995.

MACKAY, G. *The Annals of Bendigo.* Mackay & Co., Bendigo, Vic., 1867.

McKILLOP, Frank. *Early Castlemaine: The Municipal Council,* ed. G. Hocking. New Chum Press, Castlemaine, Vic., 1999; first published *Mount Alexander Mail,* 1908.

NEWNHAM, W. H. *Victoria Illustrated, 1857 & 1862: Engravings from the Original Editions by S. T. Gill & N. Chevalier.* Lansdowne Press, Melbourne, 1971.

PEARSALL, Ronald. *The Worm in the Bud: The World of Victorian Sexuality.* Penguin, London, 1971.

PRESHAW, George Ogilvie. *Banking Under Difficulties; or Life on the Goldfields of Victoria, New South Wales and New Zealand.* Edwards Dunlop & Co., Melbourne, 1888.

Prospectors' Guide (Victoria). Issued by Geo. Brown, Secretary for Mines, Govt Printer, Melbourne, 1936.

Records of the Castlemaine Pioneers. Rigby, Melbourne, 1972.

ROLLS, Eric. *Sojourners: Flowers and the Wide Sea.* University of Queensland Press, St Lucia, Qld, 1992.

ROSA, Joseph G. *The Taming of the West: The Age of the Gunfighter.* Salamander Books, London, 1993.

RUSDEN, G. W. *History of Australia.* Chapman & Hall, London; S. Mullen, Melbourne, 1883.

SERLE, Geoffrey. *The Golden Age: A History of the Colony of Victoria.* Melbourne University Press, Carlton, Vic., 1963.

SHERER, John. *The Gold-Finder in Australia.* Penguin, Ringwood, Vic., 1973; first published 1853.

STACPOOLE, H. J. *Gold at Ballarat.* Lowden, Kilmore, Vic., 1971.

STRANGE, A. W. *Ballarat: A Brief History.* Lowden, Kilmore, Vic., 1971.

SUTHERLAND, George. *Tales of the Goldfields.* George Robertson, Melbourne, Vic., 1880.

THOMAS, David. *Artists of the Bendigo Goldfields: 1852–1864.* Bendigo Art Gallery, Bendigo, Vic., 1989.

THOMAS, David. *S. T. Gill's Bendigo.* Bendigo Art Gallery, Bendigo, Vic., 1993.

TIPPING, Marjorie. *An Artist on the Goldfields: The Diary of Eugène von Guérard.* Melbourne University Press, Carlton, Vic., 1992.

Victoria the Golden: Scenes, Sketches and Jottings from Nature by William Strutt. Melbourne, Victoria 1850–1862. Library Committee, Parliament of Victoria, Melbourne, 1980.

Walhalla Chronicle — Facsimile Edition. Harrington & King, Waverley Offset Publishing Group, 1978.

WEITEMEYER, Thorvald Peter Ludwig. *Missing Friends and Adventures in Northern Queensland,* T. Fisher Unwin, London, 1892.

Websites

California's Untold Stories Gold Rush! Oakland Museum of California www.museum.org/goldrush.html

Online Archive of California. http://sunsite2.berkeley.edu/oac/

Trails to the Goldrush. www.over-land.com/trgold.html

Life on the Goldfields. www.gov.au/slv/exhibitions/goldfields

– ACKNOWLEDGEMENTS –

MY INTENTION in preparing this book was to bring together as wide a range as possible of pictorial images (paintings, engravings, photographs and ephemera) that would tell the story of the mass migration to the Australian goldfields of the 1850s.

I wanted to express the hopes and desires, the fantastic finds and devastating failures that were the stuff of legend on the goldfields. I wanted to understand why this period still holds our fascination today, to search for the meaning of this event, the impact it had on the world and the reasons why so many of our forefathers pulled up their roots and sailed halfway around the globe into uncertain future, but exhilarating adventure.

This story had to start with the rush to the California diggings. In the writing of this work I learnt that my great-grandfather went first to California, then Montana, and then onto Australia. This sent me on a fascinating journey of exploration into the electronic world of the worldwide web. Where once my great-grandfather walked, I was now surfing; the Californian Sesquicentennial celebrations of the discovery of gold in 1848 left a valuable legacy of information and images that helped me to draw out the link between the Californian diggings and the discoveries in Australia three years later.

I thank all those across the Pacific with whom I have enjoyed fruitful electronic discussions: Tracy Melings of the University of Berkeley, California; Courtney De Angelis of the Amon Carter Museum of Fort Worth, Texas; Jeff Kram of the Oakland Museum of California. All have been most generous with their time and efforts in ensuring that works requested from their collections found their way to the Antipodes.

I also acknowledge the assistance given from the other side of the world, in particular by Iain Harrison of the Birmingham Art Gallery and Museum, Birmingham, England.

I wish to thank all those who have given me such generous assistance over the time of the preparation of this book. Without the efforts of the many librarians, picture researchers, gallery curators and private collectors who have given their time and lent the works under their care, books such as this would not be at all possible.

In particular I acknowledge the generous assistance of Scott Jessop of the Burke Museum, Beechworth; Sally Routledge of Bendigo Regional Library; Karen Quinlan and Anonda Bell of the Bendigo Art Gallery; Peter Perry of Castlemaine Art Gallery & Historical Museum; Maldon Historical Museum; Gael Ramsay of the Ballarat Fine Art Gallery; Jenny Molony of the National Gallery of Victoria; Alice Livingstone of the Art Gallery of New South Wales; Oxley Library, State Library of Queensland; Jennifer Broomhead of the State Library of South Australia; Art Gallery of Western Australia; Anne Armstrong and Diane Reilly of the State Library of Victoria; State Parliamentary Library of Victoria; Marika Tolghesi of the National Library of Australia; Young Historical Museum; John Zulic, Director Creative and Design – Sovereign Hill, Ballarat, Victoria; the special collection of the library at La Trobe University, Bendigo; and Colin Bourke of Stock Photos, Melbourne.

Thanks also go to John Menzies and Marion Colman, and to the other characters of Sovereign Hill, Ballarat, whose co-operation and conversation show in their friendly portraits. I am only sorry that the photographs taken of 'Chips' were not able to be included, but the light failed us.

There are numerous individuals who have also lent works from their private collections. I thank Graeme and Lyn Bennett, late of the Diggers' Store in Campbell's Creek, Victoria, who have joined in the new rush to the Northern Territory; my father-in-law, Q. Clifford Binks, whose private collections still remain a mystery to us all, but things do appear when most needed; Frank Cusack of Bendigo, a greatly respected historian, who generously allowed the use of some images from his own works; Allan M. Nixon, another respected author of Australiana, also for permission to use photographs from his own works; Mary Thompson of Castlemaine; Doug Mills and Felix Cappy, also of Castlemaine, who lent me their prized Colt revolvers.

There are also numerous groups and individuals who have over the years given me pictures and ephemera, often for use in other projects. I have attempted to acknowledge all such images to their source; if I have failed to do this accurately I apologise. Every attempt has been made to trace the source of material and to give proper acknowledgement.

I also acknowledge the work of others who have researched this topic before me. Geoffrey Serle's *The Golden Age,* James Flett's *The History of Gold Discovery in Victoria* and Frank Cusack's *Bendigo: A History* are invaluable texts. James Lerk, another historian from Bendigo, has always been a constant and reliable source of information, and I thank him for sharing his wide knowledge whenever asked. There is also an army of authors working at the local history level who, through their brochures and smaller texts, provide a wealth of excellent resource material. I thank them all, and urge them to continue with the task of keeping our history alive.

Lastly, I thank my wife, Christine, for once again leaving me alone to follow my obsession, for holding the camera bag, wandering through endless museums with me, sitting in the car for hours as we drove through pouring rain – just to see the Lambing Flat flag, and then to turn around and drive all the way back home again.

It takes determination to bring such a book to fruition, but it also takes the support and the tolerance of family, friends and colleagues; for that support I thank you all.

Geoff Hocking, Castlemaine

LAWRENCE MURPHY,
CASTLEMAINE HOTEL.